Jan 12 53
Feb 17 53

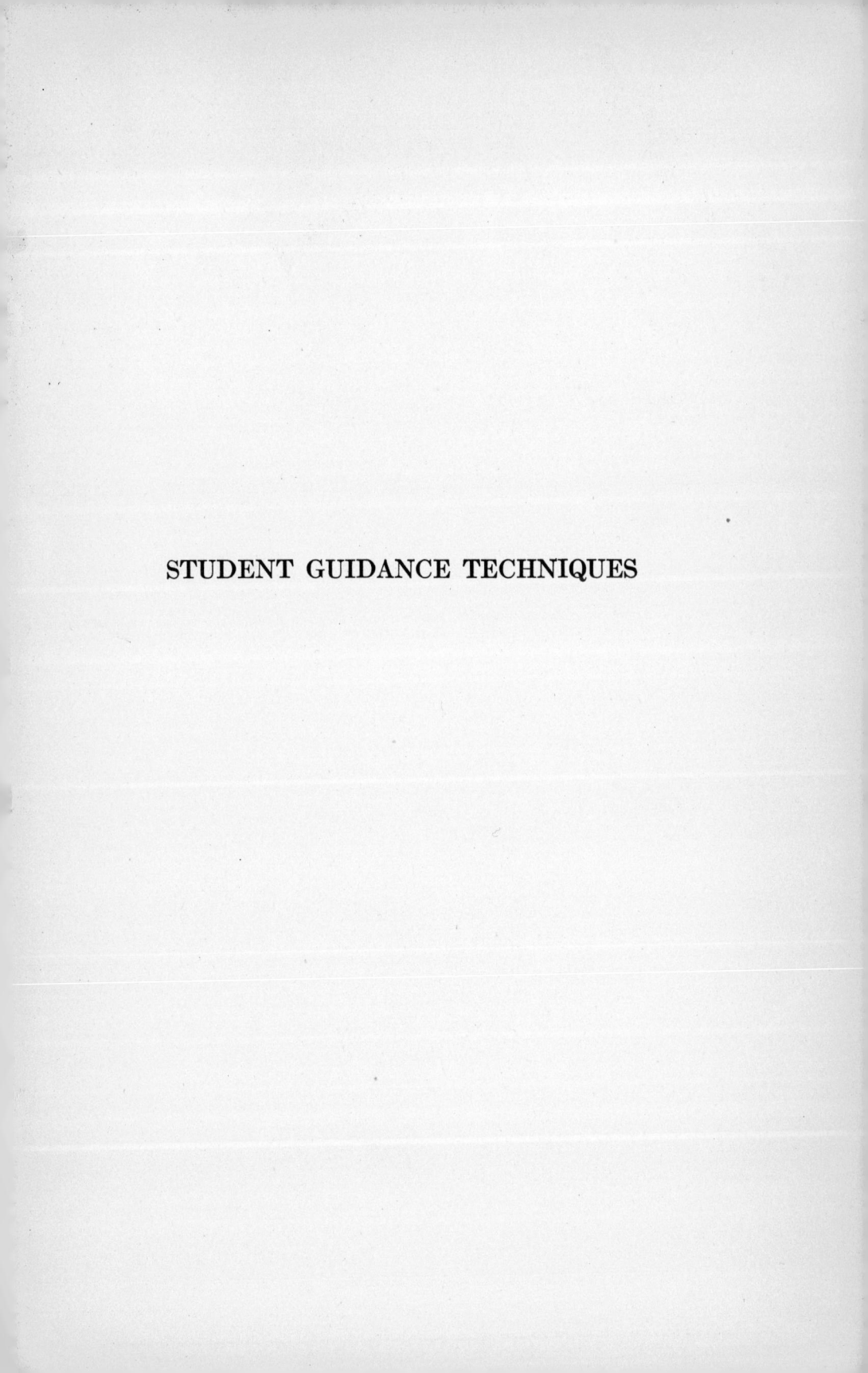

STUDENT GUIDANCE TECHNIQUES

STUDENT GUIDANCE TECHNIQUES

A Handbook for Counselors in High Schools and Colleges

BY

DONALD G. PATERSON
Professor of Psychology, University of Minnesota

GWENDOLEN G. SCHNEIDLER
Instructor in Education, Goucher College

AND

EDMUND G. WILLIAMSON
Assistant Professor of Psychology and Director of University Testing Bureau, University of Minnesota

First Edition
Third Impression

McGRAW-HILL BOOK COMPANY, Inc.
NEW YORK AND LONDON
1938

COPYRIGHT, 1938, BY THE
MCGRAW-HILL BOOK COMPANY, INC.

PRINTED IN THE UNITED STATES OF AMERICA

*All rights reserved. This book, or
parts thereof, may not be reproduced
in any form without permission of
the publishers.*

THE MAPLE PRESS COMPANY, YORK, PA.

To

THOSE WHO SEEK
TO PROFESSIONALIZE
COUNSELING,
GUIDANCE
AND PERSONNEL WORK

PREFACE

The guidance movement has reached the stage where individual diagnosis is now recognized as an essential first step in the development of an adequate guidance service for youth. The mere recognition of this fact, however, does not guarantee the translation of the idea into practice. Workers everywhere seem to be groping for the necessary technical knowledge. They are seeking dependable ways and means of diagnosing abilities, aptitudes, interests and personality characteristics which may be put at the disposal of those who desire to develop their educational and vocational plans on a rational basis of fact rather than on the irrational basis of ambition, hope and wishful thinking. The contents of this handbook, it is hoped, will partially meet this need.

In June, 1935, the authors prepared a mimeographed edition to meet the local needs of faculty counselors at the University of Minnesota.[1] In spite of the fact that this edition was written specifically for faculty counselors in a typical Midwestern university, the number of calls for it from guidance workers in other colleges and universities and even in other types of schools quickly exhausted the limited number available. In response to this demand, the authors have completely revised the mimeographed edition and have broadened its scope to cover guidance techniques in junior and senior high schools as well as at the college level.

In most collaborations it usually turns out that one of the contributors carries an undue share of the burden. This is certainly true in the present instance. To be specific, the mimeographed edition was based on the M.S. thesis worked out by Miss Schneidler during 1934–1935.[2] In the work of revising

[1] SCHNEIDLER, G., D. G. PATERSON and E. G. WILLIAMSON: *Student Personnel Procedures and Techniques Used by Faculty Counselors at the University of Minnesota*, June 16, 1935, 105 pp.

[2] SCHNEIDLER, G.: *A Manual of Student Personnel Procedures and Techniques for the Use of Faculty Counselors at the University of Minnesota.* M.S. thesis on file in the University of Minnesota Library, May, 1935.

and broadening the scope of the mimeographed edition, Miss Schneidler again carried the lion's share of the work. The preface to this handbook would be quite deficient if these facts were not explicitly set forth.

The inclusion of Two Significant Questions and Two Pertinent Replies is based on the conviction that two of the most serious obstacles to the immediate expansion of scientific guidance work are to be found in the attitudes of certain psychologists—those who would hide their light under a bushel and those who would conceal the characteristics of the student in the interests of an organismic theory. McCall's answers are appropriate and timely.

Another serious obstacle to the immediate expansion of worth-while student guidance services is to be found in the lack of technically trained workers who can be entrusted with the heavy responsibilities necessarily involved in the attempt to provide adequate guidance for youth. In a real sense, this handbook is designed to aid in overcoming this obstacle. That is to say, it is hoped that assimilation of its contents will add to the technical competency of workers on the job and of those in training. Furthermore, it is hoped that administrators will turn to these pages to obtain a first-hand acquaintance with the complexity of student guidance problems and the variety of techniques now available for their solution. Administrators who fully grasp the implications will cease appointing amateurs and laymen to guidance positions and will use personnel specifications similar to those outlined in the last chapter, in order to secure technically competent personnel workers who also possess the necessary personal qualifications to ensure effectiveness in the school situation.

Another obstacle to the development of effective student personnel programs in schools and colleges is the alleged indifference of teachers to the needs of their students. The authors believe that such indifference, when it exists, is due primarily to the fact that teachers have been unable to obtain a fairly complete picture of the ways and means that now exist for disclosing the characteristics of students as individuals. It is hoped that faculty members in high schools and colleges will welcome this handbook as a means of giving them first-hand acquaintance with available ways and means of "knowing the students." It is believed that faculty members who get this picture will find themselves increasingly eager to aid in the development of an adequate guidance service in their schools. In this way administrators, teachers and clinical guidance workers can work together to individualize the educational process.

In compiling tests, questionnaires, inventories and other techniques for inclusion, the authors were aware that their decisions were matters of judgment involving valuation. Since no completely objective basis could be found as a certain guide, their judgments with respect to what is included as well as what is excluded are open to attack. Their only defense is to state the criteria they attempted to follow, namely, reliability, validity and practicability. Furthermore, they have preferred to include only a few of the possible tests for any one purpose rather than all possible devices on the market. Doubtless they have omitted tests that should be included simply because they were ignorant of their existence or of their guidance values. Errors of this sort can be corrected if a revision is undertaken. For this reason, criticisms are welcomed.

In listing quoted prices for tests the authors have consulted catalogues and publishers' manuals. Since prices for tests may be revised from time to time by publishers and distributors, the prices contained in this handbook are not to be considered as final. Publishers' quotations should be secured before placing orders.

It has been indicated above that this handbook was prepared to meet the needs of counselors, teachers, educational administrators and students in training for personnel work. But in addition, interviewers in employment offices may find useful suggestions for improving their classification of applicants for jobs. As a matter of fact, the techniques to be used by employment managers, industrial and business personnel workers, and employment office interviewers are substantially the same as those used by personnel workers in education. However, it is recognized that workers outside educational institutions will need to adapt the suggested interpretations and uses of tests and other techniques to the particular situations in which they are working. After all, guidance is another phase of the problem of selection; hence personnel workers of all types should find useful suggestions in this handbook.

In a sense, this handbook is a companion volume to Williamson and Darley's *Student Personnel Work, An Outline of Clinical Procedures*. That book outlines the total field and discusses at length types of student problems and the clinical methods of diagnosis required to meet those problems. The present book develops in considerable detail an account of the technical diagnostic instruments themselves. Thus they supplement each other.

Grateful acknowledgment is made to Joseph E. Lepine, Charles B. Garland and H. P. Bye for assistance in reading proof and in preparing the index.

THE AUTHORS.

UNIVERSITY OF MINNESOTA,
December, 1937.

CONTENTS

	PAGE
PREFACE	vii
TWO SIGNIFICANT QUESTIONS AND TWO PERTINENT REPLIES	xvii

CHAPTER
I. INTRODUCTION 1
The Purpose of Student Guidance 1
Complexity of Student Problems 2
Functions of the Guidance Counselor 3
Annotated Bibliography and Suggested Readings 4

II. DIAGNOSTIC TECHNIQUES 6
The Interview 8
The Faculty Counselor's Diagnostic Role in Mental Hygiene . . 12
Cumulative Records 18
Recording Behavior Items 21
Measurements and Norms 27
The Purpose of Tests 31
Description of Tests 34
Administration and Scoring of Tests 40
Equivalent Forms 43
Persons for Whom Tests Are Designed 43
Norms 46
Reliability of Tests 47
Validity 50
References 51

III. SCHOLASTIC APTITUDE TESTS 52
A. Intelligence Tests at the Secondary School Level . . . 53
  1. Stanford Revision of the Binet-Simon Scale 53
  2. The Revised Stanford-Binet Scales 54
  3. Terman Group Test of Mental Ability 56
  4. Army Alpha Group Examination, Forms 5 to 9 58
  5. Revised Army Alpha Examination, Form 6, Short Form . 61
  6. Bregman's Revision of Army Alpha Examination, Forms A and B 62
  7. Pressey Senior Classification and Senior Verifying Tests . 63
  8. Otis Self-administering Test of Mental Ability, Higher Examination 66
  9. American Council on Education Psychological Examination for High School Students 68

xi

CHAPTER   PAGE
      10. Henmon-Nelson Tests for Mental Ability, High School Examination 69
      11. Additional Tests at the High School Level 71
  B. Calibration of I.Q.'s Derived from Group Intelligence Tests. 72
  C. Intelligence Tests at the College Level 74
      1. American Council on Education Psychological Examination for High School Graduates and College Freshmen. 74
      2. Ohio State Intelligence Test 76
      3. Minnesota College Ability Test 77
      4. Thorndike Intelligence Examination for High School Graduates 80
      5. Henmon-Nelson Tests of Mental Ability, for College Students 81
  D. Reading Tests. 83
      1. Chapman-Cook Speed of Reading Test. 85
      2. Minnesota Speed of Reading Test for College Students. . 87
      3. Unit Scales of Attainment, Reading 88
      4. Iowa Silent Reading Tests, Advanced 89
      5. Minnesota Reading Examination for College Students . . 91

IV. ACADEMIC ACHIEVEMENT TESTS. 95
  Junior High School 98
      1. New Stanford Achievement Test, Advanced Examination. 98
      2. Metropolitan Achievement Test, Advanced Battery. . . . 101
      3. Unit Scales of Attainment, Division 3. 105
      4. Iowa Every-pupil Tests of Basic Skills for Grades Six, Seven, and Eight. 107
      5. Progressive Achievement Tests, Intermediate Battery. . . 111

V. ACADEMIC ACHIEVEMENT TESTS (*Continued*) 114
  Senior High School and Junior College. 114
  A. English Tests 114
      1. Iowa Placement Examinations, New Series, English Training 114
      2. Cooperative English Test, Series 1. 116
      3. Cooperative English Test, Series 2. 119
      4. Cooperative Literary Acquaintance Test 120
  B. Mathematics 122
      1. Iowa Placement Examinations, Series M.T.1, Revised, A. Mathematics-training. 122
      2. Cooperative General Mathematics Test for High School Classes. 124
      3. Cooperative General Mathematics Tests for College Students 125
      4. Cooperative Plane Geometry Test. 127
      5. Cooperative Solid Geometry Test 128
      6. Cooperative Algebra Test (Elementary and Intermediate) 128

CONTENTS

CHAPTER	PAGE
7. Cooperative Trigonometry Test	129
C. SCIENCE	130
1. Cooperative General Science Test (High School)	130
2. Cooperative General Science Test for College Students	131
3. Cooperative Botany Test	133
4. Cooperative Chemistry Test for High School Students	134
5. Cooperative Chemistry Test for College Students	135
6. Iowa Placement Examinations, New Series, Chemistry Training	136
7. Cooperative Physics Test (For High School Students)	137
8. Cooperative Physics Test for College Students	138
9. Cooperative Biology Test for High School Students	140
10. Cooperative Zoology Test	141
D. Foreign Languages	141
1. Cooperative French Test	142
2. Cooperative German Test	143
3. Cooperative Spanish Test	145
4. Cooperative Latin Test	146
E. History and Social Studies	147
1. Cooperative American History Test	147
2. Cooperative Modern European History Test	148
3. Cooperative World History Test	149
4. Cooperative Contemporary Affairs Test	150
F. General Culture	153
1. Cooperative General Culture Test	153
VI. VOCATIONAL ACHIEVEMENT TESTS	157
A. Shop Courses	158
B. Home Economics Tests	158
1. Engle-Stenquist Home Economics Test	159
2. Unit Scales of Attainment in Foods and Household Management	161
3. The Minnesota House Design and House Furnishing Test	161
C. Typewriting and Stenography	163
1. Blackstone Stenographic Proficiency Tests (Typing)	163
2. Blackstone Stenographic Proficiency Tests (Stenography Test)	163
3. Stenogauge	164
D. Bookkeeping	165
1. Elwell-Fowlkes Bookkeeping Test	165
E. Trade Tests	167
1. Interview Aids and Trade Questions	167
VII. PERSONALITY TESTS AND QUESTIONNAIRES	170
A. Interest Inventories	174
1. Interest Questionnaire for High School Boys	174
2. Vocational Interest Test for Men	175

		PAGE
	3. Vocational Interest Blank for Women	181
B.	Personality, Adjustment and Attitude Inventories	183
	1. The School Inventory	184
	2. The Adjustment Inventory	185
	3. The Minnesota Inventories of Social Attitudes	189
	4. Minnesota Scale for the Survey of Opinions	193
	5. Personality Sketches	196
	6. Humm-Wadsworth Temperament Scale	197
	7. Specific Attitude Scales	201
	8. Generalized Attitude Scales	202
VIII.	SPECIAL APTITUDE TESTS	205
A.	Clerical Aptitude Tests	205
	1. Minnesota Vocational Test for Clerical Workers	206
	2. Other Clerical Aptitude Tests	209
B.	Art Talent Tests	210
	1. Art Judgment Test	210
	2. The McAdory Art Test	213
C.	Musical Ability Tests	216
	1. Seashore's Measures of Musical Talent	216
	2. Drake's Musical Memory Test	221
D.	Mechanical Ability Tests	222
	1. Minnesota Mechanical Assembly Test	222
	2. Minnesota Spatial Relations Tests	225
	3. Revised Minnesota Paper Form Board Test	227
	4. Kent-Shakow Form Boards	229
	5. MacQuarrie Test for Mechanical Ability	233
E.	Dexterity Tests	235
	1. Finger Dexterity Test	235
	2. Tweezer Dexterity Test	237
	3. Minnesota Manual Dexterity Test	240
F.	Miscellaneous Aptitude Tests	242
	1. Medical Aptitude Test	242
	2. Aptitude Test for Nursing	244
	3. Law Aptitude Examination	245
	4. Ishihara Tests for Color Blindness	247
	5. Dynamicube Test of Power to Visualize	250
	6. Staticube Test of Power to Visualize	252
	7. Mutilated Cubes Test of Power to Visualize	253
	8. Engineering Drawing Aptitude Placement Test	254
IX.	DIAGNOSIS AND TREATMENT OF EDUCATIONAL PROBLEMS	257
	Selection of Curricula and Courses	257
	Study Methods	258
	The Non-achiever and the Super-achiever	263
	Poor Scholastic Aptitude	265
	Reading Disabilities	268
	Specific Subject-matter Disabilities	270

CONTENTS

Chapter	Page
X. Treatment of Vocational Problems.	271
A. Techniques for Securing and Imparting Occupational Information	271
1. Analysis of Occupational Census Data	271
2. Local Surveys of Job Opportunities	274
3. Personal Study of Occupations	275
4. Occupational Bookshelves	275
5. Courses in Occupations.	278
6. Vocational Information Conferences	278
7. Referral of Students to Experts	279
8. Study of Classified Advertisements.	279
9. Occupational Ability Patterns.	280
B. Techniques for Appraising the Effectiveness of Guidance Programs in Schools and Colleges.	281
C. Techniques for Diagnosing Vocational Aptitudes.	282
1. Tests and Measurements.	282
2. School Curriculum.	283
3. Extra-curricular Activities	284
4. Vacation Job Experiences.	285
5. Hobbies and Recreational Activities	285
D. Treatment of Vocational Problems.	286
1. Parents.	286
2. Teachers.	287
3. Classmates	287
4. Immature Judgment of Students	287
5. Economic Pressure.	288
6. Placement Facilities	288
XI. Treatment of Personal Problems	289
A. Emotional Problems	289
B. Financial Problems.	296
C. Health Problems.	297
D. Speech Problems.	298
E. Prevention	299
XII. Guidance—A Professional Service.	300
Minimum Qualifications for a Counselor.	302
Additional Desirable Qualifications	303
Duties and Responsibilities.	304
Index	307

TWO SIGNIFICANT QUESTIONS
AND
TWO PERTINENT REPLIES[1]

I

Q. Should teachers be allowed to administer and score intelligence and educational tests and interpret results?

A. Many years ago certain specialists sought to secure a monopoly of the privilege of using standard tests by trying to persuade educators to regard the tests as possessing certain mystic properties. A few of us with Promethean tendencies set about taking these sacred cows away from the gods and giving them to mortals. Can teachers be trusted with tests? If not, then teachers ought not to be trusted with 90 per cent of their present functions. We now entrust them with the far more difficult task of teaching reading, creating concepts and building ideals. Let us not strain at a gnat when we have swallowed fifty elephants.

W. A. McCALL.

II

Q. Does an organismic conception of a child require us to dispense with educational measurement?

A. Certain extreme exponents of the organismic (often called *gestalt*) view contend that any organism is more than the sum of its parts, and that adding test scores is like trying to make a man by sticking together a head, a trunk, two arms and two legs. But a reading score cannot be properly compared to one leg. It is not a broken-off fragment of the mind. In a very real sense, a reading score tends to measure the entire organism functioning in that reading situation.

Mental measurements are essentially similar to bodily measurements. If anyone proposed to abolish the making and use

[1] *The Test Newsletter*, published by the Bureau of Publications, Teachers College, Columbia University, December, 1936.

of the measurements of pulse, temperature, blood pressure, et cetera, we would call him *crazy*, and if anyone proposes to abolish the making and use of mental measurements, he, too, should be called . . . I hesitate to say what, since somehow I must manage to live with certain of my colleagues after this is published, but surely something other than an organismic philosopher or a *gestalt* psychologist!

W. A. McCall.

STUDENT GUIDANCE TECHNIQUES

CHAPTER I

INTRODUCTION

THE PURPOSE OF STUDENT GUIDANCE

Guidance counselors are concerned with students as individuals in the process of adjusting to life. In this capacity the counselor steps out of the role of a mere teacher in order to consider the student as an integrated human being. Paradoxical as this may seem, the present educational system makes it extremely difficult for the teacher to do more than impart information and train students in a specific branch of study. In order to maintain that concern for the student as a *whole person* which has sometimes been possible in smaller educational institutions, it has been necessary in larger institutions to rely on specialists. The guidance counselor is that person who attempts to obtain a picture of all the complex lines of influence which bear down upon the individual student, in order that the student may be helped to adjust to his present problems and to plan wisely for his future activities.

Ideally, the highest aim of education is to obtain a full understanding of each student in order to adjust educational offerings to his needs so that he may be prepared for a role wherein highest achievement and satisfaction may be realized. Obviously, this demands an approach broad in conception and directed toward the whole individual. Dr. Trabue summarized the situation admirably when he stated:

From this point of view, guidance and education are intimately related. As a matter of fact, educational guidance, social guidance, emotional guidance, vocational guidance, and all other desirable types of guidance are merely different phases of a single program whose purpose is to build the happiest and most fully integrated personality possible upon the foundation with which nature and previous experience have provided the individual.[1]

COMPLEXITY OF STUDENT PROBLEMS

A guidance counselor achieves a broad conception of his duties. With most students whom he attempts to serve he is confronted, not with a single problem, but with a variety of problems concerning educational, vocational, emotional, social, economic and health adjustments. In a large proportion of cases these problems occur in groups. Seldom is the student in need of guidance concerning only one aspect of his life as a student or prospective wage earner. The counselor must be prepared to meet problems in these diverse fields and to administer educational, vocational, personal, economic and health advice. He may expect to administer these services, not only singly, but in combinations according to the needs of the student. An educational problem in most cases is linked with a vocational problem, which, in turn, often appears as the manifest symptom of a difficulty in the emotional life.

In an analysis[2] of problems presented by 371 students who had consulted counselors, the facts clearly reveal the complexity of student problems. These students presented a total of 1313 difficulties requiring attention, or an average of three and one-half problems per student. One wonders to what extent this figure would rise if all difficulties serious enough to benefit from intelligent counsel had been discovered and tabulated.

The authors state: "There is a tendency, present in about half of the cases, for certain types of problems to be associated in the same student case histories. For the most part, vocational, educational, social and health problems are associated." One-third of the students with financial problems also had social, emotional and personal problems. Nearly another two-thirds needed vocational and educational assistance. Nearly one-half of those cases whose chief problem was vocational were wrestling with educational problems also. This is objective evidence of

[1] TRABUE, M. R., "Recent Developments in Testing for Guidance," *Rev. of Educ. Res.*, 1933, 3: 41–48.
[2] WILLIAMSON, E. G., H. P. LONGSTAFF, and J. M. EDMUNDS, "Counseling Arts College Students," *J. of Appl. Psychol.*, 1935, 19: 111–124.

the overlapping of these two fields. One-fourth of those in the vocational group were coping with social and emotional problems as well. It is difficult to determine causal relationships. In some instances the student complains of vocational indecisions which are actually manifestations of fundamental personal maladjustments.

About one-half of the social, personal and emotional difficulties were associated with educational and one-fourth with vocational problems. Only 1 per cent were independent of others. Nineteen per cent were linked with health difficulties. Of the students with health problems, over one-half had also social or personal problems. Less than 1 per cent indicated no other problems.

Such facts are striking evidence of the extent to which problems overlap in the same individual. To expect that guidance could be adequate which was concerned with only one aspect of the individual would be to ignore the facts. In view of these complex interrelationships, a conception of individuals as types characterized by a single problem is erroneous. A more dynamic conception is necessary. Let us speak of specific problems, rather than of student problem types, and then realize that they combine in various patterns. Most students do not present sharp types. Each possesses his own peculiar pattern of problems and characteristics.

FUNCTIONS OF THE GUIDANCE COUNSELOR

In order to meet these varied student difficulties, the counselor must be prepared to render a number of guidance services. These may be classified as follows:
1. Educational guidance
2. Vocational guidance
3. Personal guidance (including social, emotional and leisure-time guidance)
4. Health guidance
5. Economic guidance

Since these services necessarily overlap, the counselor should consider himself a general guidance counselor. He cannot be an educational counselor without at the same time acting as a vocational and personal counselor.

In the following sections several techniques for the study of the individual will be discussed. It is only by careful analysis of both objective and subjective data that even the first steps may be taken in understanding and solving the many problems of the student. In a later section we shall also enumerate typical student problems and indicate procedures available for attempting their solution.

It is inadvisable in a handbook to discuss adequately the theory and practice of counseling. An extensive discussion of this topic is now available in Williamson and Darley's book entitled *Student Personnel Work*, in Bell's *Theory and Practice of Student Counseling*, and in Bingham's *Aptitudes and Aptitude Testing*. In addition to these basic references, the interested counselor may find the following annotated bibliography of value.

Annotated Bibliography of Suggested Readings

ALLEN, R. D.: *Inor Group-guidance Series*, Vols. I–IV, New York: Inor Publishing Company, 1934. Four volumes devoted to the description of a comprehensive educational and vocational guidance program for the schools.

American Council on Education: *Measurement and Guidance of College Students*, Baltimore: Williams & Wilkins Company, 1933. A report of the work of the Committee on Personnel Methods, describing the Cumulative Record Card, Achievement Tests, Personality Measurement, Vocational Monographs and Factors in the Character Development of College Students.

BELL, HUGH M.: *The Theory and Practice of Student Counseling*, Stanford, California: Stanford University Press, 1935. An excellent discussion of counseling, emphasizing especially the author's Adjustment Inventory.

BINGHAM, W. V.: *Aptitudes and Aptitude Testing*, New York: Harper & Brothers, 1937. Discusses aptitudes and aptitude testing from the point of view of the guidance counselor. An invaluable reference for the professional counselor.

COWLEY, W. H.: *The Personnel Bibliographical Index*, Columbus, Ohio: Bureau of Educational Research, Ohio State University, 1932. A classified, annotated index of 2183 references on all phases of student personnel work.

EARLE, F. M.: *Psychology and the Choice of a Career*, London, England: Methuen & Company, Ltd., 1933. A concise account of the role of psychology in vocational guidance.

JOHNSTON, J. B.: *The Liberal College in a Changing Society*, New York: D. Appleton-Century Company, Inc., 1931. Describes curricular developments in an arts college to meet the needs of the individual student as disclosed by personnel research work.

Koos, L. V., and G. N. KEFAUVER: *Guidance in Secondary Schools*, New York: The Macmillan Company, 1932. This book is listed here as one of the best comprehensive treatises on the principles and methods of vocational guidance in the schools.

LLOYD-JONES, ESTHER: *Student Personnel Work at Northwestern University*, New York: Harper & Brothers, 1929. An account of the centralized student personnel setup at Northwestern University.

PATERSON, D. G., et al.: "The Minnesota Personnel Program," *The Educational Record*, 1928, 9: 3–40. A description of the decentralized student personnel program at the University of Minnesota.

STRANG, RUTH: *Personal Development and Guidance in College and Secondary School*, New York: Harper & Brothers, 1934. This is an excellent comprehensive treatise on the results of investigations relating to personnel work.

———: *The Role of the Teacher in Personnel Work*, New York: Bureau of Publications, Teachers College, Columbia University, 1935. A nontechnical account of student personnel work from the point of view of the classroom teacher.

———: *Counseling Technics in College and Secondary School*, New York: Harper & Brothers, 1937. This is an excellent treatise, stressing the interview, rating scales, methods of case study and records.

———: *Behavior and Background of Students in College and Secondary School*, New York: Harper & Brothers, 1937. A valuable compendium of research findings in regard to intelligence, achievement, personality, attitudes and interests, social and economic background, use of time, and financial resources of students.

WILLIAMSON, E. G., and J. G. DARLEY: *Student Personnel Work*, New York: McGraw-Hill Book Company, Inc., 1937. An excellent comprehensive treatise on student personnel work, emphasizing points of view, principles, methods and results.

CHAPTER II
DIAGNOSTIC TECHNIQUES

Guidance is not a new phase of education. Since 1909 more or less systematic efforts have been made to bring about a harmonious adjustment between the student and the educational system. A large part of this guidance work has been concerned with educational and vocational adjustment. That is, attempts have been made to help students select an educational curriculum and a vocation which would be satisfactory and which would result in success. The favorite formula of early guidance workers consisted of three parts: (1) an analysis of occupations to determine the necessary qualifications of workers; (2) an analysis of the individual to determine his aptitudes and interests; (3) a matching of these two factors to determine the type of work for which the individual was properly qualified.

Now, this general formula of guidance should not be criticized or supplanted. Nor should there be any quarrel with attempts to analyze occupations, except that these attempts have been too local in scope and too subjective in methodology. But severe criticisms should be made of guidance workers for their naïve and rule-of-thumb methods of analyzing the aptitudes of individuals.

For the most part, these traditional methods of diagnosis have assumed that students are able to make their own analyses.[1] Students have been asked to try out various occupational activities; to make trips to factories; to interview successful businessmen; to read autobiographies of successful men; and to attend classes in occupational information. This methodology has been used, not to help students determine if they *actually possess* the necessary abilities, but to discover if they *like* a given

[1] For a critical review of 15 methods of guidance see "Methods in Vocational Guidance," by E. G. Williamson, *Proceedings of the Third Annual All State Educational Conference, University of Nebraska Publications, Educ. Monog.*, No. 9, October, 1936, pp. 68–80.

type of work and if they *think* they can do it. It is assumed that if the answer is yes to both of these questions, then the student is actually qualified for the occupation of his choice. In other words, the student is encouraged to choose the occupation he *thinks* he can do successfully. Unfortunately, the necessity of an impersonal and objective diagnosis of aptitudes has not been recognized in general practice, despite all the known facts concerning individual differences in abilities and the prevalence of irrationality in occupational choice.[2] Furthermore, Hollingworth's experiments showing the unreliability of self-estimates of ability and personality traits indicate the futility of vocational self-guidance.[3]

The newer method of guidance is based upon the assumption that students are often unable to diagnose their own aptitudes and interests and that, therefore, they need the assistance of a trained diagnostician, *in addition to* information about jobs. Such a diagnosis should be made prior to the making of an educational or vocational choice, in order that emotional attachments to impossible goals may not preclude the making of a satisfactory adjustment. Thus, this new type of guidance emphasizes the prevention of maladjustment through the choosing of goals in line with demonstrated aptitudes. Thoughtful planning rather than wishful thinking is the aim.

This point of view, that the work of skilled diagnosticians is a first step in effective guidance,[4] leads us to a review of the available techniques of diagnosis, to a critical analysis of their weaknesses and strengths and to a discussion of the ways in which they may be used to aid students in adopting achievable educational and vocational goals. This review of diagnostic techniques will cover the interview; methods of diagnosing emotional maladjustments; cumulative records as essential in diagnosis; and measurement techniques.

[2] For a survey of the development of these two points of view see *Introduction* by D. G. Paterson in *Student Personnel Work* by E. G. Williamson and J. G. Darley, McGraw-Hill Book Company, Inc., New York, 1937.

[3] HOLLINGWORTH, H. L., *Judging Human Character*, Chapter IV, pp. 45–59, Judging One's Own Characteristics, New York: D. Appleton-Century Company, Inc., 1922.

[4] PATERSON, D. G., "Individual Diagnosis—An Essential First Step," *Occupations, The Vocational Guidance Magazine*, 1937, 15: 596–597.

THE INTERVIEW

Essential to the diagnosis of the individual student and his problems is the use of record blanks and interviews to supplement facts which are amenable to more objective measurement. Personal data regarding developmental history, educational and vocational experiences, accomplishments and family background are essential to a clear understanding of any case. Whenever possible, many of these facts should be gathered before the interview by means of record forms devised for that purpose.

The interview continues to be the most subjective aspect of the diagnosis procedure. Despite its limitations, however, it is an indispensable step in the guidance program. Its purpose is threefold. It involves gathering all available pertinent facts, making a diagnosis on the basis of all the evidence and formulating an appropriate plan of action in line with the diagnosis. Treatment or practical programs usually evolve from the preliminary stages of fact finding and diagnosis. *All questions may not be settled in the interview, but to be successful, it should lead to some plan of action.* Its aim should be to serve the individual. *The counselor should serve the student, even though he may do no more than present the facts in a more objective light, thus enabling the student to see himself, his assets, his liabilities and his opportunities more clearly than he could see them unaided.* One writer urges the counselor to beware of exercising a "benevolent tyranny," but to attempt to render a real service.[5]

Paterson[6] has listed the aims of interviewing, stressing its diagnostic aspect. They are as follows:

1. Studying the time distribution of each student.

2. Investigating methods, time, place and conditions of study.

3. Studying the extent and nature of each student's participation in extra-curricular activities, aiding and urging the student to engage in those activities most in line with his own interests, abilities and needs.

---

[5] STURTEVANT, S. M., and H. HAYES, "The Use of the Interview in Advisory Work," *Teachers College Record*, 1927, 28: 551–563.

[6] PATERSON, D. G., "Finding the Individual Student and His Problems," Chapter XXXII in F. J. Allen's *Principles and Problems in Vocational Guidance*, New York: McGraw-Hill Book Company, Inc., 1927.

4. Studying each student's vocational aim, to determine its origin, its harmony with the family background and the student's real abilities.

5. Giving each student an opportunity to discuss personal problems.

We shall have more to say about the content of the interview when dealing with specific student problems in a later section. Let us now turn to a discussion of method.

Certain suggestions found in the literature regarding adequate interviewing procedure and techniques are briefly listed in outline form here:[7]

1. Planning for the interview:
    a. Provide a quiet place, free from distractions and the presence of other individuals.
    b. Gather, before the first meeting, as much evidence as possible regarding the counselee. The counselor should have rather complete knowledge of the student and his developmental history before he meets him for the guidance interview.
    c. Attempt some estimate of the problem from the available information.
    d. Plan the interview as far as it is feasible. This does not mean that the program should be formulated as early as this, since the interview, to fulfill its function, must avoid stereotyped action and, instead, become a creative experience for both counselor and counselee. In some cases, pertinent questions may be jotted down and possible suggestions kept in mind. Everything is tentative at this point. A new structure should rise upon foundations laid earlier.
2. Initiating the interview:
    a. Unless rapport is established, no interview can be successful. The counselor must take the responsibility here and adapt his methods to the personality of the student. Usually a good method is to provide an atmosphere of leisure. Allow the student to adjust to

[7] Certain suggestions have been cited in the Sturtevant and Hayes article; in W. V. Bingham and B. V. Moore, *How to Interview*, New York: Harper & Brothers, 1931; and in P. M. Symonds, *Diagnosing Personality and Conduct*, New York: D. Appleton-Century Company, Inc., 1931.

the new situation and to the personality of the counselor before touching on the student's problems. Minutes spent at the beginning of the interview may save hours of ineffectual efforts to be of service. The counselor may make the introductory remarks, at the same time aiming to gain the confidence of the student. These remarks should avoid any mention of a problem or situation which may be emotionally toned from the point of view of the student. A pleasant association is certain to start off the interview happily. Every effort should be made to put the interviewee at ease and to make him willing to talk over his problems.
   b. Attempt to take the student's point of view. Adapt your technique to the particular temperament of the student.
   c. Do not ask direct questions until it is evident that the student is ready to give the information.
3. Interviewing techniques:
   a. Begin with the student's chief interest and make this the cornerstone of subsequent conversation and planning.
   b. Attempt to determine the essential problems as early as possible.
   c. Listen to the student's story, helping him to supplement omitted pertinent facts and to keep the conversation directed on the subject. In short, be a good listener. The interviewer should refrain from registering surprise or shock at anything the student may say.
   d. Avoid the role of teacher. Put yourself on a level with the student, evidencing a sincere interest and faith in him.
   e. Be straightforward and frank and avoid the "Pollyanna" attitude.
   f. Help the student to face the facts unemotionally.
   g. Stimulate self-examination and self-appraisal. Probably the greatest service which can be rendered the student is that of presenting him with a clear and sound picture of himself, his aptitudes, abilities, interests, personality traits and motives.
   h. Attempt to get at the facts, to distinguish the relevant from the irrelevant and to see relationships.

i. Present the facts in such a way that the student may see them objectively. Open to the student a vision of the way he is going.
  j. Avoid deflation. When ambitions are out of line with abilities or opportunities, attempt a redirection of purposes to a channel which will yield substitute satisfactions.
  k. Let the suggested plans for action be those of the student, logical outcomes of a mutual seeking for the solution. The interview should invariably lead to some plan of action, although this may be only a first step in the solution of the particular problem for which the student desired consultation. The person who seeks advice usually does so because he wants to do something about a situation which he feels he cannot meet entirely alone. Action is more comfortable than indecision.
  l. Make suggestions which are specific rather than general. Suggest a particular social activity, for example, taking place at a specified time in a particular place. Avoid a suggestion that the student "should take part in more social activities."
4. Supplementing the interview: During the progress of the interview it usually becomes evident that some additional information is necessary before any program can be formulated. This information may be of different kinds:
  a. The interviewer should check with others who know the student in regard to his personality traits, interests, etc.
  b. The counselor may be asked questions regarding occupations, educational facilities or extra-curricular opportunities which he is unable to answer before further investigation.
  c. Medical or psychiatric examinations may appear desirable before intelligent advice can be given.
  d. A further check regarding grades received in elementary school, high school or college may be needed.
  e. A check with the Confidential Social Service Exchange regarding the student's contacts with social agencies in his home community may be indispensable in certain cases.
  f. Additional test results may be necessary. In these cases, it behooves the counselor to explain their purpose

so that the rapport which he has established will be carried over into the test situation, thereby increasing the chances for reliable results. The student should be told that the results of questionnaires regarding his interests, ambitions and attitudes, and tests of his native gifts and achievements will furnish additional insight into his present status and educational and vocational possibilities. He should be made to understand that they provide additional information, helpful in formulating a program. He should not be led to believe that they alone will tell the type of work best adapted to his needs. He should be informed not to expect a "pass" or "fail" mark in any, since low marks on some tests actually have significance for some occupations and are assets rather than liabilities. The fact should be stressed that the aim is to discover high points in the individual's make-up, in order to capitalize on them in choosing courses and in determining the most suitable occupational field. He should be urged to do his best on aptitude and achievement tests, knowing that he will be higher in some than in others. He should also be persuaded to answer personality tests with complete frankness, so that neither he nor the counselor will be misled.
5. Terminating the interview: The termination of the interview should be tactful but definite. It should be preceded by a brief summary of the discussion to insure that counselor and student are in accord in understanding the mutually arrived-at program. It should never be left up in the air, without definite understanding as to next steps to take on the plan of action.
6. Recording the results of the interview: Immediately following the interview, the facts should be recorded to insure an accurate account for future reference.

THE FACULTY COUNSELOR'S DIAGNOSTIC ROLE IN MENTAL HYGIENE

The following quotation will serve to introduce this discussion:

Colleges have utterly failed if they have merely imparted information and a semblance of wisdom, and have neglected the emotional lives and the conflicts of the students who pass through their halls. If college is to prepare adequately for life, measures should be taken to see that the students are mentally adapted to life as it is, instead of graduating *cum laude* and *cum* also bitterness, cynicism, inadequacy, emotionalism, paranoidism, and shoddy idealism.[8]

In this field the sins of the school are mainly those of omission. It has failed to recognize incipient personality maladjustments. Educators must take the responsibility for early diagnosis of emotional difficulties, in order that treatment may be of some assistance in effecting that ideal of complete adjustment of the individual to the environment which should be the highest aim of education.

The school situation in many cases provides the exciting causes for emotional disturbances and mental breakdowns which might never have occurred in a more protected environment. Tendencies toward moodiness, self-pity, feelings of inferiority and frustration find a fertile field here.

In many instances, the cause of difficulties lies in the frustration of drives which are so precious a part of the natural equipment of the individual. The student may not be finding satisfactions for his drives for love, companionship and approval. He may overwork one type of activity in order to compensate for the lack of expression of other impulses. The frenzy of extracurricular activities in which some students engage is a typical instance. The student who substitutes intellectual achievement for other blocked avenues of activity and expression is another example. The "dateless" girl and boy are probably far more numerous than most counselors realize and it usually requires some startling revelations, such as were made known in a study of student participation in social and extra-curricular activities at the University of Minnesota, before the administration becomes concerned.[9] Counselors must consider the whole person in order to effect satisfactory adjustments and assist students to make the most of the opportunities offered by the school. The girl or boy who is eager for some social good times and who fails to find opportunities is liable to develop some quirks of personality. One person may react by neglect of studies, or by construction of

[8] LAIRD, DONALD, "Case Studies in the Mental Problems of Later Adolescence with Special Reference to the Mental Hygiene of the College Student," *Mental Hygiene*, 1923, 7: 715–733.

[9] BROWN, CLARA M., "A Social-activities Survey," *J. of Higher Education*, 1937, 8: 257–265.

a world of fancy and day-dreams, while another may bend these surplus energies into excessive participation in activities or study. Counselors recognize the picture of the "dateless" girl who becomes the "intellectual snob."

A rather pitiable example at the college level is presented by the small-town football hero and idol who succeeds in making only the third or fourth "string" in college and who means nothing more to the campus than the ungainly student that he is. How natural for him to day-dream of stadium throngs cheering his feats of strategy and strength!

There should be no need to enumerate further cases, such as these, who have developed unfortunate traits because natural drives have been deprived of expression. The counselor is dealing with them daily.

These are rather minor emotional disturbances and may be classed together with other problems, such as worry over a home situation, studies, etc. In many such cases the understanding counselor is an adequate diagnostician and often a father confessor and healing practitioner as well. When the cause of the difficulty is evident and on the surface, the psychiatrist's assistance may not be necessary, if the counselor is able to manipulate the environment in such a way as to eliminate the primary causes and bring the student face to face with the situation in a way to lead toward intelligent, rather than emotional, reactions.

Other personality problems range in seriousness from fluctuations in moods to the degenerating mental diseases which are found only occasionally in the school population. For this more serious group, the attention of the psychiatrist is essential. The counselor should be constantly on the alert to detect these more serious disorders, which only trained psychiatrists should diagnose and treat. *The lay person must recognize his inability to diagnose or treat these cases of difficult personality adjustment.* In most cases improvement results from psychiatric consultation, treatment and modified habits of living. For a few cases of long standing, where conflict is deep-seated or dissociation of the personality progressive, even the psychiatrist may be powerless to effect a cure. At any rate, it is essential that incipient cases be discovered early, in order that the disease may not obtain too firm a foothold in disrupting the integrated personality.

It is impossible to attempt a description here of the many forms in which maladjustments become manifest in these disorders. The literature is rich with case histories, classifications and descriptions. Counselors often ask for suggestions of signs by which they may come to recognize students who are in need of psychiatric service. Psychiatrists have been reluctant to formulate specific statements, rightly contending that the lay person cannot be taught how to diagnose cases and interpret behavior in a few simple lessons. Medical, psychiatric and psychological training is necessary for adequate diagnosis and treatment in this difficult field.

Any suggestions as to symptoms of emotional disturbance would be partial and inadequate. Since they may be of some value to the counselor, however, in calling to mind some of the symptoms which might otherwise be overlooked, a list has been prepared and is here included, so that faculty counselors may be on the lookout for types of behavior calling for referral to the school psychiatrist. The presence or absence of the symptom itself is not so important as the degree to which it is displayed. Moodiness, for example, ranges all the way from normal ups and downs in temperament, which are natural results of the physical and physiological state of the organism, to marked cycles of melancholia and elation, which are typical of the serious manic-depressive psychoses. The presence of a trait in the list which we have prepared does not necessarily indicate mental ill health. We know how slight is the distinction between normality and abnormality and that these traits characterize the abnormal only as they diverge from the normal in intensity or degree.

The school psychiatrist should be connected with the school health service, so that students will come to consider his services a part of other physical health services which are accepted without emotional behavior. Despite this fact, many students retain a fear of anyone who may attempt to probe into their feelings and complexes. For this reason it is particularly necessary that extreme tact be used in suggesting that the psychiatrist be consulted. Students should be given some conception as to what to expect in this often dreaded interview. They deserve a straightforward but tactful statement regarding reasons for referral and benefits which may be expected. It is possible to tell the student that he is being referred because the counselor feels that a medical man should discuss with him certain general principles of mental hygiene which are important for students to know and practice. In cases where the student has already evidenced a desire to talk about such difficulties with the counselor, it is a simple matter to suggest an appointment with a person better equipped than the counselor to advise. In any event, it is well to avoid such terms as psychiatrist, insanity, mental disorder, psychosis, abnormal psychology and other technical terms suggestive of serious mental difficulties. It is better to use such terms as mental hygiene expert, physician who understands personality problems of students, emotional difficulties, etc.

Referral for a physical examination may be more direct and straightforward in most cases. When the health service record is not recent, it may be desirable to obtain another examination, especially when symptoms indicate a change in condition from that previously reported. An apparent general run-down condition which seems to be a factor in the student's school adjustment often needs further investigation, in order that an adequate diagnosis may be made and treatment followed. Questions relative to future occupational adjustment may require a medical check before vocational recommendations are applicable. A medical diagnosis and consulting medical service are essential in any well-rounded counseling program.

BEHAVIOR SYMPTOMS INDICATING POSSIBLE NEED FOR REFERRING STUDENTS TO A MENTAL HYGIENE EXPERT[10]

I. *Motor Disturbances*

Has facial tics and grimaces
Is given to frequent spells of dizziness
Experiences nausea and nervous indigestion
Faints frequently
Has severe shaking spells
Has spells of weakness
Has cold sweats
Constantly feels extremely tense
Has had convulsions
Has had St. Vitus Dance

[10] Grateful acknowledgment is hereby made to Charles Bird for assistance in compiling this list.

Stutters
Has temper tantrums
Is extremely distractible

II. *False Beliefs*

Feels that the world is against him
Feels that he is being watched, followed, talked about
Has exaggerated notions of his importance
Feels that life is very unreal

III. *Exaggerated Traits Having Personal Reference*

A. *Attitudes:*
  Complains of lack of sleep
  Has marked tendencies to withdraw within his own shell
  Complains often of bodily illness
  Feels lonely even when in the presence of other persons
  Has many fears and anxieties
  Worries over mental health
  Has irrational fears (of the dark, high places, open spaces, etc.)
  Worries excessively
  Experiences extreme ups and downs of mood
  Belittles own achievements excessively
  Is constantly concerned with sex problems
  Complains of extreme exhaustion

B. *Modes of Conduct:*
  Exaggerates activity in one field to the exclusion of other interests
  Has occasional attacks of somnambulism ("sleep walking; automatic and stereotyped conduct; loss of memory with consciousness of surroundings")
  Spends much time in day-dreaming
  Has experienced a nervous breakdown
  Works spasmodically and irregularly
  Cannot concentrate on the task in hand
  Hears voices and sees visions
  Possesses irresistible impulses (to scream, strike someone, etc.)
  Has at some time lost memory completely
  Frequently experiences nightmares
  Is bothered by useless thoughts

IV. *Exaggerated Traits Having Social Reference*

A. *Attitudes:*
  Is suspicious of the intentions or statements of other persons
  Assumes a "hard-boiled" attitude
  Exhibits extreme reticence
  Manifests extreme prudery
  Is touchy on various subjects
  Often expresses contempt for existing institutions and has a marked preference for one system of government or one institution

B. *Modes of conduct:*
   Is loud in his criticisms of others
   Invariably seeks the center of the stage
   Affects a peculiar gait or manner of speaking
   Is aggressive, domineering, dogmatic and supercilious
   Is constantly blaming others for his own inadequacies
   Often rationalizes or seeks to explain his conduct
   Is shy, bashful, and prefers to be alone
   Is irritable without apparent cause
   Is extremely suggestible
   Is easily moved to tears
   Avoids the opposite sex
   Shows extreme hatreds
   Exhibits many petty jealousies
   Cooperates only under constraint
   Does not accept criticism graciously

CUMULATIVE RECORDS

In introducing this topic, it is desirable to state why it is necessary to develop cumulative records as a basic tool in guidance counseling. In the first place, all data used in diagnosing students' problems have restricted reliability and validity. That is, a single impression, rating, report, test or interview, is not sufficiently reliable to permit completely valid diagnosis. Moreover, the statistical weight of many such items has not been determined. Hence, the counselor must use his best judgment as to the diagnostic significance of any particular combination of facts. To increase the validity of such a judgment, it is necessary that all available data be combined in a clinical synthesis, one fact being supplemented by another so as to yield the highest possible accuracy in diagnosis.

Moreover, the dynamic and changing character of pupils makes it improbable that single facts regarding any important characteristic will have continued validity. For example, a student's attitude does not remain the same over a period of years. Hence, it is necessary to record changes by the test technique or by the judgment method. This year's data may lack significance next year in many, but not necessarily all, cases. Pupils grow and change and these changes must be recorded, particularly those changes having to do with increased subject-matter competence, as well as with social and emotional adjustments. Thus, the continuous recording of data provides correctives for faulty diagnoses made earlier. There is also general agreement that diagnoses are improved by basing them on records of long-time exhibition of characteristics. For example, a four-year record of social timidity in high school is more significant than the first impressions of a counselor.

Other reasons for recording case data systematically may be mentioned. Any fact has more meaning and significance when it is interpreted in the light of adequate case data as a background; that is, an I.Q. has more meaning when a counselor understands the family background and developmental history of the student. A further advantage of cumulative records is found in the fact that the counselor, can save time for himself, as well as for the student, by being spared the necessity for asking numerous questions the answers to which are already recorded. Thus the interview can be devoted to diagnosis and counseling and not to inquisition. Another advantage arises because cumulative records make it unnecessary for a counselor to depend upon vague recollections of previous interviews. Because of the above reasons, each school system should install a system involving the cumulative recording of significant facts about students. The counselor should review these cumulative records before attempting to interpret any single item, whether it be a temper tantrum or a failure in algebra.

The most helpful single source of information in regard to the guidance value of cumulative records and techniques for developing them is found in the First Report of the Committee on Personnel Methods of the American Council on Education.[11] The first chapter of this report devotes 56 pages to the discussion of the need for such records and to a description of the construction and use of a model Cumulative Record Card. Many elementary and secondary schools, as well as colleges, have installed such a record card, adapting it to meet local needs.

This card consists of a record form printed on a manila folder, 8½ by 11 inches in size, which provides for summarizing, filing

[11] Chapter I, The Personal Record Card, pp. 1–56, from *Measurement and Guidance of College Students*, *First Report of the Committee on Personnel Methods*, published for the American Council on Education by Williams & Wilkins Company, Baltimore, 1933. See also, Margaret W. Moore, *The Cumulative Educational Record Form for Elementary Schools*, American Council on Education, Washington, D.C., 16 pp.

and transferring case data to other counselors and to other school units from the elementary school to the college. Within the folder may be filed loose-leaf correspondence, interview notes and other materials which are later summarized in the proper space in the folder itself. The cumulative record card should follow the student wherever he goes in the educational system.

One important part of the cumulative record card is a gridiron on which may be recorded results of cumulative and comparable testing from the elementary school through the high school and college.

The data should include, not only tests and identifying information, but records of health, social and personal development, teachers' grades and many other outcomes of education which are not now subject to objective measurement. These non-quantitative data often prove to be as important as teachers' grades, and sometimes more important.

It should be noted that the cumulative record is a method for recording data and not a substitute for such data. Actually, inaccurate data may be recorded on this form; the mere act of recording will not improve the validity of the data. The card is useful because it provides a means of recording important information and transferring it to other counselors who have contact with the student. The folder is printed so that there is adequate space for recording comparable data from year to year regarding a student's personal, emotional and school adjustment. These data have been found indispensable in the counseling of students and constitute the permanent summary of their personality development during the years in which they are under observation. The card is not a mechanical substitute for diagnosis and counseling; to yield maximum value, the data must be interpreted by trained workers. Moreover, the recording of data must not be spasmodic, that is, they should never be recorded just once and then used thereafter as though they were equally valid for the succeeding years. It is the continuous recording of data from year to year that makes a cumulative record of increasing significance and value.

Counselors may systematize the collection of interview data for inclusion in the cumulative record by using comprehensive outlines covering the major points that should be considered. The Psychological Corporation has designed an eight-page booklet, called *Aids to the Vocational Interview*, which incorporates the best features of these comprehensive outlines and in addition provides a helpful analysis of abilities in relation to occupations, together with a profile chart for recording the results of a battery of diagnostic tests. The student supplies the information called for, prior to the interview. In this way, interviewing time can be conserved, the interview itself being devoted to a discussion of the significance of the recorded facts.

RECORDING BEHAVIOR ITEMS

A brief review of the development of methods of recording behavior data for guidance purposes will reveal the importance of basing diagnoses on a comprehensive basis of fact and not on one or two "snap-shot" pictures of the individual.

One of the first methods was the rating scale, which is a standardized method of recording *interpretations* of behavior. With this technique, individuals are rated on a scale from low to high with respect to a particular trait. These ratings are, in reality, interpretations based upon observations of an individual. One of the first rating scales was that used by Sir Francis Galton for judging intelligence. One of the next improvements was that of Walter Dill Scott, who devised the *man-to-man* rating scale, each unit or step on this scale being defined in terms of a specific man known to the rater. This was a cumbersome method, but it had the virtue of being based upon concrete evidence or specific instances. It suffered from the weakness of requiring a different scale for every trait and for every rater. A modification was then made by developing the *order-of-merit* scale, in which individuals are ranked in order for each trait. This permitted intra-group comparisons, but was far from being a universal scale.

The next important modification was the *graphic* rating scale in which the traits are defined in terms of behavior. Following each definition a horizontal line permits the location of three or five degrees of the trait, each degree being defined by descriptive adjectives or phrases. After checking each trait, the rater was frequently required to submit a statement of the supporting evidence upon which his judgment was based. The supporting evidence itself is now recognized as being of greater value than the ratings. Thus, increased stress is being placed upon the recording of observations of behavior rather than the recording of inferences drawn from this behavior.

The following principles of rating adapted from Paterson's earlier summary[12] will suggest the care with which ratings must be made if they are to provide reliable and useful information:

1. Records of teachers' estimates of students should be accumulated and filed in advance of any emergency requiring such estimates as a basis of decision.

2. Estimates should be based on types of behavior that are defined unambiguously in advance.

3. Types of behavior to be rated should be defined in objective terms so far as possible and should be grouped according to the accuracy with which they can be judged.

4. Each type of behavior to be rated should refer to one type of activity carried on or to one type of result achieved by those to be rated.

5. Ratings should be confined to past or present accomplishments.

6. The behavior to be rated must be related directly to the type of work performed by those to be rated.

7. The method of recording one's ratings should be easily understood and easily complied with.

8. Estimates should be expressed in a uniform manner by all raters.

9. A statistical method of correcting for any tendency to rate too "high" or too "low" should be employed.

10. Ratings should be accepted and filed for use only from those who have proved themselves to be accurate observers.

11. Each teacher should rate his students on the first type of behavior, then, rearranging the order at random, he should rate them on the second type and so on for the remaining qualities. This will help avoid the "halo" effect in ratings.

12. As many teachers as possible should be employed in rating a given person, and an average of all the available ratings should be used as the index for that person.

Ordway and Laffan,[13] after studying the system of rating efficiency for promotion used by New York City departments,

[12] PATERSON, D. G., "Methods of Rating Human Qualities," *Annals of the American Academy of Political and Social Science*, Publication 1746, November, 1923. See also Chapter IX, Ratings Scale Methods in J. P. Guilford's *Psychometric Methods*, New York: McGraw-Hill Book Company, 1936, for a comprehensive summary of methods and errors in ratings.

[13] ORDWAY, SAMUEL H., JR., and JOHN C. LAFFAN, "Approaches to the Measurement and Reward of Effective Work of Individual Government

conclude that ratings are valuable when "substantiated by detailed evidence," that is, when they are supported by records of accomplishment instead of being mere records of vague personality traits or "mere opinions concerning the conduct or performance of the employee." Therefore, ratings should be accompanied by a detailed statement of the objective evidence on which the rater made his judgment. These authors define objective evidence as follows:

Objectivity is a matter of evidence—the kind of evidence which, in the long practice of the art of legal proof, has come to be surrounded in courts of law by rules which exclude hearsay and conclusions, guesses and suppositions and impressions. Objectivity means that facts are the only bases of values. [The authors go on to say] The subjective conclusion should not be excluded from rating considerations, but the rating should be based on the evidentiary acts and not on the conclusions.

These trends in the recording of judgments about an individual are in line with the development of the American Council on Education Rating Scale for Students, which calls for a summary of case data and observations supporting a rating.[14]

This scale consists of five questions derived from an analysis by W. E. Parker of 1000 forms and 100 questions used by 78 colleges in collecting information on personality traits of students. There is no provision for recording observations in regard to scholastic aptitude and scholastic achievement, because these data should be obtained through actual tests and measurements.

This rating scale, which may be considered the most satisfactory in use today, consists of the following questions:

1. How do his manner and appearance affect others?
2. Does he need constant prodding, or does he go ahead with his work without being told?
3. Does he get others to do what he wishes?
4. How does he control his emotions?
5. Has he a program with definite purposes in terms of which he distributes his time and energy?

Employees," *Supplement to National Municipal Rev.*, October, 1935, Vol. XXIV, No. 10.

[14] HAWKES, H. E., *Measurement and Guidance of College Students*, Chapter III, Personality Measurement, Baltimore: Williams & Wilkins Company, 1933.

STUDENT GUIDANCE TECHNIQUES

REVISION A, MAY 9, 1929
AMERICAN COUNCIL ON EDUCATION
744 JACKSON PLACE, WASHINGTON, D. C.

PERSONALITY REPORT

The information on this sheet is confidential

Name of student............................Name of institution....................

Please return this sheet to..

Selection and guidance of students are based on scholastic records of achievement, health and other factual records. Personality, difficult to evaluate, is of great importance. You will greatly assist in the education of the student named if you will rate him with respect to each question by placing a check mark on the appropriate horizontal line at any point which represents your evaluation of the candidate.

If you have had no opportunity to observe the student with respect to a given characteristic, please place a check mark in the space at the extreme right of the line.

In the rectangle below each rating scale please describe briefly and concretely significant performances and attitudes which support your judgment and which you yourself have observed.

Let your statements answer specifically the questions of the rating scale by showing how the student manifested the qualities mentioned.

Do not be satisfied with the statement of an opinion concerning matters of fact, if the facts themselves can be presented.

Select those illustrations of conduct which are consistent with the personality of the student as you have observed and understood it.

Bear in mind that from as many accurate observers as possible the college desires to secure concrete descriptions of the student's personality as exhibited in many situations and that the purpose is an understanding of the student's personality as a whole so that he and all concerned with his education may guide his development to the highest.

The following items illustrate the way in which observers have reported evidence in support of their checking of the highest answer to the second question (B):

Of a college senior: "In my course in Elizabethan drama he voluntarily built to scale models of the Blackfriars Theater and the Fortune Theater based on the work of Chambers, Albright and others and demonstrated Elizabethan methods of staging several of the plays read."

Of a college senior: "Independently collected and classified correctly one hundred type specimens of fossils found in the neighborhood of the college."

Of an eighth grade boy: "Finding in English assignment, the introduction to Burns' 'The Cotter's Saturday Night,' a reference to Robert Fergusson's 'The Farmer's Ingle' as a possible inspiration of Burns' poem, he looked up Fergusson's poem in the home library and compared it with that of Burns. At the same time, desiring to read Burns in the Scottish way he mastered the phonetic system of Sir James Wilson's 'The Dialect of Robert Burns as spoken in Central Ayrshire' which he also found in the home library, and so interested the boys of his class in the pronunciation of Scottish words that even at the end of the year the lads still called each other by appropriate Scottish nicknames and used Scotticisms which they found in Burns and Wilson."

"At the age of eleven began collecting diatoms from local ponds and streams and studying their forms under his own microscope. Now possesses collection of microscope slides, including some presented to him by scientists in Department of Agriculture and Carnegie Institution, specimens collected by Shackleton, Scott and other expeditions."

How well do you know this student?..

....
....
....

Signature   Date   Position   Address

FIG. 1.

DIAGNOSTIC TECHNIQUES

Name of student..

A. How are you and others affected by his appearance and manner?

| Avoided by others | Tolerated by others | Liked by others | Well liked by others | Sought by others | No opportunity to observe |

Please record here instances that support your judgment.

B. Does he need constant prodding or does he go ahead with his work without being told?

| Needs much prodding in doing ordinary assignments | Needs occasional prodding | Does ordinary assignments of his own accord | Completes suggested supplementary work | Seeks and sets for himself additional tasks |

Please record here instances that support your judgment.

C. Does he get others to do what he wishes?

| Probably unable to lead his fellows | Lets others take lead | Sometimes leads in minor affairs | Sometimes leads in important affairs | Displays marked ability to lead his fellows; makes things go |

Please record here instances that support your judgment.

D. How does he control his emotions?

| Too easily moved to anger or fits of depression, etc. | Tends to be over emotional | | | |
| Unresponsive, apathetic | Tends to be unresponsive | Usually well balanced | Well balanced | Unusual balance of responsiveness and control |

Please record here instances that support your judgment.

E. Has he a program with definite purposes in terms of which he distributes his time and energy?

| Aimless trifler | Aims just to "get by" | Has vaguely formed objectives | Directs energies effectively with fairly definite program | Engrossed in realizing well formulated objectives |

Please record here instances that support your judgment.

FIG. 2.

Because of the usefulness of this type of scale in student personnel work, it is reproduced in full as Fig. 1.

The most recent method developed for recording significant data not amenable to testing is called the Anecdotal Method of Recording Qualitative Data. This method calls for recording observations by the teachers of what the pupil does within or outside the classroom. The teacher records on a slip of paper significant behavior which she has observed. No interpretations and no inferences should be included and the teacher is warned to avoid the use of ambiguous, vacuous and stereotyped personality terms. In other words, she is asked to record just what she sees and hears, nothing more. This is a most important technique whereby teachers can contribute to guidance their observations which accumulate while teaching. Every guidance worker recognizes that teachers do observe many significant things happening in the school, but it has been very difficult to get teachers to report these facts to the counselor so that they might be integrated with the counselor's information.

These slips of paper with a single anecdote on them should be turned in at the central school office and filed in the cumulative record folder for each pupil. Periodically these anecdotes are abstracted, briefed and summarized in a special place on the cumulative record form.

Essential features of the anecdotal method of recording personal data have been summarized by Wood[15] as follows:

1. The observation of significant conduct and behavior by all teachers which directs the attention away from the mere teaching of facts.

2. Recording these significant observations on a sheet of paper and sending to central office for summarizing and recording on cumulative record form. At first it is suggested that each teacher try to record one anecdote a week.

3. Teachers should record every instance of behavior which attracts attention both favorable and unfavorable or which seems characteristic or even atypical of the pupil. Practice alone will show what is significant, particularly when these anecdotes are discussed in the weekly staff clinic and lined up with all other case data.

4. Teachers are asked to make these concrete anecdotes with no interpretation or coloring. Facts are a more helpful basis for diagnosis than are mere inferences.

[15] WOOD, BEN D., "The Major Strategy of Guidance," see pp. 38, 68, 101, etc., *The Educational Record*, 1934.

DIAGNOSTIC TECHNIQUES

5. Periodic staff clinics should be held for each pupil—to present, review, analyze, synthesize and diagnose or interpret all case data. At these clinics, teachers, administrators and guidance workers all participate in the process of simplifying all the case data. It is at this point that anecdotes are seen to fill the gaps in data and to check the guidance worker's diagnosis.

These three methods of recording and using counseling records, namely, the cumulative record, the rating scale and the anecdotal method, provide not only means of filling gaps in the case record, but also are convenient ways of summarizing information to be passed on to other counselors, thereby making for improved accuracy of diagnosis.

MEASUREMENTS AND NORMS

The term "individual differences" has become so firmly established in the vocabulary of present-day progressive educators that it is difficult to imagine a time when the student was not recognized in terms of the qualities and characteristics which set him apart from his fellows. Selected though a school group may be in relation to the general population, the tremendous differences among its members—differences in interests, ambitions, intelligence, special abilities, personality traits, drive, energy, etc.—are constantly apparent to most teachers who recognize the inadequacy of a two-category classification with respect to intelligence alone. These gross differences have always been present, but their significance was never so clearly defined as at present. "Individualization" is education's byword today. We hear on every hand the plea for the individualization of the curriculum. We must fit the school to the needs of the student, rather than the student to the school. "Learn the student as well as teach him," is the slogan as Ben D. Wood has phrased it. The school's reason for existence is the individual student and the school's program should be evaluated in terms of its ability to meet his needs and render service to him.

The recognition of this basic concept of individual differences has now been attained and is at present enjoying deserved consideration. The next step is to know the student better. Fitting the curriculum to the pupil presupposes an understanding of that pupil. We must recognize, not only that individual differences exist, but that these differences must be measured. Dean

Johnston,[16] when discussing "The Liberal College in a Changing Society," stressed the responsibility of the college toward understanding its students and measuring their characteristics, both native and acquired. He lists several duties of the educational system:

1. To give a richness of experience
2. To recognize individuality
3. To introduce means to discover abilities, aptitudes, personality traits, interests, etc.
4. To devise forms of educational experience
5. To measure abilities and achievements by periodical examinations

Concrete instances of attempts to individualize instruction at the University of Minnesota are numerous, an outstanding example being the University College, which was set up to provide individualized curricula for students whose educational needs are not met by existing curricula. This new departure was conceived as a method for meeting students' needs which had formerly been subordinated to the rigid requirements of the standardized curriculum. These needs were now to be considered foremost. Had the college gone no farther, its purpose would have been fulfilled only in part. The next step was to obtain a better insight into the problems, the interests, the capacities and the achievements of its students. Consequently, it has become a practice to refer these students to the University Testing Bureau in order that the educational program might be planned in harmony with their diagnosed needs and abilities.

Guidance, which should embrace educational, vocational and personal guidance, and which should be integrated with the whole educational system, should serve the individual in at least three respects. In the first place, it should enable him to obtain as objective and as clear a picture of himself as modern scientific techniques and the ingenuity of educators, counselors and special advisers are able to portray. Secondly, it should make known to him the opportunities, educational, vocational and social, which are at hand in the school environment and those existing beyond its doors. In the third place, it should attempt to guide him toward those opportunities which are available and

[16] JOHNSTON, J. B., "The Guidance Function in the Secondary Schools and Colleges," *The Educational Record*, 1933, 14: 49–62.

appropriate to his particular needs and capacities. To be adequate, guidance must follow the individual along, assisting him in his continuous process of adjustment.

The present discussion will be limited to a general description of methods and techniques which may be utilized to obtain a picture of the student.

Many efforts which have been made to understand the student have been largely subjective and it is only recently that quantitative measurement of the student has been attempted. "Mental Tests" were introduced by Cattell as early as 1890 to measure characteristics of college students and great strides in this new science have been taken since that early date. In our enthusiasm for these newer techniques, we should not lose sight of the older worth-while methods which still serve to fill in the total picture. Neither should we be overanxious to apply devices merely because they yield quantitative results. A test which yields inconsistent results or which measures something the significance of which is not known may be poorer than no measurement. It is doubtful whether the time will come when the individual, as complex as he is, will be measurable entirely in quantitative terms. The amount of data at present expressible only qualitatively will undoubtedly be reduced, but there may always remain aspects of the individual which are not objectively describable. The concept of a machine capable of grinding out involved statistics predicting the specific occupational field best suited to the individual, all of whose characteristics have been determined, is too nebulous to interest seriously the present-day counselor, although it may indeed appeal to him as a desirable labor-saving device!

A vast amount of essential data has been and will continue to be ascertained and recorded by means of the interview and record blanks. Needless to say, the amount of pertinent data which may be discovered in this way is dependent upon the skill of the interviewer and the quality of records used.

At the risk of oversimplification, we shall compare the guidance procedure and the use of test results to a person driving to some distant destination. The two points which we wish to make especially are:

1. Tests and guidance are merely aids to travel. They are the signposts and road maps which point the way and eliminate miles of unsure exploration.

2. Guidance is a continuous process en route, rather than an initial push at the beginning or at some place between the starting point and the goal.

Let us compare a person in pursuit of a vocational goal to a young man on a cross-country trip. In the first place, he starts off with a certain amount of native equipment plus the training which he has received up to that point, all of which is represented in his vehicle of travel, which may vary in quality from a "Model T" to the latest streamlined limousine. We know full well that his journey will be affected by the nature of this equipment! Shocks which must be endured by some drivers will scarcely be felt by others. All drivers will have a certain number of obstacles to overcome in the nature of narrow winding mountain roads, ferries, toll bridges, etc., but they will vary in the number of breakdowns and the seriousness of their car troubles. Our driver starts off with some conception of the direction in which he wishes to travel and the goal he plans to attain. This is true, even though he may never have visited this far country before. The locality which he decides to visit will depend upon his present equipment, his information concerning advantages in those parts, and his own particular interests. It is not unlikely that his plans will change en route and that he will decide to stop short of his original goal, or venture farther than he had at first anticipated.

Since our driver is making the trip at the present date, he will be aided along the way by the modern road posts, which give an accurate indication of mileage and direction. Desirous of taking advantage of these aids to travel, he refers to them a great many times during the trip. He would be unwise to examine them only at the starting point or later, after venturing forth without their assistance.

In a long trip, even the best of drivers is apt to deviate from the main route occasionally, either because he neglects to watch the signs or feels that his own intuition or his adviser in the back seat may be relied upon. The good driver will take advantage of these modern methods many times during the journey. When a sign reads, "Shortest route to all points west," he will take the advice seriously, since he realizes it is there to serve his interests. He knows from experience that the other route may be through many small towns, necessitating slow driving. He is careful to heed such notices as "Stop, Look, and Listen," "Slippery pavement," etc. He frequently comes upon a crossroad with signs pointing in many directions. The way he chooses depends upon the goal he has had in mind, as well as upon his past procedure. Without these guides, he is lost, but with them he proceeds upon his way feeling more assurance.

One may be certain that after such modern "road guidance," our driver would be loath to travel again without assistance or to be dependent upon the fancies and well-meant admonitions of a back-seat driver! Tests and measurements in guidance work are the road-sign and road-map equivalents that must now receive our attention.

The Purpose of Tests.—A standardized general test has been defined as "a uniform and predetermined series of tasks or situations, the performance of which has been shown to be in some measure diagnostic of an individual's capacities, attainments or habits in certain general lines."[17] This definition implies that a test is measuring a sample of behavior. The most enthusiastic advocate of tests will admit that the surest method to determine the individual's ability to succeed is to try him out in the actual situation. The question as to whether a student can grasp the concepts of a course in higher mathematics is answered by his ability to solve the problems of the course. This sure test, however, is not always either economical or practical. A sampling of behavior, requiring minutes rather than months, is often wisest from the point of view of time saved and morale maintained.

A second implication of this definition is that a test may not measure a trait directly, but rather some product, some behavior which is diagnostic of the trait. In the measurement of intelligence, for example, a direct determination is impossible, at least so far as present research has progressed. We do not measure brain weight or the ease with which a stimulus passes through the nervous system. We do not apply a yardstick to "intelligence" itself, but we measure products of that capacity. Generally, these products are things which have been learned, the acquisition of which has been conditioned by the inborn capacity which we call "intelligence." One of the best indications of abstract intelligence is vocabulary, and the measurement of the

[17] GOODENOUGH, F. L., and J. E. ANDERSON, *Experimental Child Study*, Chapter XLVI, New York: D. Appleton-Century Company, Inc., 1931.

extent of the individual's vocabulary is considered a good indirect measure of his verbal intelligence, provided, of course, that his opportunities for acquiring words have been equal to those of persons with whom he is being compared. Differences which exist among those who have had equal opportunities are taken to be representative of differences in innate ability. One can see chances for error in such an assumption, of course. Some differences may be due to causes other than "intelligence." Interest, physical energy, etc., may be partial determiners of the final result. This is one of the reasons why we cannot expect perfect agreement between tests and other criteria.

Tests may be compared with every-day methods for determining the degree to which an individual possesses a certain trait. An interview, for example, is in a certain sense a test, though unstandardized. Its purpose is to obtain an indication of the individual's behavior, general intelligence, personality and appearance. The interviewer obtains some rough measure of the extent to which the interviewee differs from people in general in respect to certain traits. The difficulty, however, is that he is very apt to be influenced by personal prejudices and the "halo effect." If the person interviewed has a pleasing appearance and personality, our estimation of his general intelligence and even aptitudes and achievements is likely to be too generous.

A test differs from an interview in that it is more standardized. One of the most widely used individual tests of general intelligence, the Stanford-Binet, resembles an interview but it is an improvement over the latter because of its rigid standardization.

In many cases the interview should be supplemented by tests which differ from it in a number of respects:[18]

1. The test situation is more controlled and is standard for all who are subjected to it.

2. The sample of behavior measured by a test is the same for all individuals.

3. Test results are judged according to the same standards for all. A scoring key cannot possibly be prejudiced against a bright young boy merely because he has not had the required number of years in school, which many are inclined to believe is the best indication of intelligence.

[18] See GOODENOUGH and ANDERSON, *op. cit.*

4. The test results stand as they have been originally set down. They do not change according to the memory of the interviewer or the general affective tone created by the interview.

5. Samples of behavior in different fields may be measured according to the test chosen. Without objective measuring sticks, the interviewer is unable to determine correctly specific aptitudes and achievements. Tests possessing only fair degrees of reliability and validity are superior to traditional, subjective methods as indicators of these traits.

The main purpose of tests is to enable more effective long-time planning for the individual. They provide a retrospective view of the past, a measurement of the present and an insight into the future achievements and capacities of the individual. This method is objective and standardized and supplies information not gained by traditional methods.

If a test could perform no other service than to measure present status, its contribution would undoubtedly be still too significant to be disregarded. To take an extreme and unlikely case for an example, if we could have less assurance than we have at present regarding the stability of a child's intelligence, if the chances were even that it would vary from normality to near feeble-mindedness over a period of years, yet knowledge of the status at the time of measurement would enable the school and the family to make certain adjustments in accordance with such insight, even though extensive planning for the future would be unwise.

The measurement of present achievement is to a considerable extent a measure of the results of learning. Such a determination of achievement is helpful in planning an educational program. The counselor will advise the student with unequal achievement in different fields to stress achievement which is highest. *Tests help individuals to visualize their strengths and weaknesses, thus enabling them to capitalize strengths.*

Aptitudes represent an important field for the investigation of present status. True aptitudes are relatively constant. They appear when the trait has matured, and are little affected by training. Usually a single measurement of an aptitude, for mechanical work, clerical work, art or music, is sufficient, if the trait has been given time to appear. Artistic aptitude seems to develop somewhat later than musical talent, for example, but both appear to remain relatively constant throughout the individual's life.

Besides the measurement of present status, tests enable us to measure growth. This concept has been often overlooked by educators and counselors. One dose of testing has been administered at certain "crises" in the life of the individual, usually at the completion of the eighth grade, the junior high school or the senior high school. These were the "jumping-off-places," periods when so-called guidance and tests were administered in an effort to make some plan to meet a particular crisis. The determination of aptitude for college work has been too much of this nature, "a single nervous act rather than a continuous progressive guidance of individuals into types of activities which best suit their capacities and needs,"[19] as Ben D. Wood has expressed it. *Tests should bring cumulative evidence to bear upon the individual's needs, capacities, interests and achievements.* A cross section of those needs at one particular time in the person's life is insufficient. Counselors will be of greater service in proportion to their knowledge and correct interpretation of the individual's past accomplishments and growth over a period of time. This calls for repeated testing and continuous counseling.

Another purpose of testing is to predict future behavior. Upon the assumption that intelligence and special aptitudes remain fairly constant, we are able to predict future behavior and to plan a course of action, over a period of time, which will lead to a specific goal in keeping with an individual's psychological, physical and social equipment.

Description of Tests.—The external form of the various tests requires little explanation. Most standardized tests are of the objective type, minimizing the necessity for interpretation on the part of the scoring clerk, and decreasing the time required for administration and scoring. Questions are arranged in different forms, including the multiple-choice, completion, single-word answer, matching, true-false, analogies, etc., types.

Tests now available for use in guidance work may be grouped for practical purposes under several headings, according to the particular traits or characteristics which they measure or uses to which they are put.

[19] WOOD, BEN D., "Basic Considerations in Educational Testing," *Rev. of Educ. Res.*, 1933, 3: 5–20.

1. *Scholastic aptitude*, or "general intelligence" tests, as they are often called, differ slightly from one another. One of the leading theories of intelligence maintains that it involves ability to think in abstract terms and, since words are the tools with which we think, they have found a prominent place in tests of scholastic aptitude. These tests are, therefore, largely verbal.

Although it is generally considered that these measures test innate capacity rather than achievement, it is difficult to measure general intelligence except as it is manifest in acquired information. T. L. Kelley[20] contends that 90 per cent of what is measured by "intelligence" tests is identical with that which is measured by achievement tests, and vice versa. Under conditions of universal compulsory education opportunity to learn becomes somewhat equalized. Hence, intelligence tests and achievement tests tend to have the same significance.

Scholastic aptitude tests have met with considerable success in enabling school authorities to predict individual school failure. Previous scholarship is a still better index. When a scholastic aptitude test is combined with previous school scholarship, however, the best single source of prediction of college failure is provided. In a study over a four-year period, Johnston and Williamson[21] found that only 4.3 per cent of students with college aptitude ratings below the 26th percentile graduated from the College of Science, Literature, and the Arts, at the University of Minnesota. Other studies with similar tests show correlations between $+.40$ and $+.60$ with school grades. It is improbable that prediction will be much improved beyond this point without measures of school success, which are themselves more reliable and valid than the present criterion of teachers' marks.

2. *Special aptitudes* have come to be recognized fairly recently but comparatively few have been analyzed and subjected to measurement. Among those most commonly thought of are aptitudes for music, art, mechanical work, clerical work and manual activities. Long before they were subjected to measurement, specific aptitudes were recognized as existing apart from

---

[20] KELLEY, T. L., *Interpretation of Educational Measurements*, Yonkers-on-Hudson, New York: World Book Company, 1927.

[21] JOHNSTON, J. B., and E. G. WILLIAMSON, "A Follow-up Study of Early Scholastic Predictions in the University of Minnesota," *School and Soc.*, 1934, 40: 730–738.

general intelligence. They have been called "talents" and "gifts," the implication being that they are part of one's natural inheritance in addition to general intelligence. Persons are differentiated by these specific factors which vary from one person to another and which are responsible not only for differences between individuals, but for trait differences in the same individual. These special characteristics are found in varying degrees and combinations in the same person. Hence, they are of great importance in vocational guidance and selection. Fortunately, occupations demand different combinations of traits. *The task is to bring together the individual possessing a particular pattern of aptitudes and characteristics and the type of work requiring a similar pattern.* To date, there has been substantial progress made in the attempt to discover "occupational ability patterns."[22]

Fundamentally, psychologists agree that special aptitudes exist, although their theories may appear to disagree. Spearman's followers refer to "specific factors" while Thorndike, Hull, Kelley and others consider them "unique traits." They are "unique" in that they are relatively independent of other traits which the individual may possess. There is only a slight positive correlation between most traits, although persons with high aptitudes in one line tend to possess above-average talent in others. An intellectually feeble person possessing artistic talent would be the exception rather than the rule.

Kelley's analyses of the interrelations of mental abilities lead him to posit the following "group factors" as basic in mental organization: verbal intelligence; numerical ability; ability to deal with spatial relations, motor abilities, musical talent, social intelligence, mechanical ability, interests and physical strength.[23] Thurstone's work in factor analysis is equally noteworthy and his announcement of the experimental isolation of seven primary abilities has aroused widespread interest.[24] These seven primary

[22] DVORAK, B. J., *Differential Occupational Ability Patterns, Bulletins of the Employment Stabilization Research Institute* 1935, Vol. 3, No. 8, Minneapolis: University of Minnesota Press.

[23] KELLEY, T. L., *Cross-roads in the Mind of Man*, Stanford, California: Stanford University Press, 1928; and *Essential Mental Traits*, Cambridge, Massachusetts: Harvard University Press, 1935.

[24] THURSTONE, L. L., *The Vectors of Mind*, Chicago: University of Chicago Press, 1935; and "The Factorial Isolation of Primary Abilities," *Psychometrika*, 1936, 1: 175–182.

abilities were disclosed by an elaborate experiment in which a battery of 56 pencil-and-paper tests requiring 15 hours of testing time was given to 240 student volunteers at the University of Chicago. These primary abilities are as follows:

N = number factor
V = visualizing two- and three-dimensional space
M = memory
W = word facility or fluency
W_2 = verbal relations
P = perceptual speed
I = induction

The fact that these seven primary abilities were found to be *uncorrelated* in the experimental population indicates the validity of the concept of relatively unique traits. The significance of this finding for purposes of *individual diagnosis* cannot be overemphasized.

Thurstone has completed the preparation of a battery of six test booklets containing 18 subtests which can be scored in such a way as to provide a *standard score* for each subject in each of the seven primary abilities. Provision is made for recording the results on a graph so as to yield a psychograph, or profile, for each examinee. The time required for all 18 tests will be approximately 3 hours. A limited research edition of the tests will be made available by the American Council on Education for use in 1938.

The practical significance of the Thurstone Battery of Tests for the Measurement of Primary Abilities must await research studies to determine the correlation between each of the Primary Ability Scores and various types of school subject-matter performance and efficiency in various types of occupations.

It would be premature to conclude that this new development in mental measurement has reached the point where we can discard the multiplicity of measuring devices which are described in the remaining chapters of this handbook. Guidance workers will continue to utilize existing measuring techniques but will be ready to utilize the Thurstone tests as a valuable addition to our testing repertoire, as soon as research results can be secured which will disclose the guidance significance of each of the primary abilities as measured. The following quotation concerning factor analysis, as it is being developed by Spearman,

Thorndike, Hotelling, Holzinger, Kelley and Thurstone, is apropos:

> The Committee on Unitary Traits, of which Thorndike is chairman, is carrying on fundamental research of great theoretical importance which may lead to revolutionary changes in the psychological tests and measurements of tomorrow. No counselor who is aware of these pioneering inquiries will dare become satisfied or completely dependent upon existing instruments of psychological diagnosis.[25]

3. *Achievement tests* are of two kinds, those which measure trade proficiency or skill and those which measure educational achievement or knowledge. Neither is able to measure achievement entirely apart from intelligence, which contributes a considerable share toward any achievement-test score. Both aim to determine differences in accomplishment among individuals. The trade-test score reveals to the employer the extent to which the applicant approaches the level of the skilled trades expert. The school-achievement test indicates to the teacher and the counselor differences in amount of acquired knowledge retained by students who have enjoyed approximately equal opportunities for acquiring that information. On the basis of these results, the school is able to place students in sections representing varying degrees of past accomplishment and probable future achievement.

The present status of students in any field of subject-matter knowledge can be determined by achievement tests. Inferences regarding their capacities cannot be made directly from the achievement-test scores, however, unless each has had a similar opportunity for acquiring the knowledge called for by the test. When past opportunities have been dissimilar, interpretation of differences in scores becomes more difficult.

The student who has had no formal training in higher mathematics but who makes an average score on an achievement test in this subject presumably has "studied on his own" and probably possesses intellectual and personality traits which account for his unusual achievement. On the other hand, there are students who have studied mathematics for several years in

---

[25] PATERSON, D. G., "Editorial Overview, Symposium on Analysis of the Individual," *Occupations, The Vocational Guidance Magazine*, April, 1934, p. 6.

formal courses but who make below-average scores when tested. These failures may be due to lack of capacity or mathematical aptitude or to other difficulties, such as lack of interest in mathematics, lack of adequate study habits, etc.

Besides their assistance in placing students in groups of like accomplishments, achievement-test results are significant in individual guidance, since they point out strong points to be capitalized. High achievement along certain lines may suggest fields for major concentration. These tests indicate what the individual has actually achieved and suggest those areas in which he is likely to make the greatest progress.

Achievement tests measure aspects of the individual which grow. Achievement varies from time to time in the same person. *By tapping these achievements at different times it becomes possible to obtain a picture of development and it is this developmental story which is so essential to an understanding of the individual.* Because measurements of development are important, it is essential that they be reliable. The unreliability of teachers' marks is now generally recognized. It is conceivable that comprehensive and carefully standardized achievement tests may some day be substituted for teachers' estimates and unstandardized tests. Until that day arrives, however, we have available excellent achievement tests for many courses and counselees may be compared in achievement with others and with their own records at different times.

4. *Interest inventories* are generally of the questionnaire form and are composed of numerous items, lists of occupations, school subjects, recreational and other activities to each of which the individual responds by indicating whether he likes, dislikes or is indifferent to the item. The greater the number and variety of items included, the more reliable the results will be.

These inventories differ somewhat from tests but they yield quantitative scores and permit comparison of the individual with known curricular, occupational and professional groups. Successful persons in the same occupation exhibit a characteristic pattern of likes and dislikes, whereas persons in different occupations have been found to differ in their characteristic pattern of interests. These similarities and differences can now be measured and comparisons can be made between individuals and groups.

Needless to say, such comparisons do not indicate the type of occupation for which the individual is necessarily best adapted, since ability is not measured by interest tests. They indicate the similarity between an individual and any particular occupational group in one respect, namely possession of a characteristic pattern of interests. This is only one indication, but a *significant* one, of the suitability of the individual for the occupation in question. There is no single magical formula which will reveal the ideal occupation for the individual!

The age at which interest-test results are significant varies somewhat among individuals, who differ in the rate at which their interests mature. Results should be significant, however, for many high school students, and for most college students. Some students, unfortunately, are slow in breaking away from adolescent expressions of interests and in developing crystallized vocational-interest patterns. Even in such cases, skillful interpretation of interest blanks may reveal significant trends.

5. *Personality traits* are necessary for success in school or occupation, yet they are most illusive traits to measure. The concentrated effort being brought to bear upon their analysis and objective description will probably be rewarded with more reliable and valid instruments and measurement techniques than we possess at the present writing. The inventories which we have, however, if properly interpreted by those who recognize their distinct limitations, are far better than judgments gained from the interview alone.

Administration and Scoring of Tests.—In describing the tests now in use, we should describe administration techniques and scoring devices.

Tests differ in the way in which they are administered. Some may be given to a group, while others must be administered individually. They may also be classified according to whether or not apparatus is involved. A great many are of the paper-and-pencil variety. Some are speed tests and others are power tests. The Thurstone Psychological Examination is an example of a power test, since there is so liberal an allowance of time that the score indicates the level of difficulty which the individual is able to reach, rather than the number of relatively easy items which he can answer correctly in a limited amount of time. The latter type is called a speed test and is represented by the Chapman-Cook Speed of Reading Test. Speed tests may be divided into two types, according to the method of scoring. In the time-limit test, an example of which is the Minnesota Vocational Test for Clerical Workers, a limited amount of time is allowed and the score consists of the amount of work accomplished in this time. In the work-limit test, an example of which is the O'Connor Finger Dexterity Test, the score consists in the amount of time required to do a specified amount of work.

Considerable discussion has been raised regarding the relative merits of speed and power tests in the field of intelligence testing. Psychologists usually consider that the degree of difficulty of the items which the individual can solve is a better measure of general intelligence than the speed with which items of equal difficulty are answered. According to a number of research findings, however, there is a high degree of relationship between speed of response and the level of difficulty of the items which are mastered. It is usually the case that those who answer the questions most rapidly are also more successful on the difficult items. "Slow" does not necessarily mean "sure."

The correct administration of psychological tests is extremely important, a trained examiner being necessary. Especially in the case of individual tests, inexperienced persons may not be depended upon to maintain standard procedure. Proper conditions for giving the test must be maintained. The examinee must be comfortable and free from distractions. The procedure for administration must be exactly uniform and in accordance with standardized directions. Good examiners realize the effects which slight changes in procedure may make. Rapport must be established before the test is undertaken. It is essential that maximum effort and cooperation be obtained from the examinee. If all these conditions are not present, the trained examiner will defer testing until standard conditions may be met.

The scoring is usually a routine clerical job for which clerks may be trained. Keys with correct answers indicate whether or not the item has been marked correctly. Objectivity is the aim in both scoring and administration, for it is this which sets off the test from less reliable methods for obtaining the same information.

Manual scoring of tests is admittedly expensive and usually involves errors. These two facts constitute a barrier to the extensive and systematic use of objective tests for guidance purposes. Many persons have attempted to overcome these obstacles by developing various mechanical scoring devices. The most promising of these attempts seems to be the recently invented International Test Scoring Machine, which is now being produced commercially by the International Business Machines Corporation.[26] The machine has been put through severe tests in a number of major testing programs and has met such tests with flying colors. In the New York Regents Inquiry, the International Test Scoring Machine was used during a period of six weeks to score approximately one-quarter million eight-page test booklets. It scored them at the rate of 935 test booklets per hour.

In addition to speed and accuracy in scoring, attention is directed to the fact that answer sheets are used, so that the test booklets themselves may be used over and over again. This represents a further substantial saving.

The machine itself is adjustable, so that the tests can be scored according to the number right, the number wrong, rights minus wrongs, rights minus one-half of the wrongs, etc., etc. The machine will also score subtests according to any desired scoring formula and will simultaneously weight these subtests in any desired manner. In addition, it will secure weighted averages. It will even be useful in research work involving multiple regression equations. In short, the machine represents a revolutionary solution to the problem of scoring objective tests.

It is safe to predict that every school of any size will promptly install one or more of these machines.[27] It is also safe to predict that standardized tests on the market will be printed so as to permit machine scoring. The same prediction may also be made with respect to informal classroom tests of the objective type, because these likewise can be subjected to the machine scoring technique. Thus, it is clear that the whole testing and guidance movement will be accelerated tremendously by the availability of this machine.

One should keep in mind, however, that such a machine, if used in the scoring of unreliable and nonvalid tests, may create an

---

[26] WOOD, BEN D., *Bull. of Information on the International Test Scoring Machine*, published by the Cooperative Test Service of the American Council on Education, October, 1936, pp. 1–12.

[27] We understand the rental price per machine will be $300 per year.

illusion in regard to the value of the test scores, merely because the scoring process is mechanically perfect. The machine, therefore, may actually increase the prevalence of inaccurate diagnoses. If this should happen, the machine will do more harm than good.

Equivalent Forms.—The provision for more than one form of a test is especially necessary in the field of achievement testing, but it is only recently that this has been recognized. Formerly, a single test result would forever stamp the individual in respect to his accomplishment in a certain field. Today, the emphasis has shifted from what has been called the "snapshot" theory of testing to the growth theory. Isolated results come to have more significance when they are accumulated over a period of time. Guidance counselors are requiring an account of facts stretching far back in the individual's history, in order that present behavior may be more adequately understood and the future more wisely planned for. Growth in achievements can be more adequately gauged when there are comparable methods for measuring that achievement at various time intervals.

Multiple forms are also necessary to guard against coaching when a test is given periodically in the same population. The American Council on Education Psychological Examinations, for example, must be provided in different forms for this reason. It sometimes becomes necessary to administer a test the second time when the reliability of the first results is questioned. The student may complain that the score is lower than a true measure because of disturbances in the testing room or for other reasons. In such cases, because of the memory factor involved, it is unwise to repeat the original test. A check is possible when more than one form is available.

Persons for Whom Tests Are Designed.—Obviously, the greater the number of measurements made on an individual, the more complete our knowledge of his behavior will become, but practical considerations often necessitate the administration of a rather limited battery of tests to the student who is being counseled. In the first place, many desirable tests, especially in the field of character traits, are not available. There are also the factors of time and expense involved. The counselor needs to make a wise selection of tests in order to gain the fullest information possible. The selection of appropriate batteries is somewhat of an art in itself, facility being gained by familiarity with the contents of the tests, their standardization, norms and occupational significance and research studies based upon them. Practice in interpretation and practical experience with tests as related to individual cases increase one's insight into their significance when applied to individual cases.

There are considerations which make some tests entirely inappropriate for certain individuals. These considerations become evident after some experience with these tools. A few general suggestions are included here, and a consultation of the reference material appearing later regarding specific tests should make clear the types of students for whom the tests are appropriate.

Tests should be applied to persons who resemble the population on which the test was standardized. One way to determine the suitability of a test for a particular individual is to consult the norms and the description of the group upon which they were based. If scores are interpreted only for college seniors in an engineering college, the test would usually be inappropriate for freshmen in an arts college.

When test results for a particular occupational group are available, individual scores should be compared with the scores made by that group. This is especially true in the case of aptitude tests which are not affected by occupational experience.

In deciding upon the appropriateness of a particular test for an individual, one should consider certain characteristics of the group on which the test was standardized, since tests are usually appropriate only for individuals who closely resemble those making up the group on whom the norms are based. Some of these considerations are listed below:

1. *Age of the Group.*—In some cases a test designed for children will yield very different results when applied to adults. The Minnesota Mechanical Assembly Test, for example, was found to be too easy for adult men and, hence, it yielded unreliable results when administered to them. Whereas it was a valid measurement of mechanical aptitude when applied to boys of junior high school age, for adults it measured acquired knowledge and did not measure this acquired knowledge as consistently as would be desirable.

2. *Sex.*—When norms are available for one sex only, results of the test when applied to the other sex can be given no objective interpretation. The Strong Interest Blank is an example. Even when applied to women planning to engage in one of the men's occupations for which norms are available, the results can be interpreted only subjectively and little assurance can be placed upon their meaning. Dr. Strong has recognized this limitation by developing a new interest test with norms for women engaged in different types of professional work.

3. *Experience.*—Achievement tests should usually be administered to persons who have had as much opportunity to acquire the information as the persons composing the norm group. A foreign language test based upon material taught in the first year of high school would ordinarily not be suitable for persons having no acquaintance with the language. In unusual cases, however, it may be desirable to administer achievement tests to persons who have had unequal opportunities for acquiring the information. In such cases, interpretation of results must be made in terms of each person's background of experience.

4. *Socio-economic Status.*—The interpretation of a "range-of-cultural-information" test, for example, differs if it is applied to a student from a home in the backwoods or to one who has had ample opportunity to gain the type of information called for. The interpretation should explain the differences found, *but it cannot explain them away.* Differences may exist, but for varying reasons.

5. *Intellectual or Educational Level.*—Results of a test meant for high school graduates may require changed interpretation if administered to college graduates. It is sometimes enlightening, however, to compare an individual's score with that of the average person higher in the educational scale. Great overlapping occurs between such artificial classifications as number of years of formal schooling.

6. *Native or Foreign Born.*—Obviously it is unfair to compare the "intelligence" of a foreign-born person possessing a language handicap with scores made by persons who have had every opportunity to acquire the word knowledge which is tested.

7. *Vocational Goal.*—Some tests are appropriate only for certain ranges of ability. The Strong Vocational Interest Blank,

for example, has been given to about thirty occupational groups in the professional and upper occupational levels. Its administration to a student with low I.Q. would be a waste of time and money.

8. *Special Aptitudes and Interests.*—Although it is true that the counselor is unable to judge entirely by interests which the individual claims he possesses, yet in many cases certain tests may be eliminated upon this basis. It is fairly easy to determine whether or not a music, art or mechanical test need be given, for example. Such a priori judgment may occasionally miss a talented person unaware of his gifts, but instances of this sort will be relatively few. In the case of a test of clerical aptitude, however, it is safer to administer it to most persons, since the possession of unusual amounts of this trait is not invariably related to overt signs or expressed interests.

Norms.—It is necessary, of course, to convert the raw numerical test scores into some other units on a universally comparable scale. Actual scores have little meaning until expressed in terms of their relationships to an actual distribution of scores made by a group of persons similar to the individual whose score is to be interpreted. Scores on different tests are ordinarily not directly comparable, but must be made comparable if direct comparisons are desired.

One device which is employed to interpret scores is the percentile rank. It is a useful technique because of its simplicity and the fact that it can be employed with most test data. A percentile score indicates the percentage of the group who make lower scores than the individual in question. A person with a score corresponding to a percentile rank of 30 on a particular test, for example, is superior in this trait to 30 per cent of the population on whom the norms were based.

For some tests, scores are not converted into percentile ranks but averages and variabilities for different groups are furnished, instead. Any score may then be interpreted by indicating its position in relation to the group or groups with which it most nearly corresponds.

Occasionally, norms are available for more than one group and, in such cases, norms for the group most similar to the individual should be employed. When the test has been applied to an occupational group fairly homogeneous with respect to the possession of the trait in question, it may be helpful to compare the student's score with the group average. This interpretation is advisable, especially when the group represents an occupational goal of the student. Men planning to enter the clerical fields of work should be compared with men in these fields rather than with men in the general population. This is especially advisable with the clerical tests, for example.

Local norms are preferable to national norms, which may not be representative of the population with whom the individual is competing. Standards in various parts of the country and in different high schools and colleges are so vastly different that national norms may be entirely misleading in respect to the local situation. When it has been impossible to compile local norms, the description of the norm group should be taken into account in interpreting results.

Reliability of Tests.—The reliability of the measurement is one of the chief concerns of test users. A test which yields different results on the same individual from one time to another is apt to be more misleading than revealing. Reliability refers to a test's ability to yield the same results upon repetition, or, in other words, the consistency with which it measures whatever it measures.

There are various methods for measuring a test's consistency. The test may be administered a second time to the same individuals. Its reliability is indicated by the extent to which those who rank in a certain position in the group on the first test maintain the same relative position upon repetition.

When equivalent forms are available, scores made by the same individuals on the two forms may be compared. The extent to which the individuals maintain the same relative position on the second test measures the consistency of the test form.

A third method for determining the reliability of the measuring device is the comparison of results on odd-numbered items with those on even-numbered items. The method is similar to that used when two forms are compared, except that the items whose reliability is under investigation are now only half the number. This tends to reduce the correlation coefficient[28] below its actual

[28] For a discussion of correlation, see T. L. Kelley, *Interpretation of Educational Measurements*, Yonkers-on-Hudson, New York: World Book Company, 1927.

value, for which a correction is often applied, by using the Spearman-Brown formula.

Since tests vary in consistency, high reliability is the first requirement demanded of a test which is to be used in work with individuals. We must be able to depend upon the stability of a test score. Other things being equal, the higher the coefficient of reliability, the more consistent the test may be considered. A correlation of .94 or above has been set by Kelley as an ideal value for tests upon which individual guidance will be based. Some lenience is allowed in practice, however, but correlations lower than .90 are now considered to be unsatisfactory. Correlations fluctuate according to the distribution of the group upon which they are based: the more variable the group, the higher the correlation. Reliabilities should be established upon relatively homogeneous groups, especially if they are to be used for individuals in a narrowly defined classification.

Since the coefficient of reliability is dependent to so great an extent upon the variability of the group measured, it is clear that reliability coefficients derived from testing different groups are not comparable unless the groups tested happen to be equally variable. Thus, standards of reliability which ignore variability are not entirely satisfactory. Furthermore, a reliability coefficient by itself does not indicate specifically the amount of unreliability in an individually obtained measurement. It is more enlightening to know the exact amount of unreliability inherent in any individual score. This can be determined by means of the standard error of estimate of a true score, the formula for which is as follows:

$$\sigma_{1.00} = \sigma_1 \sqrt{1 - r_{11}}$$

In this formula, σ_1 is the standard deviation of the distribution and r_{11} is the reliability coefficient.

The standard error of a score informs the test user in regard to the amount of error in an obtained score. It indicates the number of points by which the obtained score varies from the "true" score because of chance errors of measurement. For a detailed discussion of this measurement the reader is referred to T. L. Kelley's *Interpretation of Educational Measurement* and to Bingham's *Aptitudes and Aptitude Testing*.

In other words, since no test is perfectly reliable, it is desirable to know the extent to which an obtained score may be accepted as representative of the true score an individual would secure were he to be subjected to a large number of equivalent forms of the test. As Kelley and Bingham point out, it is erroneous to think of any test score as an absolute fixed value on a scale. It should be considered merely as an approximation. The standard error of a score permits one to note the range of the scale within which the true score probably lies. It is thus an index of reservation that must be attached to any obtained score. The smaller the standard error of a score, the greater the certainty that the obtained score can be accepted as a close approximation to the true score.

There are various reasons for the low reliability of a test. Individuals may actually vary in performance from time to time. Distractions during the test or variations in effort may account for some of those irregularities which the examiner should make every effort to control. The scoring of the test may itself be unreliable. Errors sometimes occur, even in the scoring of objective tests where subjective judgment does not enter. By checking the scoring, such possibilities are reduced to a minimum. Another cause of unreliability is in the test itself. A limited number of items in a short test may not cover sufficient ground to yield reliable results. Usually a good test may be increased in reliability by increasing its length. The larger the number of samples of behavior one obtains in the testing situation, the nearer one approaches a true indication of behavior.

The large number of tests on the market which do not conform to the desired requirement of reliability is indeed disconcerting, and for this reason the choice of tests is considerably limited. The science of psychometrics can point to other fields, also, whose measuring devices possess reliabilities which leave much to be desired. Even in the field of medicine, some measurements are extremely unreliable. Height can be accurately measured. Reliability coefficients for measurements of thickness, however, are lower than those obtained for many psychological tests. Measurements of circumference are too dependent upon the force attached to the tape! Marks of school teachers are notoriously low in their consistency, yielding correlations between .40 and .50 for single teachers.

Efforts of psychometrists are being directed toward more systematic control of variable factors and improvement in the reliability of their instruments.

Validity.—To measure a trait is one thing, but to ascertain the significance of that measurement is quite another. Merely to name a test an "intelligence" test is not sufficient. Proof must be given that it is actually measuring whatever it claims to measure. In other words, the validity of a device is a basic prerequisite to its practical application. The problem of securing an adequate outside criterion of ability against which a test may be validated is a difficult one. Few agree on a criterion for "success" on the job. Does it consist in earnings, production, estimates of proficiency by superiors or the satisfaction which the individual himself experiences?

Validity coefficients are usually considerably lower than reliability coefficients, owing in part to this inability to secure a criterion which is itself reliable and valid. Validity coefficients of less than .45, however, are usually not acceptable.

Various types of criteria have been used against which to check test scores. These may conveniently be grouped in two classes:

1. External criteria are those measurements or estimates outside the test proper which have been accepted as standards for comparison with test scores. In this group are objective measurements of work accomplished and estimates of traits made by teachers, associates and employers. It is sometimes possible, also, to compare results with those obtained upon other tests which are considered valid indicators of the trait to be measured.

2. Internal criteria must be resorted to when desirable outside criteria cannot be obtained. If the trait is one which should show progress with age and if test scores indicate fairly rapid and definite age progress, the device contains some elements of validity. In some cases reliance must be placed upon the judgments of persons who have constructed the scale. When every effort is made by subject-matter and test experts to select items which they believe to be indicative of the trait to be measured and representative of the field, validity must sometimes be assumed. This is especially true of achievement tests. Items are selected from the best textbooks and courses of study. Subject-matter specialists may also prepare suitable items. Statis-

tical techniques are then used to determine the extent to which each item contributes toward an adequate measurement of the "best," the "average," and the "poorest" students in the group.

An additional criterion sometimes resorted to is that of group differences. If contrasting groups are found to have average scores whose differences are statistically significant, then there is some basis for the assumption of the test's validity. If a group of artists ranks significantly higher on a test purporting to measure "art judgment" than a group of non-art majors in college, then the test is to some extent valid.

References

The following limited number of references dealing with psychological testing, in addition to those cited at the end of the first chapter or later in connection with specific tests, are suggestive only and are not meant to represent an exhaustive list in the field.

1. EARLE, F. M.: "The Psychological Examination," *Occupations, The Vocational Guidance Magazine*, 1934, 12: 70–74.
2. HULL, CLARK L.: *Aptitude Testing*, Yonkers-on-Hudson, New York: World Book Company, 1928.
3. KELLEY, T. L.: *Interpretation of Educational Measurements*, Yonkers-on-Hudson, New York: World Book Company, 1927.
4. McCONN, MAX: "Educational Guidance Is Now Possible," *The Educational Record*, 1933, 14: 475–499.
5. PATERSON, D. G., R. M. ELLIOTT, L. D. ANDERSON, H. A. TOOPS, and E. HEIDBREDER: *Minnesota Mechanical Ability Tests*, Chapter I, Minneapolis: University of Minnesota Press, 1930.
6. PINTNER, R.: *Intelligence Testing—Methods and Results*, New York: Henry Holt & Company, 1931.
7. SYMONDS, P. M.: *Diagnosing Personality and Conduct*, New York: D. Appleton-Century Company, Inc., 1931.
8. WOOD, BEN D.: *Basic Considerations in Educational Testing.* Reprints on request to American Council on Education, Committee on Educational Testing, 744 Jackson Place, Washington, D.C.
9. ———, and F. S. BEERS: "The Major Strategy of Guidance," *Occupations, The Vocational Guidance Magazine*, 1934, 12: 8–12.
10. YOUNG, KIMBALL: "The History of Mental Tests," *Ped. Sem.*, 1924, 31: 1–48.

CHAPTER III

SCHOLASTIC APTITUDE TESTS

Ability to manipulate and manage abstract symbols, especially word meanings and relationships, is probably the most important single factor determining academic success. For this reason, we have labeled this chapter Scholastic Aptitude Tests and have included in it information about a selected list of verbal intelligence tests and reading tests.

The counselor should recognize that success in academic school subjects is dependent only in part on "verbal intelligence." Study habits, interest in subject matter, faithfulness in carrying out classroom assignments, attitude toward teachers and the tasks they set, are all important.

Success in occupational life is, likewise, dependent only in part on "verbal intelligence." Nevertheless, in this area, verbal intelligence is increasingly important as one attempts to succeed in the higher level occupations, semi-professions and the major professions. Again, one must realize that special abilities, interests and personality factors play an important role. For these reasons, one must not look upon intelligence tests as the only important index of probable success. They measure what a person *can* do, not what he *will* do. Thus, they provide but one approach, albeit an indispensable one.

The validity of intelligence tests is determined by correlations between test scores on the one hand and school grades, teachers' estimates of intelligence and school progress on the other. Accumulated evidence points unmistakably to the importance of measured intelligence as one factor conditioning success in academic school subjects and professional types of training. Detailed evidence regarding validity will be presented in the following discussions of available tests. Since this volume is primarily a handbook, the information given is restricted to that which is essential for the selection and judicious interpretation of a limited number of tests. Additional references are given to tests not treated in this chapter, for the convenience of counselors who may wish to use any of them as supplementary guidance devices.

A. INTELLIGENCE TESTS AT THE SECONDARY SCHOOL LEVEL

1. Stanford Revision of the Binet-Simon Scale, by L. M. Terman, 1916.

Description.—The Stanford Revision of the Binet-Simon Scale has become the most widely used individual intelligence test. The tests in the scale are arranged in age levels from 3 to 18. The score which the child makes is expressed in terms of mental age. The mental age (M.A.) is then divided by the child's chronological age (C.A.) to obtain the intelligence quotient (I.Q.).

Designed For.—This test is designed for children and adults but it is most adequate for the age range 7 to 11. The norms are inadequate at the early ages and after age 11 or 12.

Norms.—The use of the I.Q. technique makes age norms unnecessary. I.Q.'s for those over age 16 are obtained by dividing M.A. by the constant 16, on the assumption that mental development ceases at age 16. Sex differences are minimal; hence, sex norms are also unnecessary. The interpretation of the I.Q. may be made by consulting the following table:

Classification	I.Q. range	Percentage distribution
"Near" genius or genius	140 and above	0.25
Very superior	120–139	6.75
Superior	110–119	13.00
Normal or average	90–109	60.00
Dull	80– 89	13.00
Borderline	70– 79	6.00
Feeble-minded	Below 70	1.00

Reliability.—Retests of the same children reported by Terman yielded a reliability coefficient of +.93. Similar retests reported by other investigators indicate a test-retest reliability of about +.88. The majority of changes in I.Q. are less than 5 points, although changes of as much as 20 or more points may occur.

On the whole, the I.Q. is remarkably constant, so that we can generalize by saying, "Bright child, bright adult; dull child, dull adult."

Validity.—Correlation between Stanford-Binet mental ages and school grade location *for a given chronological age group* (age 11 or 12) is +.80. This justifies Terman's statement that the most important single fact about a child from the point of view of the child's school career is his M.A. and I.Q. on the day he enters school. In other words, educational opportunity does not determine one's I.Q. but one's I.Q. determines what he can make of his educational opportunity. We thus distinguish between *amount of education*, as measured by years of educational exposure, and *educability*, as measured by school accomplishment.

Caution.—Individual intelligence testing is a highly technical affair. No one should attempt to give the Stanford-Binet Test unless he has received the necessary training under competent supervision.

References.—L. M. Terman, *Measurement of Intelligence*, Boston: Houghton Mifflin Company, 1916; idem, *The Intelligence of School Children*, Boston: Houghton Mifflin Company, 1919.

2. The Revised Stanford-Binet Scales, by L. M. Terman and Maud Merrill, 1937.

Description.—The 1937 revision is a radical improvement on the 1916 scale. Many more tests have been added at the lower ages and at the upper ages and two forms, *L* and *M*, are provided. The testing equipment, itself, is much more elaborate. The principle of age placement of tests yielding M.A. and I.Q. is continued.

Designed For.—This test is designed for children and adults and will be much more adequate for younger children and for adolescents and adults than the 1916 scale.

Norms.—The use of the I.Q. technique makes age norms unnecessary. A correction table for the higher chronological ages is provided so that a corrected C.A. divisor can be used in computing I.Q. for each monthly interval from 13 years 0 months to 16 years 0 months. I.Q.'s for those over age 15 years 0 months are obtained by dividing M.A. by the constant 15 on the assumption that mental development ceases at age 15. Sex differences are minimal; hence, sex norms are unnecessary. The interpretation of the I.Q. is similar to the I.Q. classifications provided for the 1916 scale. One important difference is to be noted, however. The 1937 revision benefited from the use of the technique of systematic sampling, so that the I.Q. distributions are truly representative of the white American-born populations at each age. The following table will facilitate interpretation of I.Q. and M.A. scores:

Standard score[1]	Percentile rank	I.Q., ages 2 to 18	M.A., ages 15 and over
7.50	99.4	140	21.0
7.00	97.7	132	19.8
6.50	93.3	124	18.6
6.00	84.1	116	17.4
5.50	69.1	108	16.2
5.00	50.0	100	15.0
4.50	30.9	92	13.8
4.00	15.9	84	12.6
3.50	6.7	76	11.4
3.00	2.3	68	10.2
2.50	0.6	60	9.0

[1] The standard score scale is derived by setting the mean or average of the sample at 5.00 and using tenths of the standard deviation of the distribution as the units of measurement above and below the mean.

Reliability.—The reliability of the 1937 scale should be higher than for the 1916 scale. The most noteworthy improvement is in the increased reliability for children below age 7 and for those over age 11 or 12. Evidence is presented showing that the reliability of the I.Q. varies inversely with the magnitude of the I.Q. I.Q.'s below 70 are established with much greater reliability than I.Q.'s above 70. The standard error of an individual I.Q. score is 2.2 for I.Q.'s below 70 and increases gradually to produce a value of 5.2 for I.Q.'s of 130 and over. The median reliability coefficient for twenty-one age groups is $+.91$, being lower for the pre-school ages and higher for the ages above 6.

Validity.—The validity of the 1937 scale should be as high as, if not higher than, that of the 1916 scale.

Caution.—Since the 1937 scale is more elaborate and complicated than the 1916 scale, it follows that no one should attempt to obtain I.Q.'s by its use unless he has received the necessary training under competent supervision.

Publisher and Cost.—Test materials and 25 record booklets are distributed by Houghton Mifflin Company for $10 for each form separately.

References.—L. M. TERMAN and MAUD MERRILL, *Measuring Intelligence*, Boston: Houghton Mifflin Company, 1937. Price $2.25.

3. Terman Group Test of Mental Ability, by Lewis M. Terman, 1923.

Description.—The test consists of ten parts as follows: Information, best answer, word meaning, logical selection, arithmetic, sentence meaning, analogies, mixed sentences, classification, number series. It incorporates many of the general features of other well-known scales for group testing.

The test is issued in two forms, *A* and *B*, each consisting of 185 items. Total working time for each form is 27 minutes. The time limit for each of the ten subtests is said to be more than liberal, so that power rather than speed is the chief determinant of a child's score. Because of simplicity in the procedure, the test can be given within an ordinary school period of 35 minutes.

Designed For.—The test is designed for pupils in grades seven to twelve and yields M.A. and I.Q. measurements that are strictly comparable to Stanford-Binet M.A.'s and I.Q.'s.

Norms.—Percentile norms for each grade (seven to twelve) are provided. These norms are based upon a total of 41,241 cases from California and the Middle West. It is pointed out that norms for the country as a whole would probably be slightly lower, and would probably be much lower for states having relatively poor schools or a large proportion of relatively inferior population groups. Scores made by Negro, Indian and Mexican children will usually run far below those of white children of the same grade or age. The following percentile ranks are taken from the detailed percentile norms published in the Manual:

Percentile	Scores by grade					
	7	8	9	10	11	12
100 (highest 1%)	147+	170+	181+	194+	203+	207+
75 (Q_3)	88	112	128	147	163	169
50 (median)	68	89	104	122	138	147
25 (Q_1)	51	69	81	98	112	122
1 (lowest 1%)	20	30	35	48	55	63

The conversion of a child's total score into a percentile rank for children in his same school grade does not indicate the child's *brightness*, since age is left out of the picture. For this reason, a table of Mental Age Equivalents is given in the Manual. It is desirable, therefore, to convert a child's total score into a Stanford-Binet mental age by use of the table and then to compute I.Q. by dividing M.A. by C.A., disregarding C.A. above age 16.

ABBREVIATED SCORE—M.A. EQUIVALENT TABLE

Terman Group Test Score	Stanford-Binet Mental Age
200+	19-0+
178-199	18-0 to 18-11
157-177	17-0 to 17-11
135-156	16-0 to 16-11
114-134	15-0 to 15-11
94-113	14-0 to 14-11
73-93	13-0 to 13-11
50-72	12-0 to 12-11
29-49	11-0 to 11-11
15-28	10-4 to 10-11

The median I.Q. of pupils in high school will usually be found to be above 100 because of the selective character of secondary education. The selection is so great that valid age norms cannot be derived from tests of pupils in high school. For this reason, the fact that this test is anchored to the Stanford-Binet Test through the techniques of giving the test to 306 cases who were also given the individual Stanford-Binet is of the utmost importance. Thus, I.Q.'s for this group test become meaningful, whereas I.Q.'s derived from age norms for other group tests at the high school level have their significance greatly reduced.

Reliability.—The correlation between scores on Forms *A* and *B* given to 132 ninth-grade pupils was found to be +.89 as reported by Garrett and Schneck. Willard retested 216 students with Forms *A* and *B* after an interval of 7 months (age range 12 through 19, grade range eight through twelve) and obtained a correlation of +.88 ± .01. Test-retest correlations for each age group ranged from +.72 to +.96, with a median *r* of +.83. These results compare favorably with reliability coefficients reported for the best group tests of intelligence. Since any test of intelligence always involves a margin of error, counselors should use both forms of the test given on different days and the average of the two examinations should be taken as the pupil's score. When a marked discrepancy in the score on the two forms is observed, some other group test should be used or the pupil should be examined by a psychologist.

Validity.—The test will disclose marked individual differences in intellect among pupils. In a single grade, differences of four or five years in mental age are frequent. This means that the academic work in the average school is adjusted to meet the needs of only about half of the pupils. For the remainder, the school tasks assigned are too easy or too difficult. Since mental ability and academic accomplishment in proportion to ability should be the fundamental basis for all academic grading, classification and promotion, it is clear that the counselor will find test results invaluable in bringing about a better educational adjustment for those children who are wrongly placed. Classification of pupils into different groups for special types of instruction is a desirable preliminary to differentiated secondary school curricula. If such problems are courageously faced at the beginning of the junior high school years, the problem of educational guidance in the senior high school years will become more easily solved. If adequate educational guidance is provided, the problems of vocational guidance will be greatly simplified. Although the mental test is only one of the devices that should be employed in the study of the individual as a basis for guidance, nevertheless, it is of prime importance.

Publisher and Cost.—World Book Company, 1923, Forms *A* and *B*, and manual. Price, $1.20, net, per package. Each package contains 25 tests (Form *A* or Form *B*) with manual of directions, scoring key and class record. May also be ordered from Psychological Corporation, 522 Fifth Ave., New York, at the same prices.

References.—Manual for Terman Group Test of Mental Ability, Yonkers-on-Hudson, New York: World Book Company, 1923; D. W. WILLARD, "Native and Acquired Mental Ability as Measured by the Terman Group Test of Mental Ability," *School and Soc.*, 1922, 16: 750–756.

4. Army Alpha Group Examination, Forms 5 to 9, by Division of Psychology, S. G. O., U. S. Army, 1918.

Description.—The test consists of eight subtests as follows: Directions, arithmetic reasoning, practical judgment, opposites, disarranged sentences, number series completion, analogies, information. There are 212 items in all. The directions for each subtest are printed, but the examiner also reads them orally. There is no time limit for the directions test (subjects listen to each of 12 verbal directions, recording responses immediately after each is given). Time limits are given for the remaining tests and about 45 minutes are required for the complete test. There are five alternate forms, each of which is approximately equal in difficulty.

Norms.—The following table gives norms for interpreting Alpha scores:

Army letter rating	Army interpretation	Alpha scores	Kohs-Proctor Stanford-Binet mental ages[1]	School grade equivalents	Occupational intelligence standards	Per cent of white draft in each letter grade
A	Very superior	135–212	18–0 to 19– 6	Superior record in college	Major professions	4.1
B	Superior	105–134	16–0 to 17–11	Average record in college	Lower professions and semi-professions	8.0
C+	High average	75–104	14–0 to 15–11	Capable of completing academic high school course	Technical, clerical and supervisory positions	15.0
C	Average	45– 74	12–0 to 13–11	Rarely capable of completing acad. high school course	Skilled trades, lower clerical and routine sales jobs	25.0
C−	Low average	25– 44	10–8 to 11–11	Capable of completing 7th and 8th grades	Semiskilled levels of work	23.8
D	Inferior	15– 24	10–0 to 10– 7	Capable of completing 5th and 6th grades	Unskilled levels of work	17.1
D−	Very inferior	0– 14	0–0 to 9–11	Special classes for subnormal	Capable of simple work under close supervision	7.0

[1] W. S. Miller developed the following formula for converting Alpha scores into Kohs-Proctor Stanford-Binet mental ages: $.8 \times score + 108 = M.A.$ in months.

The following grouping of occupations according to optimum intelligence levels is suggestive of the relation between abstract intelligence and occupational adjustment. One must keep in mind, however, the fact that abstract intelligence is only one of the factors involved in occupational adjustment; hence, occupational guidance solely on the basis of an I.Q. is indefensible. For this reason, the preceding table and the following table must be considered merely as a rough guide, "other things being equal."

Intelligence Level	Occupations
A	Editor, lawyer, physician, college professor, engineer (M., E., C.), diplomat, minister, technical salesman, mathematical statistician, certified public accountant, major business executive
B	Reporter, teacher (H. S. & Elem.), insurance salesman, merchant and banker, industrial chemist, private secretary, office manager, factory superintendent, draftsman, buyer. social worker, dentist, minor business executive
C+	Stenographer, bookkeeper, nurse, office clerk, small merchant, railroad clerk, teacher of special subjects (music, physical educ., arts), photographer, telegrapher, postal clerk, radio service man, foreman, druggist, typist, photo-engraver
C	Locomotive engineer, general mechanic, policeman, tool and die maker, plumber and pipe fitter, tailor, general machinist, shop mechanic, printer, painter and decorator, truck driver, bricklayer, sales clerk, boilermaker
C−	Lumberman, watchman, shoemaker, barber, sailor, factory production worker, packer, porter, domestic servant
D	Unskilled laborer, farm laborer, loader, helper
D−	Simplest type of laboring work and simple routine work under close supervision

Reliability.—For unselected soldiers in the army, the reliability coefficient is approximately .95. The probable error of a score is approximately 5 points which is one-eighth of the standard deviation of the score distribution for unselected soldiers. The reliability will be lower for more homogeneous groups, such as college freshmen or high school sophomores. For example, the reliability for sophomores in college is about +.82 (based on a series of psychology laboratory classes at the University of Minnesota).

Validity.—The correlation between Alpha and Stanford-Binet for the special sample of 653 soldiers selected as being "representative" was +.81. The correlation between Alpha I.Q.'s and Stanford-Binet I.Q.'s for 800 high school pupils and grade school children ranged from +.80 to +.92. The correlation between school-grade location and Alpha scores for children of a given chronological age (such as 12, 13, or 14) was +.81.

There is reason to believe that Alpha is an excellent test of intelligence for school pupils from 11 to 16 years of age but that it is not sufficiently discriminative for college students. Its use should be restricted, therefore, to Junior and Senior high school pupils.

Publisher and Cost.—Bureau of Educational Measurements, Kansas State Teachers College of Emporia. Price, $3.50 per hundred. All forms available. Manual of directions, $0.30, key, $0.15. Stoelting Company, Chicago, also distribute the tests at $6.75 per hundred.

References.—R. M. YERKES, and C. S. YOAKUM, *Army Mental Tests*, New York: Henry Holt & Company, 1920; W. M. PROCTOR, "The Use of Psychological Tests in the Educational and Vocational Guidance of High School Pupils," *J. of Educ. Res. Monog.*, No. 1, June, 1921, Public School Publishing Company, Bloomington, Illinois; W. M. PROCTOR, "The Use of Intelligence Tests in the Educational Guidance of High School Pupils," *School and Soc.*, 1918, 8: 473–478, 502–509; M. V. COBB, "The Limits Set to Educational Achievement by Limited Intelligence," *J. of Educ. Psychol.*, 1922, 13: 449–464, 546–555; D. FRYER, "Occupational-Intelligence Standards," *School and Soc.*, 1922, 16: 273–278; D. FRYER, and E. J. SPARLING, "Intelligence and Occupational Adjustment," *Occupations, The Vocational Guidance Magazine*, 1934, 12: 55–63.

5. Revised Army Alpha Examination, Form 6, Short Form, by C. R. Atwell and F. L. Wells, 1933.

Description.—In this revision, the Army Alpha Examination has been radically shortened and rearranged so that it is (1) easier to give and to score and (2) more appropriate for educational and business uses (items concerning the military have been eliminated). Items depending upon knowledge current only at a particular date have also been eliminated, so that the contents of the test cannot go out of date. There are four subtests: Arithmetic reasoning, opposites, following directions and analogies. A total of 120 items is included. The directions for each subtest are printed, but the examiner also reads them orally. Time limits are given for the subtests and the total working time is 13½ minutes.

Designed For.—The test is designed for superior adults and thus it is adapted for use with high-grade adults and students in high school and college.

Norms.—The standardization of the test is based on 1200 individuals scoring above 90 points on Army Alpha. For such individuals (upper quartile) the scores on the Revised Alpha are directly comparable to the original Alpha scores by means of the following abbreviated conversion table.

Revised form score	Alpha score	Percentile rating
140	212	99
130	196	99
120	181	99
110	166	98
100	151	96
90	136	93
80	121	88
70	106	82
62	94	75

Reliability.—The correlation between the Revised Alpha and Alpha *for the restricted range tested* is +.80 (N = 745). The test-retest reliability for two forms of Revised Alpha for the *same restricted range* is +.84 (N = 210).

Validity.—The validity of the Revised Alpha is undoubtedly as high as for Alpha.

<small>**Publisher and Cost.**—The Psychological Corporation, 522 Fifth Ave., New York. Price, one test, $0.06; $5 per hundred; Manual with key and norms, $0.25.

References.—F. L. WELLS, "Army Alpha Revised," *Personnel J.*, 1932, 10: 411–417.</small>

6. Bregman's Revision of Army Alpha Examination, Forms A and B, by Elsie O. Bregman, 1931 and 1935.

Description.—Bregman's Revision is a combination of the five forms of Alpha. The best questions for general use have been retained. Items depending upon dated knowledge or items involving military terminology have been excluded or modified.

Designed For.—The test is especially adapted for use with civilian adults and students in high school.

Norms.—Since scores yielded by the Revision are directly comparable to scores yielded by the original forms of Alpha, it follows that standards available for the interpretation of scores on the original Alpha Examinations may be used to interpret scores on the Bregman Revision. The following additional information in regard to school grade norms is supplied by the author.

	School grades					
	7	8	9	10	11	12
Median.....................	71	85	97	111	122	127
Quartile deviation............	14	17	18	18	18	18
Number of cases.............	1372	2841	3288	4126	1934	1429

Reliability.—As high as, or higher than, Army Alpha.

Validity.—As high as, or higher than, Army Alpha.

Publisher and Cost.—The Psychological Corporation, 522 Fifth Ave., New York. Price, $5 per hundred.

References.—E. O. BREGMAN, Manual of Directions, The Psychological Corporation, 522 Fifth Ave., New York.

7. Pressey Senior Classification and Senior Verifying Tests, by S. L. Pressey and L. C. Pressey, 1922.

Description.—The Senior Classification Test consists of four types of test items: Opposites, information, practical arithmetic and practical judgment, arranged in cycle order for convenience in giving and scoring. It is a brief examination for measuring abstract intelligence or ability to do schoolwork. There are 96 items in the test. Since the test utilizes the cycle-omnibus technique of test construction and arrangement, there are no subtest time limits, an over-all time limit of 16 minutes being allowed.

The Senior Verifying Test is designed to serve as an alternate form of the Classification Test. It consists of four types of test items: Recognition vocabulary, concept recognition, number series and letter series completion, information, arranged in cycle order. There are 96 items and the time limit is 16 minutes.

Designed For.—These two tests are adapted for use in grades seven to twelve and for unselected adults. The tests are not sufficiently discriminative for use with college students or adults of superior intelligence.

Norms.—The following age and grade norms are supplied by the authors:

Grades		7B	7A	8B	8A	9B	9A	10B	10A	11B	11A	12B	12A
Median Score	Classification	23	27	30	34	38	42	46	50	54	58	62	68
	Verifying	26	30½	33	37	41	45	49	53	57	61	65	71
Ages				11½	12½	13½	14½		15½	16½	17½		
Median score, classification				15	25	33	42		50	57	64		

Norms for gainfully occupied adults are furnished by the University of Minnesota Employment Stabilization Research Institute as follows:

Letter rating	Standard score range	Percentile range	Senior classification Men	Senior classification Women	Senior verifying Men	Senior verifying Women
A	6.5 and over	93.4–100.0	84–96	86–96	82–96	87–96
B	5.5 to 6.4	69.2– 93.3	56–83	59–85	57–81	68–86
C	4.5 to 5.4	30.9– 69.1	31–55	34–58	34–56	43–67
D	3.5 to 4.4	6.7– 30.8	13–30	18–33	17–33	26–42
E	Under 3.5	0.0– 6.6	0–12	0–17	0–16	0–25

It will be noted that the verifying test is slightly easier than the classification test for men subjects. This is probably due to practice effects since the verifying test was given after the classification test. The verifying test, however, is much easier for women subjects than the classification tests, due probably to the fact that arithmetical reasoning problems which are included in the classification test are omitted from the verifying test. Presumably, the same sort of sex difference exists at the high school level; hence, age and grade norms should be set up for boys and girls separately.

Norms for various occupational groups are available as a result of the Employment Stabilization Research Institute studies as shown in the tables on pages 65 and 66.

Reliability.—The reliability of the Pressey Classification Test can be assessed indirectly by noting the correlation between this test and the Pressey Verifying Test. For 334 men in the Standard Sample (selected to be representative of the gainfully occupied) the correlation coefficient is $+.91 \pm .01$; for 131 women, $+.90 \pm .02$. This evidence would incline one to assert that these two tests possess a highly satisfactory degree of reliability.

EMPLOYED GROUPS—WOMEN WORKERS

Occupational group	Number of cases	Classification test scores -1σ	Mean	$+1\sigma$	Classification test I.Q.'s[1] -1σ	Mean	$+1\sigma$
Office clerks, Company M....	32	66.8	77.2	87.6	112	121	131
Office clerks, rated A.........	13	62.8	75.6	88.4	109	120	131
Office clerks, rated B.........	65	55.6	70.6	85.6	103	116	129
General clerical workers......	59	54.0	69.7	85.4	100	115	128
Stenographer—typists........	180	52.5	68.7	84.9	99	114	128
Office clerks, rated C.........	91	53.8	68.2	82.6	100	113	127
Office clerks, Company N....	208	51.9	67.9	83.9	99	113	128
Office clerks, rated D.........	31	46.3	64.1	81.9	94	109	126
Routine clerical workers......	24	39.6	59.7	79.8	90	106	124
Office machine operators.....	21	40.0	59.5	79.0	90	106	122
Standard sample of women...	131	27.9	50.1	72.3	81	97	117
Retail saleswomen[2]...........	136	26.8	45.4	64.0	80	93	109

[1] In this table and in the following table for men workers the Pressey Classification scores have been converted into M.A. equivalents by means of the age norms, and these have been divided by the constant 16 to yield adult I.Q.'s, on the assumption that M.A. ceases at age 16. These I.Q.'s are roughly equivalent to Terman Group Test I.Q.'s, and these in turn are roughly equivalent to Stanford-Binet I.Q.'s.

[2] The retail saleswomen were given the verifying test only. The scores were treated as if they were equivalent to the classification test scores. Since the verifying test yields higher scores than the classification test, it is apparent that the norms given here are too high. In other words, norms for retail saleswomen would show lower scores had the classification test only been given to them.

Validity.—Repeated use of the Pressey tests in advanced classes in group intelligence testing in the College of Education, University of Minnesota, has shown that the Pressey Tests correlate as well with such standard intelligence tests as Otis, Miller, Alpha, Terman Group, etc., as each of these correlates with the other. For 57 University High School freshman, the Pressey Senior Classification Test correlated $+.92$ with the mean of nine other tests and it was found to yield higher validity coefficients (correlation with academic grades) than most of the nine standard tests used.

EMPLOYED GROUPS—MEN WORKERS

Occupational group	Number of cases	Classification test scores			Classification test I.Q.'s		
		-1σ	Mean	$+1\sigma$	-1σ	Mean	$+1\sigma$
Accountants-bookkeepers	27	57.2	72.3	87.4	104	117	130
Minor executives	26	55.7	71.2	86.7	103	116	130
Life insurance salesmen	60	49.7	66.6	83.5	97	112	128
General clerical workers	41	49.2	66.3	83.4	96	111	127
Draftsmen	20	46.2	65.0	83.8	94	110	127
Minor bank officials	31	48.0	64.4	80.8	95	109	125
Routine clerical workers	30	45.0	61.5	78.0	93	108	122
Shipping-stock clerks	23	40.6	61.0	81.4	90	107	125
Bank tellers	17	41.5	58.7	73.9	91	104	118
Retail salesmen	65	41.2	58.0	74.8	90	104	119
Policemen, rated A	31	37.9	57.7	77.5	88	104	122
Janitors, rated A	46	31.3	48.7	66.1	83	96	111
Standard sample, Men	334	23.4	45.9	68.4	77	94	113
Policemen, rated B	37	21.7	40.5	59.3	77	90	105
Ornamental iron workers	31	19.3	39.0	58.7	74	89	105
Policemen, rated C	29	17.1	38.9	60.7	73	89	107
Janitors, rated B	23	21.3	31.6	41.9	76	83	91

Publisher and Cost.—Public School Publishing Company, Bloomington, Illinois. Price, $1.25 per hundred, for either test.

References.—S. L. PRESSEY and G. S. LONG, "A New Idea in Intelligence Testing," *Ohio State University Educ. Res. Bull.*, 1924, 3: 365–368; H. J. GREEN, I. R. BERMAN, D. G. PATERSON, M. R. TRABUE, *A Manual of Selected Occupational Tests for Use in Public Employment Offices*, Minneapolis: University of Minnesota Press, 1933; J. G. DARLEY, "The Reliability of the Tests in the Standard Battery" in *Research Studies in Individual Diagnosis*, edited by D. G. Paterson, Minneapolis: University of Minnesota Press, 1934; D. M. ANDREW and D. G. PATERSON, *Measured Characteristics of Clerical Workers*, Minneapolis: University of Minnesota Press, 1934; B. J. DVORAK, *Differential Occupational Ability Patterns*, Minneapolis: University of Minnesota Press, 1935; W. S. MILLER, "The Variation and Significance of Intelligence Quotients Obtained from Group Tests," *J. of Educ. Psychol.*, 1924, 15: 359–366.

8. **Otis Self-administering Tests of Mental Ability, Higher Examination,** for Grades nine to twelve, 1922.

Description.—The Higher Examination is issued in four alternate forms, Forms *A*, *B*, *C* and *D*, alike except in specific content. The 75 items in each form are arranged as an omnibus test in order of difficulty, covering such familiar types of items as: Information, arithmetical reasoning, number series completion, opposites, analogies, proverbs, logical inference and practical judgment. The time limit for the total test is 30 minutes, although the time limit can be shortened to 20 minutes. If the 20-minute time limit is used, the resulting scores can be transmuted into terms of 30-minute time-limit scores by means of Table I in the Manual of Directions. The score is the number of correct answers.

Designed For.—This test is adapted for use in grades nine to twelve and for college freshmen. The test is probably not sufficiently difficult to provide adequate measurement of college students.

Norms.—The following age and grade norms are selected from those supplied by the author in the Manual:

Ages	12½	13½	14½	15½	16½	17½
Median score	26	30	34	38	40	42

Grades	8B	8A	9B	9A	10B	10A	11B	11A	12B	12A
Median score	30	32	34	35	37	38	40	41	42	43

Norms for 2516 college students are as follows:

Percentile	Scores
100 (highest 1%)	75
75 (Q_3)	62
50 (median)	53
25 (Q_1)	46
1 (lowest 1%)	20

Charts in the Manual permit the examiner to translate any raw score into a percentile rank, Binet mental age, or an I.Q.

The table at the top of page 68 gives Alpha equivalents and Binet M.A. equivalents for scores in the test.

Whenever a second form of the test is given after a first form, there is a practice effect of four points. Therefore, four points should be subtracted from the scores for the second form in order to make allowance for the practice effect.

Reliability.—The reliability is reported to be +.92 for grades seven to twelve.

Validity.—The evidence indicates that this test is as valid as, if not more valid than, most of the standard group intelligence tests at the high school level.

Scores in higher examination	Alpha scores	Binet M.A.'s
58–75	135–212	17– 6 to 19–6
49–57	105–134	16– 5 to 17–5
39–48	75–104	14–10 to 16–3
28–38	45– 74	12–10 to 14–8
20–27	25– 44	11– 5 to 12–8
15–19	15– 24	10– 6 to 11–3
1–14	1– 14	7–10 to 10–4

Publisher and Cost.—World Book Company, Yonkers-on-Hudson, New York. Price, including manual, 25 for $0.80:

References.—A. S. OTIS, *Manual of Directions*, Yonkers-on-Hudson, New York: World Book Company; G. M. RUCH and G. D. STODDARD, *Tests and Measurements in High School Instruction*, Chapter XII, Yonkers-on-Hudson, New York: World Book Company, 1927; A. E. TRAXLER, "Reliability, Constancy, and Validity of the Otis I.Q.," *J. of Appl. Psychol.*, 1934 18: 241–251.

9. American Council on Education Psychological Examination for High School Students, by L. L. Thurstone and T. G. Thurstone, 1936.

Description.—The 1936 edition is composed of four tests—English completion, arithmetic, analogies, opposites—and requires one hour to administer.

Designed For.—Pupils in grades nine to twelve.

Norms.—Gross score norms for 30,717 pupils in 218 high schools are as follows:

Percentile	Gross scores by school grades			
	Grade 9	Grade 10	Grade 11	Grade 12
100 (highest 1%)	190+	200+	200+	210+
75 (Q_3)	109	128	141	150
50 (median)	79	100	115	124
25 (Q_1)	58	72	85	95
1 (lowest 1%)	29	35	39	45

Reliability.—Not reported, but presumably would compare favorably with the best available standard intelligence tests.

Validity.—Not reported, but presumably would compare favorably with the best available standard intelligence tests.

Publisher and Cost.—American Council on Education, 744 Jackson Place, N.W., Washington, D.C. Price, $5 per hundred.

References.—Circular distributed by American Council on Education and reports in *The Educational Record.*

10. Henmon-Nelson Tests of Mental Ability, High School Examination, Grades seven to twelve, by V. A. C. Henmon and M. J. Nelson; 1935.

Description.—A four-page test containing 90 test items printed on the first page and the fourth page. The two inside pages do not contain test items. Instead, carbon strips are printed thereon in such a way as to record the responses made on the first and fourth pages thus providing a simple device (The Clapp-Young Self-marking Scheme) for recording correct answers which can be counted in minimum time with minimum possibilities of error. No scoring key or stencil and no intricate directions for scoring are required. The score is the total number of correct responses.

The 90 items are arranged in order of increasing difficulty. A wide variety of types of questions is used, such as: Opposites, completion, geometric analogies, word classification, number series completion, verbal analogies, disarranged sentences, recognition vocabulary and arithmetic reasoning. Each question is set up in single-choice form, the examinee selecting one of five possible answers. The time allowed is 30 minutes for the test as a whole. Three forms, A, B and C, are provided.

Designed For.—The test is designed to measure the mental ability of students in junior and senior high schools or in grades seven to twelve. A simpler form of the test is also available for use in grades three to eight and a more difficult form is available for use with college students.

Norms.—Norms are provided on the basis of 5000 cases used for standardization purposes and checked in the light of returns from the testing of 212,034 students in 29 states. Mental Age equivalents are given for each total score from 1 to 90 and a chart for converting total scores into I.Q.'s is given, but the authors caution users of the test against the M.A. and I.Q. interpretation of test scores for high school students. The authors prefer that the age and grade percentile norms be used for purposes of interpretation. The percentile norms give the decile equivalents for total score for each age from 12 to 17 and for each grade from seven through twelve. An abbreviated percentile norm table is as follows:

Percentile	Ages						Grades					
	12	13	14	15	16	17	7	8	9	10	11	12
100	70	72	76	82	86	86	68	71	73	78	80	83
80	51	53	55	60	66	68	45	48	52	61	65	68
50	37	40	42	47	52	55	35	37	41	50	54	58
20	25	27	28	31	35	41	24	27	30	39	42	46
1	8	10	13	14	15	17	12	14	16	22	26	29

There is a three-point increase in average score for Forms A and B, when B is given within a week after A is given. This practice effect is greatest with students who are not "test-wise."

Reliability.—The corrected odd-even reliability coefficients range from +.91 to +.94 for each age group from 12 through 17 and from +.88 to +.90 for each grade group from seven through twelve. The probable error of a raw score (total score) is three points for each age and grade group. The correlation between Forms A and B for 178 pupils in grade 10 was +.897 ±.01.

Validity.—The care with which the tests were constructed is cited as one type of evidence regarding validity. Two hundred fifty items were prepared and submitted to experienced teachers for criticism. This reduced the number to 202. These were divided into two forms and given to some 500 students. Each item was then analyzed and only those items were retained which were proved to differentiate between pupils of known superior and known inferior mental ability. The two forms of 90 items each were then constructed from the items having the best predictive value. Similar care was used in the construction of Form C.

Correlations between the Henmon-Nelson Tests and other standard intelligence tests (Terman Group, Otis Self-administering, American Council Psychological Examination, Kuhlmann-Anderson, and Illinois) were computed. These correlations range from +.72 to +.88 for single grade groups. In one study when the two forms of the Terman Test and two forms of the Henmon-Nelson Test were administered and the I.Q.'s averaged, the correlation was +.93 for one group of 144 junior high school pupils and +.94 for another group of 97 junior high school pupils. Other evidence of this sort shows that the correlation rises when the Henmon-Nelson Test is correlated with two such standard intelligence tests. This is interpreted to indicate the validity of the Henmon-Nelson Test, since the correlation increases as the validity of the criterion (other tests) improves. Incidentally, this type of evidence should be a warning to counselors not to be content with a single I.Q. (P.R., M.A. or Total Score) on one form of a test. It suggests the desirability of basing I.Q.'s on two or more forms of a given test or on two or more different tests.

Evidence is also presented by the authors to indicate that the M.A.'s and I.Q.'s produced by the Henmon-Nelson Tests are closely equivalent to the M.A.'s and I.Q.'s produced by use of the Terman Group Test of Mental Ability, the Otis Self-administering Test and the Kuhlmann-Anderson.

Publisher and Cost.—Houghton Mifflin Company, Boston, New York, Chicago, Dallas, Atlanta and San Francisco. Price forms A, B, C, 25 for $0.75.

References.—*Teacher's Manual* (revised) by V. A. C. HENMON and M. J. NELSON, published by Houghton Mifflin Company.

11. Additional Tests at the High School Level.

a. Miller Mental Ability Tests, A and B, World Book Company, Yonkers-on-Hudson, New York.

b. Dearborn Group Intelligence Tests, Series II, C and D, Educational Test Bureau, Minneapolis, Minnesota.

c. Haggerty Intelligence Examination, Delta 2, World Book Company, Yonkers-on-Hudson, New York.

d. Kuhlmann-Anderson Intelligence Tests by F. Kuhlmann and R. G. Anderson, Educational Test Bureau, Minneapolis, Minnesota.

e. Unit Scales of Aptitude by M. J. Van Wagenen, Forms A, B, C, D, E, Educational Test Bureau, Minneapolis, Minnesota.

f. National Intelligence Tests, Scales A and B, prepared under the auspices of the National Research Council, by M. E. Haggerty, L. M. Terman, E. L. Thorndike, G. M. Whipple, and

R. M. Yerkes, World Book Company, Yonkers-on-Hudson, New York.

g. Multi-mental Scale, by William McCall, *et al.*, Bureau of Publications, Teachers College, Columbia University, New York.

h. California Test of Mental Maturity, Advanced Battery, Grades 9–14, by Elizabeth T. Sullivan, Willis W. Clark, and Ernest W. Tiegs, Southern California School Book Depository, Ltd., 3636 Beverly Blvd., Los Angeles, California.

B. CALIBRATION OF I.Q.'S DERIVED FROM GROUP INTELLIGENCE TESTS

Laymen (and even psychologists) are frequently confused by instances where a pupil's I.Q., derived from several group tests, appears to vary markedly. Miller has shown that such fluctuations, for the most part, are due to the non-comparability of such I.Q.'s. This non-comparability arises from the fact that the age norms for the different group tests have been derived from non-comparable groups of adolescents. There is urgent need for a National Bureau of Standards for Mental Measurement which would standardize each test on systematically defined standard populations, so that results for one test could be compared accurately with results from any other test. Lacking such a Bureau of Standards, Dr. W. S. Miller developed a chart for transposing I.Q.'s derived from different tests to a common base. He used the Terman Group Test of Mental Ability as a base because it was the only group test standardized in such a manner as to yield I.Q.'s comparable to the Stanford Revision of the Binet Scale. His method provided comparability by giving a battery of group tests to a group of 57 high school pupils. Kefauver (and later, Finch) has elaborated

EQUIVALENT GROUP TEST I.Q.'s

Terman A	Army Alpha	Delta 2	Miller A	Pressey Senior Class.
70	68	61	52	60
85	83	80	75	77
100	101	102	101	95
115	117	122	126	113
135	139	149	158	137

SCHOLASTIC APTITUDE TESTS

Miller's technique, providing tables of equivalent I.Q.'s for a number of group tests. I.Q. equivalents for several I.Q. levels, as published by Finch, are presented in the table on page 72.

The following data are given to illustrate the value of this technique in minimizing the variation of I.Q.'s derived from different group tests given to an individual pupil:

Pupils tested	Alpha	Pressey Senior Class.	Delta 2	Terman	Miller	Range of I.Q.'s
Pupil *A*:						
Original test I.Q.'s......	117	110	126	121	137	27
Stanford-Binet I.Q. equivalents..........	112	111	116	117	118	7
Pupil *B*:						
Original test I.Q.'s......	99	89	104	100	95	15
Stanford-Binet I.Q. equivalents..........	97	96	100	97	95	5
Pupil *C*:						
Original test I.Q.'s......	114	104	113	112	119	15
Stanford-Binet I.Q. equivalents..........	110	107	106	109	108	4
Pupil *D*:						
Original test I.Q.'s......	128	111	125	129	149	38
Stanford-Binet I.Q. equivalents..........	122	112	115	125	125	13

In view of the facts presented above, it should be clear that I.Q.'s derived from different group tests are *not* comparable. For this reason, counselors should insist that mental test results recorded on pupils' cumulative record cards should always include the date of the test and the *name and form* of the test. It would also be well to give, in addition, the Stanford-Binet I.Q. equivalent.

The difficulties mentioned in this section would not be overcome by abandoning the I.Q. as a method of reporting mental test scores. Scores from different tests reported as percentiles, as S.D. units or what not would *not* be comparable unless the different tests were standardized on the same defined populations. Hence, the urgent need for a National Bureau of Standards for Mental Measurement. Standardization to provide comparability of physical measurements has been achieved by the U. S. Bureau of Standards and similar agencies. There is equal need for a similar agency of standardization to provide comparability of mental measurements.

References.—W. S. MILLER, "The Variation and Significance of Intelligence Quotients Obtained from Group Tests," *J. of Educ. Psychol.*, 1924, 15: 359–366; G. N. KEFAUVER, "Need of Equating Intelligence Quotients Obtained from Group Tests," *J. of Educ. Res.*, 1929, 19: 92–101; F. H. FINCH, "Equating Intelligence Quotients from Group Tests," *J. of Educ. Res.*, 1935, 28: 589–592.

C. INTELLIGENCE TESTS AT THE COLLEGE LEVEL

1. American Council on Education Psychological Examination for High School Graduates and College Freshmen, by L. L. Thurstone and T. G. Thurstone, 1929, and annually thereafter.

Description.—This test was constructed to provide an adequate measure of intelligence for high school students and college students. It is more difficult than tests designed for the secondary school level.

There are five parts to the tests. Printed directions for each part constitute a section of each test and are included in the time limits. The total test requires one hour. Its make-up may be seen from the following tabular arrangement:

Type of test	Number of items	Time limits (in minutes)
Completion test	40	10
Arithmetical reasoning	20	20
Artificial language	30	13
Nonverbal analogies	29	10
Same or opposites	33	7
Total	152	60

Designed For.—The test has been used extensively to test high school seniors in state-wide testing programs and to test freshmen in hundreds of colleges and universities, throughout the country. It is sufficiently difficult to discriminate the higher levels of intelligence found among college students. It is designed to furnish an objective measure that will permit a counselor to distinguish between a student's mental ability and his high school preparation and his "classroom industry."

Norms.—National norms are published annually in the April issue of *The Educational Record*.

Institutional differences are so great as to justify Terman's oft-quoted statement that there is a college for almost every level of intellect. The following data for two "highest score" institutions, for a "middle-score" institution and for the two "lowest scoring" institutions are as follows:

Institution code number	Number of students	Gross scores Q_1	Median	Q_3
1	89	230.3	254.5	279.8
2	338	209.3	240.0	270.8
112	235	147.9	183.4	219.1
264	156	93.0	116.7	147.7
265	88	55.7	82.0	111.4
All colleges	56,895	143.1	183.6	223.4

The following data indicate that important differences between types of colleges also exist:

Type of college	Number of students	Q_1	Median	Q_3
204 four-year colleges	44,925	146.6	187.7	227.6
31 junior colleges	4,737	133.2	168.1	206.2
31 teachers colleges	7,233	131.9	169.6	207.2

The published norms give gross scores for each percentile for each subtest, as well as for the test as a whole, and also give Tables of Equivalent Scores for Succeeding Annual Editions of the Test.

Reliability.—Thurstone reports the Spearman-Brown coefficient of correlation based on odd versus even scores as being +.95. Similar reliabilities for the subtests range from +.81 to +.98.

Validity.—An average of the coefficients of correlation between total scores on the test and college grades during the freshman year in over 50 colleges is about +.50. There is some basis for believing that the test is a better indicator of future academic achievement in arts colleges than in schools of business or pharmacy.

Publisher and Cost.—American Council on Education, 744 Jackson Place N.W., Washington, D.C. $7 per 100.

References.—L. L. THURSTONE and T. G. THURSTONE, annual reports in April issue of *The Educational Record*, published by The American Council on Education.

2. Ohio State Intelligence Test, by H. A. Toops.

Description.—There are 19 different forms (not statistically comparable). The questions are composed of items in arithmetical reasoning, same-opposites, analogies, number completion and paragraph meaning. Exhaustive research has been carried on by Dr. Toops in developing test items on the basis of item analysis and new forms. A special feature of the last three forms is the scoring device involving the use of prepared answer sheets and a stylus. This greatly increases the speed and accuracy of scoring. Forms 18 and 19 are work-limit tests usually completed within two class periods.

Designed For.—The test may be used for all years of high school and is difficult enough for advanced college students. The various forms have been used for many years in the annual state-wide testing of Ohio students in high schools and colleges.

Norms.—Extensive normative data are made available by the author with the purchase of tests or when tests are sent to him for scoring. The following norms are for freshmen in Ohio colleges on Form 18:

Percentile	Total Score
100	124
75	88
50	70
25	54
1	27

Reliability.—The author reports the following coefficients of correlation (one form versus another form) for four separate studies: .90, .91, .88 and .91. One college (Muskegon, Ohio) reported a corrected coefficient of .94.

Validity.—The author reports validity coefficients of between .55 and .60 for Form 17 with first-year scholarship in college. Form 18 yielded coefficients of .60 to .70 in five of the six larger colleges of Ohio State University. The average validity coefficient for four groups of high school students was .62 for Form 18 and .66 for Form 19. Additional data may be found in numerous bulletins of the Ohio College Association.

Publisher and Cost.—H. A. Toops, Ohio State University, Columbus, Ohio. Form 19: $0.10 per test, including test booklet and answer pad. The test booklets may be used indefinitely: new answer pads (one for each student) $0.06 each. Special prices for earlier forms of the tests may be obtained by writing the author. One stylus, for recording answers on the answer sheet, is supplied with each test.

References.—H. A. TOOPS, *A Catechism on a State-wide Testing and Guidance Program* (Mimeographed), Columbus, Ohio: Ohio State University; 1934–1935 (Tenth) Annual Report of the Committee on Intelligence Tests for Entrance, *Ohio College Assoc. Bull.* 97; H. A. EDGERTON and H. A. TOOPS, "Academic Progress," *Ohio State University Studies, Contributions in Administration*, 1, 1929, Columbus, Ohio: Ohio State University Press.

3. Minnesota College Ability Test, by D. G. Paterson, 1924.

Description.—This test was constructed for use in the annual testing of high school seniors and college freshmen in Minnesota. It was used during the period 1924 through 1928. There are four parts:

Subtests	Number of items	Time limits (in minutes)
Completion (revision of Moore's test)	30 (times 5)	10
Opposites (multiple choice)	120	10
Recognition vocabulary A (Multiple choice)	120	15
Recognition vocabulary B (Multiple choice)	120	15
Total	510	50

Designed For.—This test has been used particularly to select freshmen in The College of Science, Literature, and The Arts in The University of Minnesota. It was administered to high school seniors to provide a partial basis for advising such students regarding their plans to attend college.

Norms.—The following table shows differences among average test scores of freshmen in colleges of The University of Minnesota for the years 1926 to 1928 inclusive:

College		September, 1926	September, 1927	September, 1928
Agriculture, Forestry and Home Economics	No. Mean S.D.	137 217.94 55.62	167 215.07 56.82	186 231.69 56.87
Chemistry	No. Mean S.D.	48 264.69 57.20	65 255.12 60.69	50 268.60 53.09
Education (4-year curricula)	No. Mean S.D.	48 206.25 56.50	114 213.82 56.77	117 217.24 55.54
Engineering	No. Mean S.D.	281 237.41 58.76	331 237.44 61.24	411 241.30 59.21
Mines	No. Mean S.D.		28 243.75 51.59	16 241.88 49.14
Nursing	No. Mean S.D.		116 215.04 50.10	111 205.61 61.27
Pharmacy	No. Mean S.D.	32 197.81 68.37	15 189.50 51.78	21 223.93 61.69
S.L.A.	No. Mean S.D.	1349 242.84 59.19	1377 248.03 58.19	1556 254.61 62.31
Total	No. Mean S.D.	1918 238.65 59.95	2226 240.15 59.52	2481 246.47 62.50

Reliability.—The corrected odd-even reliability for the total test given to 522 college freshmen is +.94 with a sigma of 51.9.

The correlation between Vocabulary *A* and Vocabulary *B* was .88 for 1467 college freshmen.

Validity.—This test was used, together with high school scholarship, as a basis for advising and selecting freshmen in the Arts College of the University of Minnesota. As a result of this use, the mean score of Arts College freshmen increased in magnitude in succeeding years and the standard deviation decreased, a condition which produced changes in the validity coefficients as shown in the table below. This fact illustrates the important principle that validity coefficients, as well as test norms, are highly specific to the personnel and admission program obtaining in any college; hence the interpretation of test data must be made in terms of local educational conditions.

Year	N	Mean total score	Mean percentile rank	S.D. total score	Correlation with college grades
1926	792	248.0	53	58.3	.50
1928	993	254.5	56	58.7	.45
1934	951	278.9	72	48.9	.39
1935	827	281.0	73	52.1	.43

This test, together with high school grades, was used by Dean J. B. Johnston in his extensive series of studies in the identification of college freshmen unable to get satisfactory grades in the Arts College of the University of Minnesota. Studies of freshmen enrolling in the years between 1921 and 1928 show a remarkable degree of validity of this use of test data. A very low percentage of students with low test scores and low high school grades graduate from the university, despite continued residence far beyond the normal four-year period.

Publisher and Cost.—This test is not copyrighted; it may be used by other colleges without restrictions.

References.—J. B. JOHNSTON, *The Liberal College in a Changing Society*, New York: D. Appleton-Century Company, Inc., 1930; *idem*, *Who Should Go to College?* Minneapolis: University of Minnesota Press, 1930; *idem*, and E. G. WILLIAMSON, "Follow-up Studies of Early Scholastic Predictions in The University of Minnesota," *School and Soc.*, 1934, 40: 730–738; E. G. WILLIAMSON, "The Decreasing Accuracy of Scholastic Predictions," *J. of Educ. Psychol.*, 1937, 28: 1–16.

4. **Thorndike Intelligence Examination for High School Graduates,** by E. L. Thorndike, 1919 to date.

Description.—This is one of the most elaborate tests on the market. One of its distinctive features is the extensive fore-exercise provided to familiarize the student with the types of items included in the test itself. Part I consists of nine subtests of the following types: Directions, arithmetic computation, arithmetic reasoning, information, same-opposites and word meaning. Part II consists of six subtests of the following types: Completion, algebra problems, technical and general information. Part III contains eight tests of ability to read and comprehend different paragraphs.

The test requires about 3½ hours. The unusual amount of time required is due to the large number (460) and variety of test items and also due to Thorndike's desire to produce a power test in which the speed factor is reduced to a minimum. Scoring is done by keys and stencils. New, but equivalent, forms are issued annually.

Designed For.—The test is designed for high school graduates and college freshmen and is purposely pitched at such a high level of difficulty as to permit adequate measurement of individual differences in abstract intelligence among college students.

Ben D. Wood reports mean scores and standard deviations for a number of colleges and universities. Striking institutional differences are revealed by this comparison. For example, freshman men who "pass" their first semester work in one college are just barely equal in average Thorndike score to those who "fail" in another college. Typical results are as follows:

Institution	Number tested	Mean score	Standard deviation
A	350	81	13.3
E	294	71	16.7
J	400	52	16.0

Reliability.—The correlation between the scores obtained by the same group of college students on two forms of the Thorndike test is about +.85. In view of the narrow range of talent among those tested, Wood rightly estimates that the reliability of the test, if it were administered to students in grades nine through thirteen, would be +.95 or better.

In spite of the narrow range of talent tested at the college level, the probable error of a true score on the Thorndike test is only about 3 points.

Validity.—Numerous studies report correlations between Thorndike test scores and college marks (usually freshman marks) ranging from +.37 to +.67. In view of the care with which the examination was constructed, together with the variety of items included, one is inclined to accept the test as being one of the most valid intelligence tests at the college level. Wood's data indicate that the Thorndike test is more valid for predicting scholarship than Regent's Examination grades, secondary school grades, and College Entrance Examination Board marks.

Publisher and Cost.—Teachers College Bureau of Publications, Columbia University, New York. Price, $0.75 per test.

References.—E. L. THORNDIKE, "Intelligence Examinations for College Entrance," *J. of Educ. Res.*, 1920, 1: 329–337; RUTH STRANG, *Personal Development and Guidance in College and Secondary School*, Harper and Brothers, 1934; BEN D. WOOD, *Measurement in Higher Education*, especially Chapters III, IV and V, pp. 22–106, Yonkers-on-Hudson, New York: World Book Company, 1923.

5. Henmon-Nelson Tests of Mental Ability, for College Students, by V. A. C. Henmon, and M. J. Nelson, 1932.

Description.—The description of these tests parallels the description of the tests for high school pupils by the same authors (see p. 69). The only difference between them is in the difficulty of the items. Two forms, *A* and *B*, are available. The time allowed is 30 minutes.

Designed For.—The test is prepared for use with high school seniors and college students.

Norms.—Percentile norms are provided for each year in college on the basis of scores made by 5500 students in colleges and universities of varying sizes in different parts of the United States. None of the schools in which the tests were given for normative purposes utilizes a selective admission policy. The norms, therefore, are representative of colleges and universities that accept all high school graduates who apply. The percentile norm table gives the decile and quartile equivalents for total score. An abbreviated percentile norm table is as follows:

Percentile	Freshmen	Sophomores	Juniors	Seniors
100 (highest 1%)	70	71	76	80
75 (Q_3)	51	53	56	58
50 (median)	44	46	48	50
25 (Q_1)	37	38	40	41
1 (lowest 1%)	19	21	23	24

There is a two-point increase in average score for Forms A and B, when B follows A on successive days.

Reliability.—The correlation between Forms A and B given to 171 freshmen was $+.89 \pm .01$. The probable error of the total raw score is slightly more than 2 points.

Validity.—The technique of test construction used in devising the high school tests was also followed in preparing the college test. A total of 224 carefully prepared items were divided into two forms and given to 500 college students. Only items which proved to differentiate between superior and inferior students (as measured by a comprehensive battery of intelligence tests and achievement tests) were retained. The 180 items having the highest predictive value were then divided into two equivalent forms of 90 items each.

Correlations between the Henmon-Nelson Test and the American Council Psychological Examination, 1931 edition, were $+.77 \pm .03$; $+.68 \pm .02$; and $+.76 \pm .02$ for three studies involving college freshmen in a state university and in two teachers colleges. In a fourth study of college freshmen, the Henmon-Nelson Test was found to correlate $+.79 \pm .03$ with the Otis Test, Higher Examination, Form A. The authors interpret these correlations as being relatively high, in view of the narrow range of talent involved. One might add, however, the range of talent as measured by these tests in these four studies is undoubtedly far greater than would be found in a college or university in which selective admission is practiced.

The correlation between test score and first-semester grades in a teachers college was found to be $+.60 \pm .03$.

Drake and Henmon report a study of 618 liberal arts freshmen at the University of Wisconsin for whom the following measures were available: Percentile rank in high school graduating class (based on scholarship grades for four years); American Council Psychological Examination; Cooperative English Test I; and Henmon-Nelson Test for College Students. The following correlations between each of these four measures and freshmen grade point average were secured:

> Freshman grades and high school percentile.......... +.60
> Freshman grades and American Council Test......... +.58
> Freshman grades and Cooperative English Test I..... +.54
> Freshman grades and Henmon-Nelson Test.......... +.48

The authors found that the combination of high school scholarship percentile rank with one of the other tests increased the correlation with freshman grade average to a significant degree. They report that the Henmon-Nelson test when combined with high school percentile gives almost as high a correlation as does the American Council Test when combined with high school percentile, and therefore they conclude that the use of the former test is justified, especially so in view of the difference in cost.

Publisher and Cost.—Houghton Mifflin Company, Boston. Price of forms A and B, 75 cents per package of 25.

References.—L. E. DRAKE and V. A. C. HENMON, "The Prediction of Scholarship in the College of Letters and Science at the University of Wisconsin," *School and Soc.*, 1937, 45: 191–195; *Teacher's Manual*, 1932, by V. A. C. Henmon and M. J. Nelson, published by Houghton Mifflin Company.

D. READING TESTS

Differences among individuals in speed of reading and in ability to comprehend the printed page are probably as great as are differences in academic capacity. Since these differences are likely to affect favorably or unfavorably the adjustment of the individual, their extent should be determined in a well-rounded clinical study of the student.

Remedial work with students having serious reading and spelling disabilities should be undertaken only by those who are competent to diagnose and treat such cases. The work of Grace Fernald in Los Angeles indicates the complexities and difficulties in this field, as well as the remarkable results that can be achieved. She has shown that highly beneficial results can be obtained at the college level, even though the reading deficiency may have existed throughout the school history of the individual.[1] For these reasons, the guidance counselor must be on the alert to discover those students in high school or in college who need such expert diagnostic service and remedial treatment. The measurement of reading speed and comprehension is an obvious first step.

Even though the results of remedial treatment at the high school and college levels should be negligible, yet there would remain sufficient reasons for utilizing reading tests in a guidance program. To know how widely divergent an individual's achievement in reading comprehension and reading speed is from the average for his group should yield significant insight for educational guidance purposes. Even if no improvement at all could be expected, the student could at least be guided into those courses of study which would not strain his ability at its most vulnerable point. Courses requiring a great deal of reading could be avoided, and others chosen which happened to be more in line with abilities. There are probably as great differences among course requirements in the matter of quantity of reading required as there are differences among students in the ability to profit from such courses.

There is an additional reason for employing measurements of reading ability. A number of studies show that a considerable percentage of high school and college students who make serious efforts to improve their reading status are able to accomplish some measure of improvement. Drills in reading for speed, as well as comprehension, often make for improvement. Improvement in word knowledge is presumably an important factor in any general increase in reading accomplishment—hence, systematic vocabulary drills may be desirable.

Most important, perhaps, in coping with the general problem of reading efficiency is the factor of motivation. If the counselor can bring the student to the point where he is anxious to increase his achievement in reading, important progress towards increased reading skills can be made. Measurements of reading speed and comprehension should, therefore, have a definite place in the clinical program of guidance, although competent psychological

[1] FERNALD, GRACE M., and HELEN B. KELLER, "On Certain Language Disabilities, Their Nature and Treatment," *Mental Measurement Monog.*, Series 11, August, 1936, Baltimore: Williams & Wilkins Company.

diagnosticians should be consulted for intensive remedial work with students having serious reading disabilities.

1. **Chapman-Cook Speed of Reading Test,** 1923, by J. C. Chapman and S. A. Cook.

Description.—As the name indicates, the test was designed for the purpose of measuring speed of reading. The material consists of simple English sentences arranged in 30 paragraphs with 30 words in each paragraph. In the second half of each paragraph one of the words is obviously incorrect. To insure that the examinee reads for comprehension, he is checked by being required to locate the incorrect word and cross it out. A preliminary drill is provided before the test proper, which requires only 2½ minutes of time. Examinees are told to work as fast as they can. It has been found advisable to decrease the time allowance to 2 minutes when college students are examined on this test.

Two forms, *A* and *B*, have been constructed. Form *B* is slightly more difficult than Form *A*, in order to counteract any effects of practice resulting from the administration of Form *A* first.

When used at the high school and college levels, this test measures speed of reading rather than comprehension, since the vocabulary is so simple for more advanced students that practically all of them make no errors in locating the word which should be crossed out. Research with other tests, where speed of reading and comprehension of the same material are adequately measured, indicated that there is a close relationship between the speed with which an individual reads and his comprehension of the subject matter. Usually fast readers are those who grasp the meaning of the material most readily. On the whole, speed of reading is related to intelligence to some degree, but this does not hold in all cases.

Since rapid reading is a desirable trait for a college student to possess, the question of increase of reading speed with training is a pertinent one. The indications are that it can be increased, but probably not so much as 50 to 100 per cent in individual cases, according to a study reported in Bird's *Effective Study Habits.* One group of about 250 students improved after training, on the average, 16.5 per cent, as measured by this speed of reading test. Individuals, of course, vary in their ability to change their habits of reading.

Designed For.—The test was originally designed to measure speed of reading in elementary school pupils. It has since been applied to students at the college level, since it differentiates among students at this level as well.

Norms.—The authors furnish, with their directions for administering the test, percentile norms for grades four through eight, based upon the 2½-minute time limit. The median scores made by students in these grades are presented below, together with the median scores of high school and college students who were examined with the 2-minute time limit. The scores are merely the number of paragraphs read as determined by the last paragraph in which the incorrect word was crossed out.

Group	Median Score
Fourth grade	7.5
Fifth grade	10.4
Sixth grade	12.8
Seventh grade	14.5
Eighth grade	16.0
High school seniors (2260)	17.5
University arts freshmen (1415)	20.0

Reliability.—The correlation between the two forms has been found[2] to be $+.896 \pm .01$, an indication that one form of the test, when administered to individuals, yields sufficiently consistent scores.

Validity.—Because this test differentiates persons on the basis of the speed with which they are able to read these simple paragraphs, we cannot generalize and claim that it is a test for speed of reading of more difficult material. The indications are that reading skills are quite specialized and that individuals are inconsistent in the speed with which they read material of different degrees of difficulty.

Publisher and Cost.—Educational Test Bureau, Inc., 720 Washington Ave., S.E., Minneapolis, Minnesota. Price, 25 for $0.40.

References.—CHARLES BIRD, *Effective Study Habits*, New York: D. Appleton-Century Company, Inc., 1931; MILES A. TINKER, "The Relation of Speed to Comprehension in Reading," *School and Soc.*, 1932, 36.

[2] LITTERER, O., "An Experimental Study of Visual Apprehension in Reading," *J. of Appl. Psychol.*, June, 1933.

2. Minnesota Speed of Reading Test for College Students, by Alvin C. Eurich, 1936.

Description.—The two forms of this test which measures speed of reading require 6 minutes each of working time. Directions and sample paragraphs are given on the first page. The material is comparable in difficulty to reading material which the student meets in college. For this reason, the test probably is superior to the speed of reading tests in which the material is very simple, since speed of reading varies with the complexity of the material read. The examinee is instructed to read through as many of the 38 paragraphs as possible, drawing a line through the one absurd statement, which is located near the end of each paragraph. This affords a check, to make certain that the student has actually read that material for comprehension. One credit is given for each paragraph that is correct.

Designed For.—The test is most appropriate for students at the college level. Since grade norms have been established for some high school groups, it can be administered to those students as well.

Norms.—Percentile norms based upon University of Minnesota sophomores and juniors, as well as standard scores, are available for both forms of the test and are given in detail in the test manual. For illustrative purposes, norms for Form *A* are abbreviated below:

Raw score	Percentile	Scale value
31	95.24	66.5
23	76.79	57.5
20	53.87	51.0
16	27.68	44.0
8	4.76	33.0

Percentile norms are available for other grade groups as well. Grade norms for college graduates and juniors and high school seniors allow a rough indication of the grade level of an individual's score. The grade norms for Form *A* are as shown in the table on page 88.

Reliability.—The average reliability of a single form of this test was found to be .85 when the reliabilities between Form

A and Form B were calculated for six homogeneous grade groups of students from the seventh grade through college graduate students. When both forms of the test are administered, thus doubling the length of the test, the reliability would increase to .92.

Grade	Median score	Q_3	Q_1
College graduates	23.5	28.3	18.5
College juniors	22.6	26.1	19.2
High school seniors	18.4	20.8	14.1
High school sophomores	15.1	18.5	12.1

The test has been found to measure speed of reading at the seventh-grade level as reliably as it measures it at the college level, despite the relatively greater difficulty in content for younger children.

Validity.—When scores on this test were correlated with scores on the Chapman-Cook Speed of Reading Test with college juniors as subjects, the correlations ranged from .63 to .76, indicating that the two tests are measuring similar functions.

Publisher and Cost.—University of Minnesota Press, Minneapolis, Minnesota. Price, $2.75 per hundred; specimen set $0.35.

References.—A. C. EURICH, *The Reading Abilities of College Students*, Minneapolis: The University of Minnesota Press, 1931.

3. **Unit Scales of Attainment—Reading.** Division 4, Grades 9–12, by M. J. Van Wagenen, 1933.

Description.—Reading comprehension apart from speed is measured by the single choice questions following the eight paragraphs of this test. The subject matter of the paragraphs includes materials in the social and natural sciences. The examinee's ability to grasp the main idea of the paragraph and to understand and interpret the material read is measured. About 45 minutes are allowed. There will be published six forms of the test.

Designed For.—This particular test is designed for grades nine through twelve. Norms are available for students as low as the seventh grade, however. It is the reading section of

Division 4 of the Unit Scales of Attainment which is not yet on the market at the present writing.

Comparable reading tests for the lower grades are available as separate tests or as parts of the regular battery of the Unit Scales of Attainment.

Norms.—Raw scores may be transmuted into C-score values. C-scores indicate the level of difficulty which the examinee can reach and get half of the items correct.

By entering the C-score on the Class Record sheet it is a simple matter to read off the reading age, the mental age, and the grade-level equivalent of the score. Norms have been devised from large samples of cases. An abbreviated table of norms based upon 25,000 cases tested in 1936 is given below:

C-score	102	99	96	93	89	85
Grade	12A	11A	10A	9A	8A	7A

Reliability.—No reliability coefficients are supplied. Instead, probable errors of measurement are furnished. The approximate error in the C-score on this test is about 2.5 to 3.5 C-score points, or about the size of the gain made by an individual in a half-year's growth. If a more reliable measurement is desired, it is suggested that more than one form be administered in order to increase the number of items.

Validity.—The contents of this test have been carefully checked with subject-matter and test experts and in addition only those items were included which differentiated upper grade pupils from lower grade pupils and pupils making high scores on the test as a whole from those making low scores.

Publisher and Cost.—Educational Test Bureau, Minneapolis, Minnesota. Price, 25 for $0.75; specimen set, $0.20.

References.—M. J. VAN WAGENEN, *Directions for Administering and Scoring Unit Scales of Attainment—Reading*, Educational Test Bureau, Minneapolis, 1933.

4. Iowa Silent Reading Tests. Advanced Tests, by H. A. Greene, A. N. Jorgensen, and N. H. Kelley, 1927.

Description.—This test measures, in 35 minutes of testing time, a wide range of skills necessary in effective reading of the type required in high school and college. There are six tests with subtests and two forms.

Test 1 measures ability to comprehend the meaning of paragraphs dealing with subject matters in science and in English. The examinee is instructed to read a selection and then to demonstrate comprehension by answering questions on the material. The answer is given by selecting and designating the numbered and bracketed passage in the paragraph which contains the answer.

Knowledge of word meaning is determined in Test 2 by single-choice types of items in the fields of social science, science, mathematics and English.

Test 3 measures the ability to comprehend the organization of paragraphs. The examinee is asked to select the phrase following the paragraphs read which most nearly expresses the central idea of the paragraph. In the second part, the examinee outlines paragraphs read by placing in outline form numbers corresponding to bracketed phrases in the paragraph.

Test 4 is a modified true-false test, measuring comprehension of the meaning of sentences.

Test 5 measures the examinee's ability to locate information in a sample index.

The last test measures rate of reading rather than comprehension.

Designed For.—This test may be administered to students from the first year in high school through the first year in college.

The Elementary Test is designed for grades four to nine. Diagnosis is even more important in the lower grades, where there is more possibility for results from remedial treatment. In the upper grades, knowledge of achievement is equally helpful in guidance.

Norms.—The authors furnish complete grade and percentile norms for the subtests and for the battery as a whole. These norms were based upon about 6000 students distributed approximately equally among the grades from the ninth through the thirteenth. The results were obtained at the end of the school year.

For illustrative purposes, abbreviated percentile norms are given on page 91 for the total score on the first five tests, measuring "comprehension," and for the sixth test, measuring "speed" of reading:

Percentile	Tests 1–5 Grades					Test 6 Grades				
	9	10	11	12	13	9	10	11	12	13
99	160	168	180	190	205	52	56	58	59	60
75	100	116	134	147	169	33	35	36	37	38
50	80	93	109	123	145	26	29	30	31	32
25	59	70	83	96	118	20	23	24	25	26
1	29	34	44	53	83	8	10	12	13	14

Reliability.—The authors reported corrected odd-even reliability coefficients and probable errors of scores, obtained on different groups of students tested within a single grade range. These coefficients vary somewhat with the group used but, on the whole, are quite acceptable. Especially may the test as a whole be considered a reliable device. The lowest corrected correlation for the first five tests as a unit was found to be .95 for a twelfth-grade group. The probable error of that group's score was 5.73.

For Test 1 the coefficients ranged from .84 to .91; for Test 2, from .87 to .94; for Test 3, from .86 to .94; for Test 4, from .59 to .95; for Test 5, from .80 to .90.

Validity.—According to the authors, "validity may be expressed in terms of the extent to which the test sets up a situation calling into play the use of the skills or abilities which experienced observers consider fundamental to success in the given field." This particular measure meets with the authors' criterion of validity, as they describe its method of construction.

Publisher and Cost.—World Book Company, Yonkers-on-Hudson, New York. Price, 25 for $1.40; manual of directions, $0.08; key, $0.03; class record, $0.02; specimen set, $0.20.

References.—H. A. GREENE, A. N. JORGENSEN, and N. H. KELLEY, *Iowa Silent Reading Tests. Advanced Test. Manual of Directions*, Yonkers-on-Hudson, New York: World Book Company, 1931.

5. Minnesota Reading Examination for College Students, 1930, by M. E. Haggerty and A. C. Eurich.

Description.—This test was designed to measure comprehension in reading, and requires less than an hour to administer.

Test I is a recognition vocabulary test. Test II consists of ten paragraphs, followed by objective questions on the material contained in the paragraph. The time allowed for this second part is ample so that comprehension, aside from speed, is measured. Printed directions precede each part and a few samples and trial exercises are given to assure understanding of the directions. Two comparable forms, A and B, have been constructed.

Designed For.—The title of the test is in a way a misnomer, since it may be administered to students in all high school grades, as well as college years. Norms have been established at these levels and may be found in the Examiner's Manual. Its greatest usefulness will probably be with students who are failing or who present problems of adjustment to the curriculum. Suggestions regarding concentrated vocabulary drill, enrollment in "How to Study" courses, etc., might profitably be based on objective evidence such as is furnished by the test.

Norms.—Percentile and standard score norms are furnished in the Examiner's Manual for Test 1 and Test 2, Form A, for university freshmen and high school seniors. Percentile and standard score norms are also furnished for scores on either form of the test as a whole for college sophomores, juniors and seniors. Median scores and Q_1 and Q_3 scores are furnished for the ninth, tenth, eleventh, and twelfth grades and for college juniors and seniors on Test 1 and Test 2 of Form A.

The median percentile scores for some of these groups are listed below for illustrative purposes:

Group	Test I Form A	Test II Form A	Total test Form A	Total test Form B
College juniors and seniors	41	18		
College sophomores, juniors, seniors	..	..	91	94
University freshmen	33	15		
High school graduating seniors	33	14		
12th grade	39	15		
11th grade	27	14		
10th grade	24	13		
9th grade	21	11		

Reliability.—The reliability for Test I is as high as that characterizing many tests used for individual diagnosis. The reliability of Test II is somewhat lower and should not be considered apart from the vocabulary score in diagnosing reading comprehension. A fairly reliable measure is obtained when both parts are used. The reliability coefficients reported by Dr. A. C. Eurich are as follows:

Group	Method	Test I	Test II	Total
283 high school seniors	Corrected odd-even	.93	.69	
216 college juniors and seniors	Retest	.91	.78	.86

Validity.—Since there is no readily accessible outside criterion against which to check this type of test, to determine whether or not it is actually measuring "reading comprehension," it was necessary to select items which would by their very nature be valid indicators of "reading comprehension." The authors point out that recognition of words is a necessary element in comprehension. Likewise, the answering of questions based upon paragraphs read seems to be analogous to situations in which one must "comprehend" reading matter. The authors listed the factors of the test that are similar to "comprehension" and these are given below as evidence of validity:

1. The test requires a knowledge of how to read.
2. The test requires a knowledge of vocabulary.
3. The test requires an understanding of the authors' organization of thought.
4. The same mechanics of reading, such as eye movements, are involved in the test as in the usual reading situations.
5. The test requires of the reader a background of experience to enable him to understand the content of the passage.
6. The test requires the ability to analyze the passage.

As the authors also point out, the test differs from the ordinary reading situation only in the increased motivation in the test situation, the artificiality of the situation and the brevity of the reading matter and its divorce from its proper setting.

There is a fair degree of relationship between the test and measures of academic intelligence but the correlations are not so high as to indicate that both are measuring exactly the same traits. We may say that this test is measuring "reading comprehension," while other tests are measuring "college aptitude," knowing of course that such titles are artificial and that some similar traits are measured by both tests. There is also a fairly high correlation between this test and scholarship in college and in high school. The relationship was +.48 for 128 college juniors and seniors and +.54 for 285 high school seniors.

Publisher and Cost.—University of Minnesota Press. Price, $6 per hundred.

References.—A. C. EURICH, *Reading Abilities of College Students*, Minneapolis: University of Minnesota Press, 1931; A. C. EURICH and M. E. HAGGERTY, *Examiner's Manual. The Minnesota Reading Examination for College Students*, Minneapolis: University of Minnesota Press, 1935.

CHAPTER IV
ACADEMIC ACHIEVEMENT TESTS

The measurement of achievement has been associated with educational practice for many years. It is not surprising, therefore, to discover that marked progress in improving measuring devices in this field has taken place. Achievement testing, like intelligence testing, developed earlier and has progressed faster in the schools than has the measurement of aptitudes, attitudes, interests and personality traits. This is mainly so because educators have always emphasized intellectual growth and academic achievement. Since subject-matter achievement has been a primary goal of the school, it is natural that educators should have welcomed methods for measuring relative degrees of scholastic accomplishments. These methods fitted naturally into the traditional scheme of academic credits, units, requirements, etc.

Educational philosophy more recently is emphasizing individual differences and individual "adjustments," rather than "standards" of accomplishment to be met by all alike. This shift in emphasis means that the administrative and supervisory use of achievement tests is being replaced by the practice of using them as basic tools in the guidance of individual pupils. Along with this new point of view, there have been introduced other tools for gaining insight into students' aptitudes, interests, personality traits, etc, which make it increasingly possible for educators to adapt educational facilities to the needs of students.

The purpose of achievement tests now is to determine not so much whether the student has "passed" or "failed" as it is to determine how he ranks in relation to his fellows who have enjoyed equal amounts of "exposure" to teaching and in what aspects of his schooling he has shown the greatest and the least relative amounts of progress. Thus the measurement of past achievement tends to be used as a gauge for future accomplishment.

The counselor needs to know more than the actual present or past accomplishment of the student. In planning for his future training he needs to know the individual's capacity for further development. It is possible to infer aptitude from achievement. Even though the test itself may not be an "aptitude" test in the usual sense of the term, achievement scores may nevertheless yield indications of aptitude. When the test items cover material to which everyone has had an approximately equal exposure the differences obtained are indicative of capacity. There is a very fine line separating achievement and aptitude tests, since the two types appear to be measuring about the same thing, if previous exposure is approximately equal. Thus, an achievement-test score increases in significance when it is interpreted in the light of the individual's exposure to the information included. Given equal opportunities for acquiring the facts of a given subject matter, some of the differences among individuals may be attributed to native differences in capacity for acquiring those facts. It is true that all the differences may not be due to differences in innate ability, but for practical purposes, interpretations of this type can be made. A student who has had general science, botany, biology, physics and chemistry in high school and who makes an average score on a general science achievement test, for example, probably possesses much less aptitude for scientific work than an individual with the same score who has been "exposed" to far less formal science training.

The major purpose of these tests, then, should be to help in judging students in regard to their educational and vocational decisions. There are other uses for achievement tests beyond those for guidance. They may be used for students in admission, promotion and graduation. It is quite legitimate in some situations to set minimum standards of accomplishment. The student with low achievement scores will benefit if prevented from enrolling in courses beyond his capacity.

One important use of achievement tests is in the prediction of scholarship. It has been shown that the one best single indication of future scholarship is past scholarship.[1] Relative high

[1] See WILLIAMSON, E. G., *The Prediction of College Scholarship*, unpublished report, University Testing Bureau, University of Minnesota, 1937; also, SEGEL, DAVID, "Prediction of Success in College," *U.S. Office of Education Bull.*, 1934, No. 15, U.S. Government Printing Office, Washington, D.C., 1934.

school scholarship (rank in graduating class based on past grades for three or four years) is the single best index for the prediction of college scholarship. Due to the fact, however, that high school scholarship has such different meanings from one school to another, it is better to use achievement-test scores if a single index is to be used. Furthermore, a battery of achievement tests is superior to a single test of academic intelligence in predicting scholarship. There is some evidence, however, that an intelligence test such as the American Council on Education Examination or the Ohio State Psychological Examination is superior to high school grades and general achievement-test scores in the case of women students. For men, however, the high school grades and achievement-test scores are the best predictive measures. If several tests are available, a better measure of prediction is obtained by combining achievement-test results with relative high school scholarship than by using one academic aptitude test and high school grades. The best index, of course, would be based upon relative high school rank, a scholastic aptitude test and a battery of achievement tests.

There are two general types of tests in this field: general achievement tests and diagnostic tests. There seems to be no hard and fast line of demarcation, but the difference is a matter of the reliance which may be placed upon test scores. Most of the measures of achievement are of the general type, in that they yield a single score representing the individual's relative achievement in the general field being measured. When the test is divided into sections measuring different aspects of the general subject-matter, and when these separate scores are sufficiently reliable, then the test becomes a diagnostic device. The main difference between the two types is that the general test only samples the parts of the whole field in such a way that reliance may not be placed upon scores on any one part alone. With the diagnostic test, it becomes possible to discover the particular aspect of the achievement field in which the examinee is relatively lower or higher, thus making it possible to determine the parts of the subject matter which need special remedial treatment or which may be considered as fields for major concentration.

One of the requirements of a good achievement test is that it be supplied in several comparable forms. This makes it possible to apply a comparable measuring stick at different periods during a person's development and thus obtain a picture of his growth in the trait measured. This developmental picture in objective terms is essential to complete diagnosis and is more dependable than the cross-section picture obtained by one short test applied at one specific point of time.

The technique used in constructing the best achievement tests at the present time cannot be described here. The tendency is for the work to be done by centralized agencies which can assure proper attention to the requirements of test construction. Generally subject-matter experts join with test experts in the work. Attempts are made to assure the validity of the instruments by the careful selection and construction of items. Objectives of courses are determined by reference to widely used curricula and textbooks and items submitted for approval to curriculum experts and teachers.

It would be impracticable to include here a description of all well-standardized achievement tests applicable to junior and senior high school and college students. Those which are described represent some of those more widely used and are representative of the more reliable tests. Achievement tests for junior high school will be described in this chapter. Tests for senior high school and junior college will be presented in the next chapter.

JUNIOR HIGH SCHOOL

1. New Stanford Achievement Test, Advanced Examination, 1929, by T. L. Kelley, G. M. Ruch and L. M. Terman.

Description.—The New Stanford Achievement Test, Advanced Examination, with its five forms, V, W, X, Y and Z, is a revision of the 1923 test. It is designed to measure achievement in elementary school subjects. The ten individual tests are available separately or as a part of the 24-page battery. The nature of the test is revealed by the tabular description of the subtests as shown in the table on page 99.

The time allowed is usually ample, thus testing power rather than speed. Two and one-half hours of actual working time are required, but the gross time needed would be 15 or 20 minutes longer. The authors recommend four sittings to complete the battery.

ACADEMIC ACHIEVEMENT TESTS

Sub-test number	Name	Nature of items	Number of items	Time allowed (in minutes)	Subject matter tested
1	Paragraph meaning	Completion	80	25	Reading comprehension
2	Word meaning	Multiple choice	80	10	Vocabulary
3	Dictation	Oral	108	15	Spelling
4	Language usage	Multiple choice	74	10	Word usage and grammar
5	Literature	Multiple choice	80	10	Acquaintance with literature
6	History and civics	Multiple choice	80	10	Acquaintance with social studies
7	Geography	Multiple choice	80	10	Acquaintance with geographical information of social importance
8	Physiology and hygiene	Multiple choice	80	10	Functional information in anatomy, and physiology related to principles of hygiene
9	Arithmetic reasoning	Short mathematical responses	40	20	Interpretive ability rather than mere computation
10	Arithmetic computation	Mathematical responses	60	30	Computation of various types of samples of successive degrees of complexity

Designed For.—Pupils from grades four through nine can be given this advanced battery. For most of the battery, the test questions are the same for pupils of these different levels. This means that the more advanced students are responding to a number of lower level questions which do not serve to differentiate them, while the younger pupils are faced with many problems which prove too difficult for them. The wide variety of questions in this case appears to be disadvantageous, since the number of suitable questions for a homogeneous group on a high, average or low level becomes too small to measure as reliably as is desirable for work with individuals.

Norms.—For interpretive purposes, "raw test scores" are converted into "equated scores," each of which corresponds to an educational age, a chronological age and a school grade norm. These converted scores can be easily read off from the Educational Profile Chart which is printed on each test booklet. Thus it is possible to determine the chronological age as well as the school grade for which the test score obtained is typical. The norms are based on large numbers of pupils in representative schools in selected parts of the country. The authors state that the age norms are "far more significant" than grade norms and prefer to use these, since the grade in which a pupil is located may be due to many factors extraneous to that of subject-matter accomplishment. A further refinement of the age norms which has not been used in this test is that of furnishing age-at-grade norms, or norms for different ages at various grade levels. Another limitation of the test is that percentile norms are not furnished for each grade. These are usually more meaningful and dependable for interpretive purposes than the grade norms.

The Educational Profile Chart provides a graphic method for comparing an individual's scores on the various tests of the battery with scores of the average for his group. It also makes it easy to see the fields in which the person excels, as well as those in which he may need remedial attention. A word of caution is necessary, however. One must keep in mind the fact that the reliability of the separate subtests is not always so high as it should be for individual diagnosis.

A Class Analysis Chart provides a graphic means for representing the distribution and central tendency of the class scores for the separate tests, as well as for the total scores.

Reliability.—The test as a unit is highly reliable. The authors show a correlation of +.94 obtained for the total score for 143 ninth-grade pupils. A number of the individual tests. however, are not so reliable as they should be for use in individual guidance and, in this respect, the Metropolitan Achievement Test appears to be a superior instrument, since it contains many more questions for each separate test.

Validity.—Validity rests upon the character of the content and was assured by the painstaking methods used in constructing and selecting items. Detailed studies of textbooks and courses of study preceded the preparation of items. These were then rated by competent judges and tryouts were undertaken. The final selection of items was based upon statistical item analysis.

Publisher and Cost.—The World Book Company, Yonkers-on-Hudson, New York. Prices: tests, $0.08, each; directions for administering, $0.07; key, $0.07; class analysis chart, $0.03; guide for interpreting, $0.15.

References.—T. L. KELLEY, G. M. RUCH, and L. M. TERMAN, *Guide for Interpreting New Stanford Achievement Test,* Yonkers-on-Hudson, New York: World Book Company, 1929; T. L. KELLEY, G. M. RUCH, and L. M TERMAN, *Directions for Administering New Stanford Achievement Test,* Yonkers-on-Hudson, New York: World Book Company, 1929.

2. **Metropolitan Achievement Test, Advanced Battery,** 1933, by R. D. Allen, H. H. Bixler, W. L. Connor, F. B. Graham, G. H. Hildreth and J. S. Orleans.

Description.—The Metropolitan Achievement Tests also measure the achievement of pupils in elementary school subjects. The questions are divided into four batteries: the two primary batteries and the intermediate battery are appropriate for the first six grades, and the advanced battery, which will be described here, is designed for seventh- and eighth-grade children. There are five nearly comparable forms of the intermediate and advanced batteries, thus making it possible to measure individual growth by comparable measures over a period of several years. The authors have listed some of the purposes for which the tests may be used as follows:

1. To provide a more objective and reliable basis for classification and grouping for instructional purposes.
2. To provide a more objective and reliable basis for promotion.
3. To help the teacher evaluate her teaching methods objectively.
4. To give the supervisor an objective basis for helping the teacher to improve her instruction.
5. To diagnose the deficiencies of pupils as a basis for remedial work.
6. To evaluate achievement in terms of ability.

The main objective should be to adjust the work of the school to the attainments and aptitudes of the pupil. These objective and reliable methods are superior to the nonstandardized traditional methods. High school counselors will find the tests useful in guidance, since the accomplishment of pupils in various subject-matter fields in the elementary grades will provide valuable clues with respect to probable future accomplishment in high school. Not only will general level of achievement be revealed but, what is frequently of more importance, special abilities and disabilities will also be revealed. Both kinds of facts are essential for wise educational and vocational planning.

The advanced battery is made up of nine tests, covering the subjects most commonly taught at this level: reading, arithmetic, English and social studies. The type of question varies from one test to another and may vary within a single test. For the most part, completion, short-answer, multiple-choice and matching questions constitute the various types used.

In the reading test, the pupil supplies omitted words or answers questions on short paragraphs read in a way to indicate that he has been able to select the given facts, draw conclusions or comprehend the thought. Test 2 is a recognition vocabulary test of the multiple-choice variety. Test 3 measures arithmetic fundamentals, such as adding, subtracting, multiplying and dividing whole numbers and fractions and the interpretation of graphs. Test 4 covers different types of arithmetic problems calling for the application of arithmetic to the solution of practical problems. Test 5 is divided into three parts, measuring language usage, punctuation and capitalization and grammar. In the first part the pupil must supply in a given sentence the correct form of a word which is often used incorrectly. The second part calls for supplying correct punctuation marks and capitalization in sentences in which they have been omitted. In the grammar section, the pupil must indicate his knowledge of types of sentences, sentence structure, parts of speech and the grammatical reasons for specific examples of correct usage. Test 6 measures by the multiple-choice technique the pupil's acquaintance with a wide range of literature to which he may have been exposed. Test 7 includes multiple-choice items in the fields of history and civics, and Test 8 covers questions in geography. Test 9 consists of a list of 50 spelling words dictated by the examiner.

The total time for the battery of 9 tests is about 4 hours, including the time for directions, etc. The authors recommend that the battery be divided into four sittings of about an hour each, in order to eliminate fatigue. The time limits for the individual tests are liberal, thus making the test one of power rather than speed. Explicit directions for administering and scoring are supplied by the publishers.

Designed For.—The advanced battery is appropriate for seventh- and eighth-grade pupils in the public schools. It has been used extensively in the independent schools as well, but due to the fact that these students are advanced about one year on the average, in terms of national public school grade norms, separate norms for independent schools have been published by the Educational Records Bureau.

School Administrators may find it worth while to administer the battery near the end of the eighth grade, in order to collect valuable data which will facilitate the placement of students in sections in high school courses appropriate to their achievement in the fundamental subject-matter courses of the elementary school. Knowledge of test scores will save teachers many hours of effort in determining the level of achievement of new pupils and will help to assure better adaptation of the school to the pupil.

The test results may be found of use in occasional cases where indications of past attainment are not available. Transfer students' scores should be compared with norms developed in the school to which the transfer is made. Occasionally there may be persons, possibly of more mature age, who wish to enroll in high school without having completed the formal requirements of the elementary schools. Objective-achievement tests will enable the school to judge the individual case.

The supervisor's manual contains valuable information on methods of diagnosis and remedial treatment for specific subject-matter deficiencies which characterize some students.

The test has a wide range of applicability, thus making it appropriate for seventh-grade pupils of low achievement as well as eighth-grade pupils of exceptionally high achievement.

Norms.—The test authors urge users to develop their own norms for local use, since pupils' scores have more meaning when compared with students of their own population than when compared with a national norm, which is made up of a composite of scores on students from widely scattered schools with varying standards and types of pupils. The authors furnish three types of norms, however, although they prefer to have the local authorities set up their own standards. Explicit directions for developing local norms are provided in their supervisor's manual.

Grade and age equivalents, as well as percentile norms for each grade, are furnished for test scores. Grade equivalents are based on about 6000 subjects and represent the average score in each grade for each school subject. The percentile norms for the separate tests for each of the grades are supplied in the supervisor's manual. Grade equivalents for scores are obtained by reference to the individual profile chart printed on the last page of each test booklet. It is necessary only to locate the score on the individual tests and then read across to the school grade for which the score is typical. Age equivalents are listed for each grade and tenth of a grade, thus making it possible to determine the age in years and months for which any test score is average. A further advantage of these tests is that the grade equivalents for all tests are comparable, since the tests were standardized on the same group of subjects.

The individual profile chart is a very convenient method for recording a pupil's scores in such a way that the interpretation in terms of grade and age equivalents is apparent at once. It also enables one to see at a glance those subjects in which the student is especially weak or in which he excels. There is also a class analysis chart on which the grade equivalents for each pupil and for each test are recorded. This makes it possible to see the class distribution for each subject and a profile may be drawn connecting median grade equivalents for each test, thus enabling the teacher to analyze the accomplishments of the class in relation to national or local norms.

Reliability.—The authors furnish detailed information on the consistency with which their batteries of tests measure achievement at the different grade levels, for each test separately as well as for the battery as a whole. They present their data in terms of probable errors of an individual's scores and in terms of correlation coefficients obtained by administering Forms A and B of the test to the same persons. The detailed data are given in the following table:

Grade	Total average	Test 1	Test 2	Test 3	Test 4	Test 5	Test 6	Test 7	Test 8	Test 9	Number tested
Probable Errors of a Pupil's Score in Months												
7	2.2	3.6	3.2	3.2	3.5	2.5	3.0	3.6	3.0	1.9	213
8	2.0	4.1	2.9	3.0	3.2	2.1	3.4	3.7	3.2	1.7	201
Coefficients of Correlation between Form A and Form B												
7	.92	.82	.87	.88	.84	.84	.86	.85	.87	.95	213
8	.95	.84	.86	.87	.91	.86	.79	.82	.77	.90	201

Considering that these indications of reliability were secured on relatively homogeneous groups of students, the reliability of the measurements, even for the subtests, is surprisingly high, indicating that profiles may be used with reasonable accuracy.

Validity.—The test's validity, as with so many of the achievement tests, rests mainly on its content. Here, again, validity is assured by the painstaking steps followed in construction. Before attempting to construct questions, the aims and content of courses of study in many representative school systems were studied. Preliminary research was carried on to insure the inclusion of questions for the various aspects of the different subjects.

Over 8000 questions were then compiled for use in grades four through eight. These were reduced to about 5000 after conference with subject-matter experts. The questions were then divided into five preliminary forms and administered to 10,000 pupils in a large number of representative schools. Much careful statistical work followed, until the tests reached their present form. They have since been accepted as "measuring what they purport to measure" by persons who are familiar with the content of courses of study as well as those concerned with the structural and statistical criteria.

Publisher and Cost.—World Book Company, Yonkers-on-Hudson, New York. Prices: complete Advanced Battery test, $0.08; directions for administering, $0.07; key, $0.07; class analysis chart, $0.06; supervisor's manual, $0.80. For prices on other batteries and partial batteries or separate tests, see World Book Company catalogue.

References.—*Supervisor's Manual, Metropolitan Achievement Tests*, Yonkers-on-Hudson, New York: World Book Company, 1936; *1934 Achievement Test Program in Independent Schools*, New York: Educational Records Bureau.

3. **Unit Scales of Attainment, Division 3,** 1933, by M. E. Branom, L. J. Brueckner, A. M. Jordan, P. Cutright, W. A. Anderson, M. G. Kelty, A. Dvorak and M. J. VanWagenen.

Description.—Division 3 of the Unit Scales of Attainment is appropriate for students in the seventh and eighth grades. Division 1 should be used for grades three and four and Division 2 for grades five and six. Primary divisions are also provided for the first three grades. Four forms will eventually be available for each division, and at the present date forms *A* and *B* have been printed. The time limits for the tests are not rigid but may be shortened or lengthened. The usual time allowed is 3 hours, divided into four periods of 45 minutes each.

The feature which distinguishes this battery of achievement tests is the scaling technique employed in building the tests. Each item has a difficulty value which is known. The distances between test items of known difficulty are kept constant, thereby resulting in a scale with equal units of measurement. It thus becomes possible to determine the level of difficulty which the individual achieves in any trait being measured. The authors claim that this technique permits the measurement of *absolute achievement*, whereas unscaled tests, consisting of items of unknown difficulty, can yield only scores having significance relative to group achievement. The C-score used is independent of the time required and indicates the level of difficulty at which one-half of the items are answered correctly.

There are ten sections in each form. The reading test contains eight paragraphs of increasing difficulty. The examinee responds to single-choice questions regarding the main point of the paragraph and its details. The geography section involves single-choice items calling for specific information in the field. The literature, elementary science and American history tests likewise call for facts by the single-choice type of question. Arithmetic achievement is measured by a section of verbal problems and another on fundamental operations in arithmetic. There is a spelling test of 40 words. English punctuation, capitalization and usage are measured by having the pupil detect and correct errors.

Designed For.—The third division of these scales is designed particularly for seventh- and eighth-grade students. It should be of especial value for students who transfer from the elementary school to high school at the close of the eighth grade. Such an objective measurement would be a valuable supplement to elementary school marks in aiding the new school administrators concerned with the student's proper placement, guidance and subsequent adjustment.

Norms.—An individual profile chart permits ready determination and recording of chronological age, grade and mental age equivalents of C-scores for the individual tests. The C-score is merely located for each section of the battery and the equivalent read off from the chart by following the horizontal line across to the column of norms. The norms in use were developed on 8500 normal school children in many different sections of the country.

Reliability.—The test when used as a whole yields sufficiently consistent results for use in individual guidance. The probable error of the average of individual scores is 2 months, which means that there is a fifty-fifty chance that the individual's "true" score on the test as a whole would vary from his obtained score by no more than 2 months of mental age in either direction.

The specific achievement scales are not long enough, however, to be sufficiently reliable for purposes of advising individual pupils with respect to the accomplishment in the specific subject-matter tests. The error involved in some of these individual tests amounts to as much as the gain in achievement scores which the average student makes in half a year in school.

In order to obtain a reliable measurement for the special subject fields included, the authors have prepared longer tests covering achievement in arithmetic, literature, geography, American history and elementary science. The contents of these analytical scales are similar to those of the scales in the various forms of the battery and employ the same unit of measurement. Further information may be obtained from the publisher.

Validity.—The items in the separate tests have been compiled and approved by subject-matter experts after careful study of textbooks and courses of study. In addition to this, items have been included only when they differentiated between upper and lower grades of students and between students making high scores on the test as a whole and those making lower scores.

Publisher and Cost.—Educational Test Bureau, Inc., 720 Washington Ave., S.E., Minneapolis, Minnesota, or 3416 Walnut Street, Philadelphia, Pennsylvania. Prices: 25, including 25 individual profile charts and class record sheet, for $1.50; manual, $0.25.

References.—*Unit Scales of Attainment, Directions for Administering and Scoring*, Educational Test Bureau, Inc., Minneapolis, Minnesota, and Philadelphia, Pennsylvania.

4. Iowa Every-pupil Tests of Basic Skills for Grades Six, Seven and Eight, 1936. E. Horn, M. McBroom, H. A. Greene, F. B. Knight, E. F. Lindquist.

Description.—The Iowa Every-pupil Tests of Basic Skills represent a new departure in achievement testing in that they propose to measure the basic skills necessary for success in junior and senior high school rather than achievement in a specific curriculum subject which is taught in a particular grade. The acquisition of these tool skills in arithmetic, language, reading and work-study extends over a period of years and determines to a great extent subsequent school success, according to the authors. They have carefully analyzed the four main achievement fields, reading, work-study, language and arithmetic into twenty-three basic skills and then devised items for each skill which will measure in a reliable way the pupil's ability to apply these skills in a test situation. In all, there are 718 specific items in the 48 pages to which the examinee must react. The total test requires 4 hours 24 minutes of actual testing time. The time should be divided into two or three periods to counteract fatigue. The gross time required is around 5 hours.

The analytical aspect of the battery is an advantage to the teacher in the practical situation who is concerned with correcting defects found in individual pupils with respect to these specific skills. A special section in the test manual is devoted to specific suggestions for remedial work in each of the specific skills being measured. The authors hope, however, that their analysis will operate as a stimulus toward a clearer understanding of skills involved in these subjects in order that prevention may supplant the need for cure.

The first basic skill, silent reading comprehension, is measured by four parts of Test A and Part 1 of Test B. The first part of Test A is a measure of paragraph comprehension and requires the examinee to select from several sentences the one which expresses the main idea of a paragraph in selections which the examinee is asked to read. In the second part, organization of ideas is tested, the questions being based, as in the first part, upon three selections read. Part 3 measures understanding of significant details and Part 4 tests ability to comprehend the total meaning of a selection read. A practice exercise assures understanding of directions by the pupils. Although the vocabulary section is located as the first part of Test B, it is functionally important in the comprehension of reading. It is a recognition vocabulary test, with the words to be defined presented in phrases or short sentences.

The other five parts of Test B are concerned with basic study skills, such as comprehension of maps, reading graphs and charts, use of basic references and the use of the index and the dictionary.

Test *C* measures basic language skills. Part 1 is a spelling test in which the pupil writes the designated words which are contained in sentences dictated by the examiner. In Part 2 the examinee shows his ability to distinguish sentences from phrases. In the third part he indicates errors in capitalization and in Part 4 he corrects punctuation in a list of sentences. Part 5 contains sentences with errors in English usage which must be corrected by the pupil. His ability to apply his knowledge, rather than knowledge of formal rules in grammar, is being tested.

Test *D*, which measures basic arithmetic skills, is composed of four parts. Part 1 measures ability to add, subtract, multiply and divide whole numbers, fractions and decimals and to deal with percentages and denominate numbers. Part 2 presents verbal problems for solution. Parts 3 and 4 test knowledge of verbalized rules and vocabulary in arithmetic and ability to make proper corrections in arithmetic computations.

A new form of this test is available in the spring of each year, at least until 1940, at which time five comparable forms will have been produced.

Designed For.—The tests were originally designed for survey purposes for sixth-, seventh- and eighth-grade pupils in the State of Iowa, but they are made available to other groups shortly after the annual "every-pupil testing program" in Iowa has been completed. The norms are established in the early part of each year. These norms are based for the most part on pupils in schools located in Iowa or neighboring states in communities with populations of from 1000 to 50,000. They are characterized by the authors as "Middlewestern" norms, but can be used in other sections of the country, especially when supplemented by norms developed locally.

Because of the very wide range of accomplishment found in these skills among sixth-, seventh- and eighth-grade students, there is necessarily an equally wide range of difficulty among the items, thus making the test appear rather difficult to students who make low scores.

Norms.—The authors furnish three types of norms: Grade norms, age-at-grade norms and percentile norms. They are based on 28,409 pupils in the sixth, seventh and eighth grades of 240 school systems. The grade norms indicate, for each of the four tests and for the vocabulary section, the grade and fraction of a grade for which the scores are typical. The age-at-grade norms indicate for these same tests the typical scores made by pupils of different chronological ages in each half-grade from the second semester of the fifth grade to the second semester of the eighth grade. Percentile norms are provided for each part and the total test and are set up on the profile sheet for recording individual scores in such a way as to be immediately read off from the chart when the score is located on the chart. These profile charts are especially useful in recording graphically the pupils' achievement in these basic skills in relation to other pupils and in presenting a striking picture of his high points and weaknesses on the various skills being measured.

The authors recommend the use of the percentile norms because of their ease in recording and the soundness with which they may be interpreted. These percentiles indicate the percentage of pupils of the same grade population who score lower. This is a more meaningful interpretation than that which is given by grade norms. Grade norms merely indicate the school grade for which an individual's score would be "typical."

Reliability.—No statistical evidence of the test's reliability is presented by the authors who cite past experience to substantiate their claim of adequate reliability. There is every reason to believe that this battery with its 718 items is highly reliable, but it would be desirable to know the extent of the probable error of the score, even though it be small. One suspects that the test is sufficiently reliable, in its individual parts, and as a whole, to make possible decreasing its length to some extent.

Validity.—The authors define validity as "the extent to which a test sets up situations calling into play the use of skills which experienced and qualified observers consider fundamental to success in the given field." Since their battery meets the criterion which they have set up in their definition of validity, they have not sought further evidence of the "extent to which the test measures what it purports to measure." Since outside criteria are so difficult to find in this field of measurement, the authors allow the acceptance of this battery as a valid device to depend upon an examination of its content. Courses of study and textbooks have been thoroughly investigated and the skills required for scholastic success at this level carefully analyzed before trying out the items constructed on the basis of such study and analysis.

Publisher and Cost.—Bureau of Educational Research and Service, Extension Division, University of Iowa, Iowa City, Iowa. Prices: four-test battery, $0.20; copies of tests separately, $0.06 each; profile charts for individual pupils, $0.01 each; directions for examiner and manual supplied with order of tests. Prices subject to discount for quantities.

References.—*Manual for Administration and Interpretation of Iowa Every-pupil Tests of Basic Skills*, Bureau of Educational Research and Service, Extension Division, University of Iowa, Iowa City, Iowa, 1936.

5. Progressive Achievement Tests, Intermediate Battery, 1934, by E. W. Tiegs and W. W. Clark.

Description.—The Progressive Achievement Tests aim to measure accomplishment in the basic skills of reading, language and arithmetic. Batteries are available for the primary, elementary and advanced levels, as well as for the intermediate seventh, eighth and ninth grades. They measure achievement in the learning skills rather than information covering the more formal content of courses of study. Such basic skills are more universally included in the curriculum than are some of the other subject-matter courses.

The authors stress the diagnostic aspect of their tests, which feature enables teachers to refer directly to the specific aspects of the learning skill in which the tested pupil may be weak and thus needs remedial work. They list in each test the elements into which they have analyzed the larger skills, indicating the specific test questions which have been included to measure these particular elements.

The tests are available in three forms at the intermediate level and in two forms at the advanced level for high school students and college freshmen. They come either bound together in the complete battery or in separate sections for the tests of reading vocabulary and comprehension, arithmetic reasoning and fundamentals, and language.

The intermediate and advanced batteries require approximately $2\frac{1}{2}$ hours of time. This is the time allotment suggested by the test authors, but considerable leeway is allowed, thus making the test one of power rather than of speed.

Each of the five tests has a number of subsections. The test of reading vocabulary, which contains 90 multiple-choice items, samples the vocabulary of mathematics, science, social science and general literature.

The reading comprehension test, composed of 55 items, measures ability to follow written directions, familiarity with the vocabulary and skills necessary for reference work, and ability to interpret meanings. This last ability is gauged by the examinee's success in answering multiple-choice questions following paragraphs which are read.

The arithmetic reasoning test includes 55 items, covering number concepts, symbols and rules, equations and problems. Arithmetic fundamentals are measured by 80 problems in arithmetic, including addition, subtraction, multiplication and division. An attempt is made to determine whether the student understands the various techniques required in those operations.

The 110 items of the fifth test of the battery are designed to measure various aspects of language usage. The ability to capitalize, punctuate, select correct grammatical constructions and complete sentences, classify words according to the parts of speech which they represent, spell and write legibly, is measured.

Designed For.—The intermediate battery is appropriate for students of the junior high school grades, seven, eight and nine. The advanced battery is designed for use in the four years of high school and the first year of college. It probably has special value in the case of those students suspected of weakness in one of these fundamental skills before engaging upon a program of remedial work.

Norms.—Age and grade norms are provided for scores on the five tests separately, the two reading tests, the two arithmetic tests and the total score on the five tests. These norms were established on the basis of scores made by 1100 students in grades six, seven, eight and nine in nine schools. A diagnostic profile printed on the cover page of the test booklet enables one to read off the grade placement directly as soon as the score for the individual test is checked on the scale provided.

In the advanced battery, in addition to the grade placement norms, percentile norms are provided for each test and subtest for students of each of the grades for which the test is appropriate.

Reliability.—The authors report high odd-even coefficients of reliability, but these have been obtained for a two-grade range, which fact would tend to produce higher correlations than might have been obtained had the more severe one-grade range been employed. These correlations range from $+.89$ to $+.95$ for the five subtests. The reliability for the test as a whole is $+.97$. Unfortunately we have no indication of the consistency with which the subsections are measuring the elements which are presumably being tested. Since the test has been emphasized as a diagnostic device, these smaller units should stand up under the consistency criterion. If they do not, because of inadequate sampling or too few items, the diagnostic value of the test is decreased. In the diagnostic analysis of learning difficulties, the authors list the elements which are measured under the twenty-one different subtests. Some of these elements are represented by only one, two or three test items. The reliability of measuring these elements must be considerably less than that reported for the test as a whole, and yet diagnosis rests upon this analysis of responses to small groups of items.

Validity.—The authors base their claim to the test's validity upon the fact that items were carefully selected to represent the basic and most crucial elements of the skills being measured. They report also that success in content work may be predicted much more accurately from the total score on this test than from an intelligence test.

Publisher and Cost.—Southern California School Book Depository, Ltd., 3636 Beverly Blvd., Los Angeles, California. Prices: Intermediate Battery, any form, 25 for $1.25; Advanced Battery, Form *A* or *B*, 25 for $1.50.

References.—*Manual of Directions, Progressive Achievement Tests*, Los Angeles, California: Southern California School Book Depository, Ltd., 1934.

CHAPTER V

ACADEMIC ACHIEVEMENT TESTS.—(*Continued*)

Senior High School and Junior College

A. ENGLISH TESTS

1. **Iowa Placement Examinations, New Series, English Training**, 1925, by M. F. Carpenter, G. D. Stoddard and L. W. Miller.

Description.—The authors claim that the test measures "the most important factors in English which can be tested by objective techniques." They emphasize the fact that results should not be used for predictive purposes only, but should assist the instructor in adapting the teaching to the needs of the individual student. The test results should make it possible, not only to predict subsequent success in English more accurately, but also to make success more possible of attainment.

This revised test includes two forms, X and Y, both consisting of four parts and requiring 40 minutes of time.

Part I is a spelling test in which the student is told to detect and correct the misspelled words in a given list (a combination of the recognition and recall techniques of measurement).

Part II tests knowledge of sentence structure and punctuation.

Part III is a test of grammar in which the individual indicates whether or not each of the 50 sentences is right or wrong.

In Part IV the individual's ability to recognize the correct meaning of words is tested.

Designed For.—The test has been most widely used for high school seniors and entering college freshmen. It is claimed that "this examination should give as adequate information about the student's place and needs in the course as the instructor ordinarily acquires by the end of the first semester under the traditional methods of instruction."

Norms.—The authors furnish norms for a large group of students.

Percentile	Scores	
	Form X	Form Y
100	186	184
75	140	128
50	106	95
25	67	60
1	16	16

Reliability.—The test's consistency is especially high, making it possible to consider an individual's score as a highly reliable indication of his usual performance on material of the kind included. The authors report a coefficient of +.96 for 150 students. The probable error of the score is 6.1.

Validity.—Because of the way in which the test was constructed, it may be considered a valid tool. All items were checked by test and subject-matter experts and the general character of the scale was based upon recommendations made by various committees on curricula. Textbooks and courses of study were analyzed to make certain that the test would be measuring important aspects of the typical college freshman English course.

Achievement on the test was checked with subsequent achievement in first-year college English, to determine more specifically the extent to which it was measuring what it was expected to measure. Despite the fact that other factors, such as the unreliability of instructors' grades and unmeasurable individual differences in effort and other personality traits, tend to lower any relationship which might exist between test and subsequent classroom achievement, yet the measured agreement was good. It predicts success in a specific subject, English, about as well as a pure vocabulary or intelligence test predicts success in general academic courses. The specific subject-matter test should supplement the general measure of scholastic aptitude when achievement in a particular subject-matter field is being predicted. In summarizing research studies, Segel reports a median coefficient of .40 between this test and grades in college English.

A test of this nature is more successful in predicting high achievement and failure than relative standings between these two extremes. Ninety-six per cent of a given group of freshmen making scores in the upper quartile on the English Training Test passed their first quarter work in English, and only 57 per cent of those in the lowest quartile on the test succeeded in the course work.

These tests are also useful for the remedial treatment of individuals. When there is a discrepancy between an individual's general intelligence rating and his English achievement, and the former rating is good, the student will probably show marked improvement when given special assistance with reading and study methods. Many students in the lower brackets on this achievement test might profit from a course in how to study.

Publisher and Cost.—Bureau of Educational Research and Service, University of Iowa, Iowa City, Iowa. Price, $3.50 per hundred, including manual of directions and keys.

References.—G. D. STODDARD, "Iowa Placement Examinations," *University of Iowa Studies in Education*, 1925, Vol. 3, No. 2, 103 pp.; L. W. MILLER, "An Experimental Study of the Iowa Placement Examinations," *University of Iowa Studies in Education*, 1930, Vol. 5, No. 6, 116 pp.; DAVID SEGEL, "Prediction of Success in College," *U.S. Office of Education Bull.* 1934, No. 15, U.S. Government Printing Office, Washington, D.C., 1934.

2. Cooperative English Test. Series 1, by S. A. Leonard, M. H. Willing, V. A. C. Henmon, W. W. Cook, D. G. Paterson and F. S. Beers.

Description.—There are three parts, requiring 95 minutes in all.[1]

Part I measures English usage. In the first section of this part, the student is required to detect errors in punctuation, capitalization, sentence structure and spelling, and to make the necessary changes. In the second section he is asked to select the best sentence from groups of four which are given. In the third section he is expected to make changes in given sentences according to specified instructions.

Part II is a spelling test in which the examinee selects the misspelled words from the groups of four words listed in each item.

Part III is a vocabulary test in which the individual selects

[1] Beginning with 1937, a 40-minute form will be published in addition to the longer forms.

from among five words that one which is nearest in meaning to a given word.

A new and comparable form is published each year.

Designed For.—Series 1 is somewhat more appropriate for college students than is Series 2, but it may be administered to students as low as the seventh grade. The test results should be of considerable service in determining the individual's need for remedial work in English. In some cases, advice regarding the choice of a major subject, especially in the field of English or a related one, would be more sound if these English achievement scores were available.

This quantitative measurement should prove useful in the case of transfer students or others for whom it is difficult to determine achievement in the fundamentals of this subject, either because records are not comparable or because formal preparatory training in English has been limited. In some cases it may be desirable to obtain a measure of a foreign student's achievement with the English language before course suggestions are offered.

Norms.—National norms are available for the usage, spelling and vocabulary sections separately, and for scores on the total test for each grade from the seventh through the senior year in college.

Total Score Norms for Different School Grades
(1935 form)

Percentile	7	8	9	10	11	12	13[1]	14[1]	15[1]	16[1]
100	171	175	197	208	212	227	245	251	250	260
75	34	60	83	102	119	141	165	178	186	197
50	24	34	57	74	90	105	134	149	159	172
25	15	22	35	48	66	80	105	118	129	141
1	4	7	14	18	26	33	48	49	53	60

[1] End-of-year norms; a more complete set of norms is published by the Cooperative Test Service.

It is advisable for colleges to establish local norms for this test, since there is considerable variation in the distribution of scores in different colleges. The authors cite facts which show differences among various professional goal groups also. For example, it was found that majors in journalism are superior in their performance on the total test and on the spelling section, their average on the total test exceeding about 70 per cent of the total group of students. The law, teaching, medicine, ministry and architecture group means, on the other hand, cluster around the average for all students, while the average for agriculture students is in the lowest one-fifth of the distribution for the unselected group and the percentile obtained by the average engineering student exceeded only about 38 per cent of the general college population.

Reliability.—The separate parts, as well as the test as a whole, are unusually reliable and may be used with individuals. For example, the 1935 form has the following corrected odd-even reliability coefficients:

Test	Coefficient	Sigma of distribution
Usage	.96	20.73
Spelling	.95	15.07
Vocabulary	.95	21.42
Total score	.98	52.23

Validity.—The Cooperative Test Service reports a correlation of +.54 between *average college grades* and English scores for 2000 to 3000 students in 27 colleges. The correlation between *average college grade in English* and the English test is .48.

There is some evidence from an unpublished study made at the University of Minnesota in connection with the sectioning of English classes that the score on this total test ranks second as a prognosticator of ability to do good work in English, the best prediction being obtained by a combination of high school grades and vocabulary test scores. Other evidence of the validity of this test is given in the reports of the Cooperative Test Service.

We may conclude that this test is a good indicator of success in both English courses and college work in general.

Publisher and Cost.—Cooperative Test Service, 500 West 116th Street, New York. Price, each test $0.05, less discount for quantities.

References.—*Tables of Norms and Reliability Coefficients*, Cooperative Test Service, September, 1935; see reports of the College Sophomore Testing Program in *The Educational Record* for October of 1932, 1933, 1934, 1935, and 1936.

3. Cooperative English Test, Series 2, by M. F. Carpenter, E. F. Lindquist, D. G. Paterson and F. S. Beers.

Description.—There are two parts, requiring 75 minutes in all. Part I measures usage and spelling. The examinee is directed to find and correct errors in spelling, grammar, capitalization and punctuation, which occur in six prepared compositions. Part II consists of a recognition vocabulary test. A new and comparable form is published each year.

Designed For.—The tests may be given to students from the seventh grade through the senior year in college.

Test results should be of aid in placing students in English sections or in determining the advisability of further studies or remedial work in English. The test is used in Minnesota for these purposes in the annual state-wide testing of high school seniors and college freshmen, conducted by The University of Minnesota Testing Bureau for the Association of Minnesota Colleges.

Norms.—National norms are available for the two parts separately and for the test as a whole for students from the seventh through the twelfth grade.

TOTAL SCORE NORMS FOR DIFFERENT SCHOOL GRADES
(1935 form)

Percentile	Grades					
	7	8	9	10	11	12
100	181	188	220	227	235	253
75	40	63	85	113	138	156
50	24	40	58	76	99	119
25	13	21	36	48	68	83
1	1	4	11	14	25	32

Reliability.—The test in its entirety, as well as the separate parts, yields highly consistent results, as shown by the corrected odd-even reliability coefficients in the table at the top of page 120.

Validity.—Results from this total test constitute one of the best indications of ability to do good work in college English. According to an unpublished study made at the University of Minnesota there is a coefficient of correlation of .37 between achievement on this test and general achievement in arts college

Test	Coefficient	Sigma of distribution
Usage........................	.97	25.99
Spelling......................	.97	14.90
Vocabulary....................	.95	19.73
Total.........................	.99	56.35

work during the first quarter in residence. Although this relationship is not high, it was higher than that found to exist between first-quarter grades and a pure vocabulary test for a group of 827 Minnesota freshmen. When combined with other achievement tests and high school scholarship, a very satisfactory basis for predicting college success and failure is provided. In this same unpublished study, the following correlations were found between the English test and English grades for the first year in the arts college:

Average English grade................ .38 for 708 students
Average composition grade............ .41 for 696 students
Average literature grade.............. .37 for 333 students

Publisher and Cost.—Cooperative Test Service, 500 West 116th Street, New York. Price, each test $0.05, less discount for quantities.

References.—*Tables of Norms and Reliability Coefficients*, Cooperative Test Service.

4. Cooperative Literary Acquaintance Test, by F. S. Beers and D. G. Paterson.

Description.—The test was designed to measure the student's general acquaintance with the field of literature from ancient to contemporary times. The test requires 45 minutes and includes a variety of questions requiring a knowledge of characters, plots, quotations, authors and subject matter, over a wide range of literature. New and comparable forms are provided each year.

Designed For.—Students in any year of high school or college may be given this test. Its use is especially recommended for those students contemplating a major in English, journalism or the languages.

Norms.—National norms are available for the 4 years of high school and college. Different professional goal groups are significantly differentiated on the basis of the scores made on this test as shown below:

Number	Goal group	Median percentile
143	Journalism	75
110	Ministry	62
155	Law	56
...	Teaching	54
204	Medicine	45
76	Engineering	38

The following national norms are published by the Cooperative Test Service:

NORMS FOR DIFFERENT SCHOOL GRADES
(1935 forms)[1]

Per-centile	Grades							
	9	10	11	12	13	14	15	16
100	81	92	132	150	180	167	160	180
75	26	40	52	68	70	80	72	101
50	19	29	36	52	50	60	59	73
25	14	20	26	37	33	41	41	48
1	4	7	8	13	10	12	13	13

[1] End-of-year norms.

Reliability.—The test meets the standard requirements for reliability. The odd-even coefficients of reliability are .95 (21.75 sigma of distribution) and .96 (31.60 sigma of distribution).

Validity.—The individual items have been validated by including only those items to which persons making high scores have responded more successfully. The following validity coefficients were found for arts college freshmen in an unpublished study at the University of Minnesota.

    Average first quarter grade............ .37 for 827 students
    Average English grade................ .43 for 708 students
    Average literature grade.............. .49 for 333 students

Additional evidence of validity is given in the Reports of the College Sophomore Testing Program.

Publisher and Cost.—The Cooperative Test Service, 500 West 116th Street, New York. Price, each test $0.05, less discount for quantities.

References.—"The 1934 College Sophomore Testing Program," *The Educational Record*, October, 1934. See also, other reports in the same journal for 1932 to 1936.

5. See discussion on pages 111–113, Chapter IV, regarding the Progressive Achievement Tests. Sections of the advanced battery on reading vocabulary, reading comprehension and language are printed separately. These tests of basic skills in reading and language are appropriate for high school students and college freshmen.

B. MATHEMATICS

1. **Iowa Placement Examinations, Series M. T. 1, Revised, A. Mathematics—Training,** 1925, by G. D. Stoddard and E. W. Chittenden.

   Description.—Forty minutes of working time are required for the four parts of this examination. The purpose of the test is to measure the skills necessary for success in college mathematics. Part I tests various simple skills in the fundamentals of arithmetic. Part II tests knowledge of fundamental operations in algebra. Part III calls for true-false responses to items in geometry and Part IV calls for short answers requiring training in high school mathematics. Forms *A* and *B* are available.

   Designed For.—According to the authors, "this examination should give at the end of two hours as adequate information about the student's place and needs in the course as the instructor ordinarily acquires at the end of the first semester under the traditional methods of instruction."

   It should be administered to students who have had the advantage of formal or informal training in high school algebra and geometry.

   The results should be of value to the counselor in determining the advisability of further training in mathematics. The authors also claim that directed study given to students in the lower levels of mathematical achievement produces worth-while results in salvaging failing students.

   Norms.—Percentile norms based on several thousand cases are furnished in the manual for Forms *A* and *B*.

Local norms may be developed for special groups of students. For example, freshmen entering the University of Minnesota engineering school were found to make higher scores on this test than students in general as represented in the national norms presented by the authors. The condensed norms below for Form A make this clear and indicate the need for comparing the student with the particular group with which he is competing academically.

Scores made by groups of freshmen:

Percentile rating	225 U. of M. engineering freshmen	4437 freshmen
99	69	63
70	56	42
50	49	33
30	43	26
1	21	5

Reliability.—Consistent results on individuals are made possible by this measure. The authors report a coefficient of +.88 when Form A was administered to 100 students whose standard deviation on the test was 10.4.

Validity.—Some assurance of the validity of this test is given by the fact that items were included only after careful study of textbooks and courses of study and after securing the approval of persons competent to judge their individual validity and representativeness.

Further assurance of validity is given by the extent to which test scores are related to achievement as measured by first semester grades in mathematics. Of over 1000 students whose test scores were checked against first semester grades, 61 per cent of those in the lowest tenth on the test and only 7 per cent of those in the highest tenth failed to pass the course in mathematics. A large percentage of the failures could have been spared the ordeal by counseling with the aid of this measuring device before the student had entered upon a course not suited to his background of training.

This mathematics training test appears to predict success in **first-year** college mathematics as well as many intelligence tests predict general scholastic achievement. Furthermore, there is evidence that the test is measuring something other than general intelligence.

The following correlations between scores and first-quarter honor-point ratios are reported by Northby for engineering freshmen at the University of Minnesota:

	1928	1931
High school scholarship	.55	.65
Iowa Mathematics Training	.55	.70

Publisher and Cost.—Bureau of Educational Research and Service, University of Iowa, Iowa City, Iowa. Price, $3.50 per hundred, including manual of directions and key.

References.—G. D. STODDARD, "Iowa Placement Examinations," *University of Iowa Studies in Education*, 1925, Vol. III, No. 2, 103 pp.; L. W. MILLER, "An Experimental Study of the Iowa Placement Examinations," *University of Iowa Studies in Education*, 1930, Vol. V, No. 6, 116 pp.; H. P. HAMMOND and G. D. STODDARD, "A Study of Placement Examinations," *University of Iowa Studies in Education*, 1928, Vol. IV, No. 7; A. S. NORTHBY, "Prediction of Scholastic Success in the College of Engineering and Architecture," in *Minnesota Studies in Articulation*, University of Minnesota, Committee on Educational Research, 1937, pp. 42–49.

2. Cooperative General Mathematics Test for High School Classes, by H. T. Lundholm and L. P. Siceloff.

Description.—This test measures information acquired in high school courses in algebra, plane and solid geometry and trigonometry. The three parts, which include questions of the short-answer and multiple-choice variety, require an hour and a half of working time. Comparable forms are constructed each year.

Designed For.—The test may be administered to students who have had two years of high school mathematics or its equivalent. These test results are useful in counseling college freshmen, as they afford a partial basis for determining the appropriate level of course work in mathematics to be attempted. Some students will have retained so little that a repetition of work is desirable, whereas others score high with less formal training. For students with more mathematical training, the General Mathematics Test for College Students is more appropriate.

Norms.—National norms for high school students with two, three, and four years of study are available as well as norms on college freshmen obtained for a limited number of colleges which have used the test. At the University of Minnesota, for example, local norms have been established for Science, Literature and the Arts freshmen and for engineering freshmen. The median scores for arts college and engineering freshmen were 30 and 56 respectively. The national median for high school seniors is 49.

END-OF-YEAR NORMS
(1935 form)

Percentile	Years of study			Entering college freshmen
	2	3	4	
100	56	82	98	120
75	31	44	54	70
50	22	31	44	44
25	16	23	30	28
1	8	10	13	12

Reliability.—The test yields very consistent results. The corrected odd-even coefficient is .96 (21.71 sigma of distribution).

Validity.—Scores on this test are somewhat related to average college grades in the freshman year of the arts college as indicated by a correlation of +.37 obtained in an unpublished study at the University of Minnesota on 827 arts college students. The correlation with average mathematics grades was .44 for 264 freshmen in the arts college.

Publisher and Cost.—The Cooperative Test Service, 500 West 116th Street, New York. Price, each test $0.04, less discount.

References.—*Tables of Norms and Reliability Coefficients*, Cooperative Test Service.

3. Cooperative General Mathematics Test for College Students, by H. T. Lundholm and L. P. Siceloff.

Description.—This test was designed to obtain a measure of the student's general acquaintance in the field of mathematics. The four parts, which require 2 hours of time with short-answer and multiple-choice responses, include problems in algebra, plane and solid geometry, trigonometry, analytics and calculus. New forms are provided each year.

Designed For.—It is not the purpose of this particular instrument to measure the achievement of students majoring in mathematics. Instead, its purpose is to yield an approximate indication of the mathematical background of the average arts college student. It is appropriate for sophomores and upper classmen.

Norms.—National norms for all four classes of students are available, but the test has been used most extensively with college sophomores.

END-OF-YEAR NORMS FOR ARTS COLLEGE STUDENTS
(1935 form)

Percentile	Freshmen	Sophomores	Juniors	Seniors
100	120	146	160	160
75	52	54	72	64
50	32	38	47	37
25	21	25	34	23
1	2	7	12	3

Reliability.—The corrected odd-even coefficient of reliability is .97 (28.77 sigma of distribution).

Validity.—Valid results are insured because of the test's construction.

In a study of different sophomore goal groups, significant differences in averages were apparent as indicated below. Since such differences are in line with expectations, they constitute further evidence of validity.

Group	Number	Approximate average percentile
Engineering	219	90
Medicine	188	67
Law	138	58
Teaching	927	53

See reports of the Cooperative Test Service for more extensive data on validity.

Publisher and Cost.—Cooperative Test Service, 500 West 116th Street, New York. Price, each test $0.05, less discount.

References.—"The 1933 College Sophomore Testing Program," *The Educational Record*, October, 1933; *Tables of Norms and Reliability Coefficients*, Cooperative Test Service.

4. Cooperative Plane Geometry Test, by J. A. Long and L. P. Siceloff.

Description.—The three subtests, requiring 90 minutes in all, are composed of true-false, multiple-choice and short-answer items designed to gauge information in plane geometry. Comparable forms are constructed each year.

Designed For.—The test may be administered to students who have had a course in plane geometry in high school, to determine whether or not they should repeat the work in college before taking advanced courses. Achievement-test results may indicate that a more advanced course is better suited to the abilities of some students who are not able to present evidence of formal training in geometry.

Norms.—Individual scores are interpreted by reference to national norms for high school students who have had one year of study in plane geometry.

Percentile	Score
100	99
75	42
50	29
25	18
1	3

Reliability.—The corrected odd-even coefficient of reliability is .94 (21.35 sigma of distribution).

Validity.—Careful construction and inclusion of pertinent items only have produced a valid measuring device.

Publisher and Cost.—Cooperative Test Service, 500 West 116th Street, New York. Price, each test $0.04, less discount.

References.—*Tables of Norms and Reliability Coefficients*, Cooperative Test Service.

5. Cooperative Solid Geometry Test, by H. T. Lundholm, J. A. Long and L. P. Siceloff.

Description.—The purpose of this test is to measure achievement or information retained from course work in solid geometry. The questions, which include true-false, short-answer and multiple-choice types, require 90 minutes of time. New forms are provided each year.

Designed For.—Students who have studied solid geometry for a half year in high school or its equivalent may be given the test.

Norms.—National norms for students with a half year of formal training form the basis for the interpretation of the individual's score.

Percentile	Score
100	95
75	53
50	34
25	17
1	1

Reliability.—The coefficient is sufficiently high to justify its use with individuals. The corrected odd-even coefficient is .87 (17.45 sigma of distribution).

Validity.—Only items which are themselves valid have been included in the scale, thus insuring the validity of the entire test.

Publisher and Cost.—Cooperative Test Service, 500 West 116th Street, New York. Price, each test $0.04, less discount.

References.—*Table of Norms and Reliability Coefficients*, Cooperative Test Service.

6. Cooperative Algebra Test (Elementary and Intermediate) by J. A. Long, L. P. Siceloff and H. T. Lundholm.

Description.—The test is designed to measure ability in elementary algebra through quadratics. Ninety minutes are allowed for the three parts containing short-answer and multiple-choice problems in pure and practical algebra. Comparable forms are provided each year. Separate tests are published for elementary and intermediate algebra.

Designed For.—Students who have had one year of high school algebra or its equivalent may take this test. It may be used as a partial basis for assigning grades in first-year algebra or for determining the advisability of continuing in mathematics.

Norms.—National norms are available for high school students and college freshmen. The following norms are provided for end-of-year testing:

Percentile	Elementary (1 year)	Intermediate (1½ to 2 years)
100	107	107
75	50	55
50	37	42
25	24	31
1	4	5

Reliability.—Taken as a whole, the test may be considered very reliable. The elementary test has a corrected odd-even coefficient of .95 (21.79 sigma of distribution); the intermediate test has a coefficient of .95 (18.30 sigma of distribution).

Validity.—According to an unpublished study by Dr. P. O. Johnson of 72 freshmen in the College of Agriculture, Forestry and Home Economics at the University of Minnesota, there was a somewhat higher relation between grades and this test than between grades and a vocabulary or general intelligence test, and the indications are that achievement scores combined with high school marks will predict college achievement in this college better than the so-called intelligence test.

Publisher and Cost.—Cooperative Test Service, 500 West 116th Street, New York. Price, each test $0.04, less discount.

References.—*Tables of Norms and Reliability Coefficients*, Cooperative Test Service.

7. Cooperative Trigonometry Test, by J. A. Long and L. P. Siceloff.

Description.—Achievement in high school trigonometry, requiring a half year's study, is measured by this test which takes 90 minutes of time for its two parts consisting of short-answer and multiple-choice problems. A comparable form is issued yearly.

Designed For.—Students who have studied trigonometry in high school may be tested.

Norms.—The Test Service publishes national norms for high school students with a half year of training.

Percentile	Score
100	99
75	53
50	39
25	27
1	3

Reliability.—Consistent results may be expected. The corrected odd-even coefficient of reliability is .92 (16.05 sigma of distribution).

Validity.—The test appears to be measuring what it is designed to measure.

Publisher and Cost.—Cooperative Test Service, 500 West 116th Street, New York. Price, each test $0.04, less discount.

References.—*Tables of Norms and Reliability Coefficients*, Cooperative Test Service.

8. See discussion on pages 111–113, Chapter IV, regarding the Progressive Achievement Tests. Sections of the Advanced Battery on Mathematics Reasoning and Mathematics Fundamentals are printed separately. These tests of the basic skills in mathematics are appropriate for high school students and college freshmen.

C. SCIENCE

1. Cooperative General Science Test (High School) by O. E. Underhill and S. R. Powers.

Description.—The test, requiring 90 minutes for its two parts, is designed to measure general achievement and information resulting from a year's study of general science in high school. The multiple-choice items sample information in the fields of physics, chemistry, biology, physiology, botany and geology. New forms are provided each year.

Designed For.—Students who have had a course in general science in high school or its equivalent may be given this test. This form is appropriate for college freshmen and the Cooperative General Science Test for college students is better adapted to the upper-class level.

Norms.—National norms for high school students and for entering college freshmen may be used.

Percentile	High school students	Entering college students
100	133	200
75	59	73
50	47	55
25	37	40
1	15	16

Reliability.—Consistent results may be expected for individuals. The corrected odd-even coefficient is .89 (18.94 sigma of distribution).

Validity.—The test may be accepted as a valid measure of information in general science. The relationship between scores and general honor-point ratios is positive, but not high. An unpublished report made at the University of Minnesota shows a correlation of +.22 for 827 arts college students.

The following coefficients were found for arts college freshmen:

Average grade in biological sciences.... .43 for 282 students
Average grade in zoology.............. .41 for 218 students
Average grade in botany............... .43 for 75 students
Average grade in physical sciences...... .36 for 265 students
Average grade in chemistry............ .32 for 194 students

Publisher and Cost.—Cooperative Test Service, 500 West 116th Street, New York. Price, each test $0.05, less discount for quantities.

References.—*Tables of Norms and Reliability Coefficients*, Cooperative Test Service.

2. **Cooperative General Science Test for College Students,** by C. J. Lapp, A. W. Schindler, H. W. Farwell, G. M. Kay, W. J. Eckert, F. L. Fitzpatrick and V. H. Noll. (The group of persons preparing the test has varied somewhat from year to year. The above persons are responsible for the 1936 form.)

Description.—This test was designed for liberal arts students to obtain a rough measure of their general cultural background and acquaintance in the field of science. In an hour of testing time it samples the fields of elementary science, meteorology, biology, botany, physics, chemistry, astronomy and geology. The questions are concerned for the most part with practical and familiar situations the understanding of which involves some scientific principle or fact. New and comparable forms are available each year.

Designed For.—This test is more appropriate for arts college sophomores and upperclassmen than for majors in the sciences. Formal training in the subject matter of the various sciences is not a prerequisite to the taking of the tests, although it will of course influence the score. Limited formal training accompanied by a high score is evidence of special interests or aptitudes along scientific lines. For freshmen, the test for high school students is more appropriate. The test should usually be given to students considering medicine or engineering, since these groups are very much above the general college average in respect to achievement in general science.

Norms.—National norms are available for freshmen and sophomores and less adequate norms have been established for the other classes.

END-OF-YEAR NORMS
(Arts college students)

Percentile	Freshmen	Sophomore	Junior	Senior
100	160	170	200	180
75	65	63	86	75
50	47	47	63	55
25	32	33	43	40
1	5	8	12	10

Striking differences among different sophomore professional-goal groups have been found. Average approximate percentiles for several of these groups are reported as follows:

Number	Group	Average percentile
481	Medicine	84
118	Engineering	80
122	Ministry	54
238	Law	52
41	Journalism	45

Reliability.—The test yields results which are consistent for the individual student. The corrected odd-even coefficient is .93 (26.21 sigma of distribution).

Validity.—Results of correlating scores on the 1933 form with grades received by a large number of students from different colleges indicate that the relationship between achievement on a general science test and college achievement is positive (.24), but lower than that obtaining between grades and scores on the Cooperative General Culture and English tests. There is a large sex difference on this test, men scoring, on the average, much higher than women. This may possibly be accounted for by the fact that men may have had more formal training in the sciences. Additional evidence of validity, in terms of differentiation of groups of students, is given in the reports of the Cooperative Test Service.

Publisher and Cost.—Cooperative Test Service, 500 West 116th Street, New York. Price, each test $0.05, less discount for quantities.

References.—"The 1934 College Sophomore Testing Program," *The Educational Record*, October, 1934.

3. Cooperative Botany Test, by F. K. Butters, P. O. Johnson, F. P. Frutchey, R. B. Gordon, C. W. Horton, H. C. Sampson, L. H. Tiffany and R. W. Tyler.

Description.—There are three parts to this provisional form, as follows, but as yet only Part C has been fully standardized:

Part I covers four informational objectives of elementary botany: (1) information; (2) terminology; (3) identification of structures; and (4) identification of functions. 120 minutes.

Part II covers two scientific-method objectives of elementary botany: (1) interpretation of experiments; and (2) application of principles. 90 minutes.

Part C is a composite test which covers two informational objectives and one scientific-method objective of elementary botany: (1) information; (2) terminology; and (3) application of principles. 120 minutes.

Designed For.—Students should have taken at least the elementary course in college botany before taking this test.

Norms.—Norms from eleven different colleges are available for Part C only and these have not been established on a greater number than 277 students. No doubt more extensive norms will be forthcoming later.

Percentile	Score
100	220
75	133
50	105
25	78
1	40

Reliability.—When Part C is considered in its entirety, it is a reliable measure for use with individuals. The corrected odd-even coefficient is .93 (38.96 sigma of distribution).

Validity.—An attempt was made to include only those items which meet the objectives set for the course, and this is one of the factors making for the test's validity.

Publisher and Cost.—Cooperative Test Service, 500 West 116th Street, New York. Price, each part $0.05, less discount for quantities.

References.—*Tables of Norms and Reliability Coefficients*, Cooperative Test Service.

4. Cooperative Chemistry Test for High School Students, by V. H. Noll and S. R. Powers.

Description.—Achievement in high school chemistry is measured by this test, requiring 90 minutes and covering the material taught in high school chemistry, such as chemical terms, reactions, valences, formulas, equations, etc. New and comparable forms are provided each year.

Designed For.—The test is appropriate for students who have had the equivalent of one year of high school chemistry.

Norms.—National norms are available for high school students who have one year of chemistry.

Percentile	Score
100	217
75	142
50	115
25	88
1	25

Reliability.—The test is a reliable measure. The corrected odd-even coefficient is .95 (38.31 sigma of distribution).

Validity.—Items are included only when considered by experts in the field to be of essential importance in elementary chemistry.

Publisher and Cost.—Cooperative Test Service, 500 West 116th Street, New York. Price, each test $0.04, less discount for quantities.

References.—*Tables of Norms and Reliability Coefficients*, Cooperative Test Service.

5. **Cooperative Chemistry Test for College Students**, by B. C. Hendricks, O. M. Smith, F. P. Frutchey, A. G. Horney and R. W. Tyler.

Description.—There are three parts to this battery of tests, as follows:

Part I covers three informational objectives of elementary chemistry: (1) information; (2) terminology; and (3) symbols, formulas and equations. 120 minutes.

Part II covers two scientific-method objectives of elementary chemistry: (1) interpretation of experiments; and (2) application of principles. 90 minutes.

Part C covers two informational objectives and one scientific-method objective: (1) information; (2) terminology; and (3) application of principles. 120 minutes.

Designed For.—Students who take this test should have had the elementary course offered in chemistry in college. It may be used in individual cases to help determine the advisability of continuing in college chemistry courses.

Norms.—The most adequate national norms are for Part C of this provisional test as the norms for Parts I and II do not include a sufficient number of cases as yet.

Percentile	Total score		
	Part I	Part II	Part C
100	447	175	280
75	211	135	155
50	162	120	121
25	125	107	87
1	67	57	40

Reliability.—As a whole, the test may be considered a reliable measure, although Part II and two of the subsections in Part C should not be used alone, because of inadequate reliability. The corrected odd-even coefficients are as follows:

Test	Coefficient	Sigma of distribution
Part I	.96	48.64
Part II		
Section 1	.78	14.26
Section 2	.51	9.03
Part C		
Section 1	.92	27.36
Section 2	.88	10.96
Section 3	.77	11.42
Total	.95	45.02

Validity.—Because of its construction and the fact that items were selected in order to cover the objectives of the course in elementary chemistry, the test may be considered a valid one.

Publisher and Cost.—Cooperative Test Service, 500 West 116th Street, New York. Price, each part $0.05, less discount for quantities.

References.—*Tables of Norms and Reliability Coefficients*, Cooperative Test Service.

6. Iowa Placement Examinations, New Series, Chemistry Training, 1925, by J. Cornog, G. D. Stoddard and L. W. Miller.

Description.—There are two forms of this examination, which requires about 50 minutes to administer. Part I contains true-false items of knowledge of fundamentals of chemical processes. Part II requires the examinee to determine valences, write out formulas, balance equations and match formulas with chemical terms. Part III tests knowledge of applications of chemistry. Part IV calls for the solution of problems in chemistry.

Designed For.—Ordinarily this test is administered to graduating high school seniors and entering college freshmen to determine the student's ability before placement in college chemistry. A course in high school chemistry or its equivalent should be a prerequisite to taking the test.

Norms.—Percentile norms are furnished by the authors in the manual of directions as shown in the table on page 137.

Reliability.—Both forms, X and Y, are sufficiently reliable for individual comparisons, the coefficient for 150 students being +.91 for Form X and .89 for Form Y.

Percentile	Scores	
	Form X	Form Y
100	135	133
75	85	84
50	63	66
25	43	49
1	11	12

Validity.—Textbooks and courses of study were analyzed in the construction of the items and experts in subject matter and test construction were employed to assure the validity of the final product.

Hammond and Stoddard's study of the average grades received by 634 students during the first semester of college indicates that the test results, especially at the extremes, can be depended upon to predict subsequent grades. For example, of those in the upper decile, 70 per cent made A or B grades, 30 per cent made C or D grades and none failed during their first semester. Of those scoring in the lowest decile on the test, only 8 per cent made A or B grades, 62 per cent made C or D grades and 30 per cent failed.

In summarizing research studies on this test, Segel reports a median coefficient of .54 between this test and college grades in chemistry.

Publisher and Cost.—Bureau of Educational Research and Service, University of Iowa, Iowa City. Price, $3.50 per hundred.

References.—H. P. HAMMOND and G. D. STODDARD, "A Study of Placement Examinations," *University of Iowa Studies in Education*, 1928, Vol. 4, No. 7; *Manual of Directions, Iowa Placement Examinations*, Bureau of Educational Research and Service, University of Iowa, Iowa City; G. M. RUCH and G. D. STODDARD, *Tests and Measurements in High School Instruction*, Yonkers-on-Hudson, New York: World Book Company, 1927, 381 pp.; DAVID SEGEL, "Prediction of Success in College," *U. S. Office of Education Bull.* 1934, No. 15, U. S. Government Printing Office, Washington, D. C.

7. Cooperative Physics Test For High School Students by H. W. Farwell.

Description.—Ninety minutes of time are required for this test, composed of multiple-choice items which are designed to measure information acquired in the high school course in physics. New forms are provided each year.

Designed For.—Students who have had the one year of physics offered in high school or its equivalent may be given this test.

Norms.—National norms are available.

Percentile	Score
100	154
75	84
50	65
25	49
1	19

Reliability.—The desired standard for reliability has been met. The corrected odd-even coefficient is .94 (25.96 sigma of distribution).

Validity.—Validity is inherent in the measure.

Publisher and Cost.—Cooperative Test Service, 500 West 116th Street, New York. Price, each test $0.05, less discount for quantities.

References.—*Tables of Norms and Reliability Coefficients*, Cooperative Test Service.

8. Cooperative Physics Test for College Students, by H. W. Farwell, C. J. Lapp, F. Palmer, J. T. Tate and A. G. Worthing.

Description.—Achievement in the subject matter of physics is measured by six tests, printed separately and requiring different time limits as indicated below:

Mechanics	60 minutes
Heat	30 minutes
Sound	20 minutes
Light	40 minutes
Electricity	50 minutes
Modern Physics	25 minutes

Comparable forms issued each year make possible the measurement of growth of achievement in this field.

Designed For.—These tests usually should be administered only to students who have had some training in physics. Occasionally they may be appropriate for promising students who have not had the prerequisites for advanced courses in physics but who seem to have acquired a knowledge of the field. Counselors may wish to suggest the test for students who seem to have an unusual grasp of the subject, in order that a quantitative estimate of achievement may be furnished their instructors and more individual treatment arranged. Results on these achievement tests may prove helpful when the student is considering the advisability of taking advanced work. In the case of poor students, comparison with national norms presents the picture in an objective light so that he can see the desirability of a program more compatible with his abilities.

Norms.—National norms are available for each test for men and women students separately, since the latter secure lower scores on the average on parts of the battery.

END-OF-YEAR NORMS FOR COLLEGE SOPHOMORE MEN COMPLETING ONE OR TWO SEMESTERS OF COLLEGE PHYSICS[1]
(1935 form)

Percentile	Mechanics	Heat	Sound	Light	Electricity	Modern physics
100	51	30	16	35	43	19
75	25	19	9	16	23	7
50	18	14	7	11	17	3
25	12	10	4	8	12	1
1	1	2	1	1	3	1

[1] Separate norms are provided for women.

Reliability.—The mechanics test is the only one of the group which, alone, meets the criterion of reliability for individual comparisons, the corrected odd-even correlation being +.90 for 300 students. Results on the other tests singly should not be used for comparing individuals, but should be used only in conjunction with the other tests in the complete battery.

Test	Coefficient	Sigma of distribution
Mechanics	.90	10.80
Heat	.83	6.23
Sound	.70	3.88
Light	.69	5.54
Electricity	.83	8.01
Modern Physics	.75	3.72

Validity.—The test items themselves meet the standards of validity. They were carefully constructed by physics professors and test experts with a view toward including diagnostic items sampling the entire elementary course work in the fields tested.

The percentages of students succeeding on each item were calculated and these figures indicate that the test samples abilities at all levels. Items were also analyzed to determine the extent to which they differentiated between the high- and low-scoring groups and only those with good validity indices were incorporated in the final forms.

Correlations between scores and grades in the courses were high, indicating that the tests are measuring achievement which physics teachers consider essential.

Publisher and Cost.—Cooperative Test Service, 500 West 116th Street, New York. Price, each test $0.02, less discount for quantities.

References.—"The 1933–1934 College Physics Testing Program," *The American Physics Teacher*, 1934, Vol. 2, No. 3, Supplement.

9. Cooperative Biology Test for High School Students, by T. L. Fitzpatrick and S. R. Powers.

Description.—The test was designed to measure achievement resulting from one year of high school biology, and is composed of multiple-choice and matching questions, requiring an hour and a half of working time. A comparable form is issued each year.

Designed For.—Most students taking this test should have completed one year of biology in high school. Some indication of relative achievement is helpful when advanced work is being considered.

Norms.—National norms for high school students with one year's study in biology are available.

Percentile	Score
100	157
75	101
50	82
25	65
1	28

Reliability.—The reliability of the test has been shown to be adequate. The corrected odd-even coefficient is .93 (24.62 sigma of distribution).

Validity.—The items were carefully constructed and analyzed as to difficulty and ability to differentiate between low- and high-scoring students.

Publisher and Cost.—Cooperative Test Service, 500 West 116th Street, New York. Price, each test $0.04, less discount for quantities.

References.—*Tables of Norms and Reliability Coefficients*, Cooperative Test Service.

10. Cooperative Zoology Test, by W. M. Barrows, F. P. Frutchey, J. W. Price, L. H. Snyder and R. W. Tyler.

Description.—There are three parts to this test as follows:

Part I covers four informational objectives of elementary zoology: (1) Information; (2) terminology; (3) identification of structures; and (4) identification of functions. 120 minutes.

Part II covers two scientific-method objectives of elementary zoology: (1) Interpretation of experiments and (2) application of principles. 90 minutes.

Part *C* is a composite test which covers two informational objectives and one scientific-method objective of elementary zoology: (1) Information; (2) terminology; and (3) application of principles. 120 minutes.

Designed For.—Students who have had a year's course in college zoology may take the test.

Norms.—For the 1935 provisional form, norms are available only for Part *C*. Other norms will be published later.

Percentile	Score
100	240
75	133
50	101
25	74
1	24

Reliability.—Figures on reliability have been reported only for Part *C* and they are acceptably high, indicating that the test may be considered sufficiently reliable for use with individuals. The corrected odd-even coefficient of the total score is .93 (40.14 sigma of distribution).

Validity.—The construction of the test attests to its validity.

Publisher and Cost.—Cooperative Test Service, 500 West 116th Street, New York. Price, each part $0.05, less discount for quantities.

References.—*Tables of Norms and Reliability Coefficients*, Cooperative Test Service.

D. FOREIGN LANGUAGES

NOTE.—The attention of counselors is directed to the availability of the standardized objective-achievement examinations in foreign languages, prepared by the Modern Foreign Language Study, American Council on Education. These tests have been used primarily for placement purposes. They are distributed by The World Book Company, Yonkers-on-Hudson, New York.

1. Cooperative French Test, by G. Spaulding and P. Vaillant.

Description.—Multiple-choice responses are called for in this test of achievement in French reading, vocabulary and grammar. One and one-half hours are required for its three parts. A new form is issued each year. Junior forms are available for use in the junior high schools.

Designed For.—Since different norms are furnished for groups with training in French varying from one year in high school to four years in college, the test is appropriate for these levels. Since achievement in any given class varies so greatly, it should be of service in determining the actual level of achievement, in order that the student may be assigned to the proper training course. This should be of special service to the counselor in recommending placement in a course to a student entering college, especially when some time has elapsed since his last high school course in the language. A few hours spent in testing may save hours of wasted effort in courses either below or above the student's ability.

Norms.—The Cooperative Test Service furnishes each year national norms based on students with one, two, three and four years of training in high school and college French.

End-of-year Norms by Years of Study (Total Score)
(1935 form)

Percentile	High school students with				Entering college freshmen with			College students with			
	1 year	2 years	3 years	4 years	2 years	3 years	4 years	1 year	2 years	3 years	4 or more years
100	220	266	265	266	250	260	270	230	260	268	270
75	71	128	172	204	143	195	233	98	144	187	235
50	51	99	142	184	108	162	201	73	111	145	212
25	35	75	114	161	77	135	170	53	83	107	166
1	5	24	60	74	21	48	72	14	30	29	102

Reliability.—The entire test as well as the single parts meet the requirements for reliability very satisfactorily as shown by the following corrected odd-even reliability coefficients:

Test	Coefficient	Sigma of distribution
Reading........................	.97	20.69
Vocabulary.....................	.96	20.36
Grammar.......................	.94	21.24
Total score....................	.98	57.51

Validity.—The construction of the test is adequate evidence for the validity of the instrument.

Publisher and Cost.—Cooperative Test Service, 500 West 116th Street, New York. Price, each test $0.05, less discount.

References.—*Norms and Reliability Coefficients*, The Cooperative Test Service.

2. **Cooperative German Test,** by M. V. Hespelt, E. H. Hespelt and G. Spaulding.

Description.—The three parts, measuring achievement in German reading, vocabulary and grammar, require an hour and a half of time in which the student responds to the items by selecting one of five choices given for each item. A new form is provided each year and junior forms are available for use at the junior high school level.

Designed For.—The test is appropriate for students who have had from one to three years of high school or college German. Results should be useful in placing students in classes concordant with their abilities. Some students are more advanced because of outside experience with the language and should be placed according to actual achievement rather than years of study. Others with high school training rank low enough to make repetition of an elementary course desirable.

Norms.—The student's score may be interpreted by reference to scores made by high school and college students in schools scattered across the country who have had from one to three or more years of training.

END-OF-YEAR NORMS BY YEARS OF STUDY
(Total score for 1935 form)

Per-centile	High school			Entering college freshmen with		College students with[1]		
	1 year	2 years	3 years	2 years	3 years	1 year	2 years	3 or more years
100	152	233	276	235	225	230	265	257
75	74	122	167	136	163	109	126	183
50	48	81	135	95	136	70	87	126
25	25	56	106	69	103	47	53	82
1	3	22	40	10	28	5	10	33

[1] One year of high school German equals one-half year of college study.

Reliability.—A reliable index of ability is represented by the individual's score. The corrected odd-even coefficients are as follows:

Subtest	Coefficient	Sigma of distribution
Reading..........................	.96	18.16
Vocabulary.......................	.96	18.02
Grammar.........................	.93	19.33
Total test........................	.98	53.24

Validity.—An unpublished study made by George V. Moser in 1933 at the University of Minnesota substantiates the claim which has been made for the test's validity on the basis of its scientific construction and standardization. A correlation of +.69 was obtained between the German test score and grades in German 3 and 4 for 123 students. This relationship is high, especially since the reliability of teachers' grades as indicators of achievement is known to be low. With few exceptions, those students scoring high on the test received the higher grades in their course work. This achievement test in German was found to be a much better indicator of success in the German course than the College Aptitude Test or high school scholarship.

Further indication of validity is secured by the extent to which groups with varying amounts of German training are differentiated by the test scores. Marked differences were found between the averages of groups who had had three quarters of German and those with four quarters. There is always some overlapping between these groups, showing that some students with fewer quarters of study have actually achieved as much as others with more "exposure" to the subject matter of the course. This point argues in favor of sectioning students on the basis of actual accomplishment, as measured by an achievement test, rather than upon mere "time serving."

Publisher and Cost.—Cooperative Test Service, 500 West 116th Street, New York. Price, each test $0.05, less discount.

References.—*Tables of Norms and Reliability Coefficients,* Cooperative Test Service.

3. Cooperative Spanish Test, by E. H. Hespelt, R. H. Williams and G. Spaulding.

Description.—Ninety minutes are required for the three parts which aim to measure achievement in Spanish reading, vocabulary and grammar. Comparable forms are issued yearly.

Designed For.—Students who have studied Spanish in high school or college from one to three years may be given this test. It should be of value in placing the student in the class in college Spanish which is most appropriate to his level of accomplishment.

Norms.—Norms are supplied for students who have had one, two and three years of high school Spanish and also for students with one, two and three years of Spanish in college.

END-OF-YEAR NORMS BY YEARS OF STUDY (TOTAL SCORE)
(1935 form)

Per-centile	High school students with			Entering college students with		College students with		
	1 year	2 years	3 years	2 years	3 years	1 year	2 years	3 or more years
100	94	199	249	235	245	280	235	271
75	59	110	137	137	195	102	112	198
50	41	84	113	105	167	77	86	162
25	30	56	99	77	117	48	56	109
1	9	16	57	11	62	3	13	23

Reliability.—The indications are that the test yields very consistent results.

Test	Coefficient	Sigma of distribution
Reading.....................	.97	15.53
Vocabulary..................	.92	15.15
Grammar....................	.95	21.85
Total score.................	.98	52.70

Validity.—Validity of the test is assured as a result of its careful construction.

Publisher and Cost.—Cooperative Test Service, 500 West 116th Street, New York. Price, each $0.05, less discount for quantities.

References.—*Tables of Norms and Reliability Coefficients*, Cooperative Test Service.

4. Cooperative Latin Test, by J. C. Kirtland, R. B. McJimsey and B. M. Allen.

Description.—This test is designed to measure achievement in the study of Latin. An hour and a half is required for the three parts, which test knowledge of Latin vocabulary, grammar and reading. New forms are supplied each year.

END-OF-YEAR NORMS BY YEARS OF STUDY (TOTAL SCORE)
(1935 form)

Percentile	High school students with				Entering college students with	College students with	
	1 year	2 years	3 years	4 years	2 years	3 years	4 or more years
100	174	221	242	294	210	246	271
75	68	115	167	190	104	156	186
50	54	96	144	158	71	128	153
25	37	74	118	139	45	90	114
1	14	31	50	75	4	44	41

Designed For.—Persons who have had one year of high school Latin or more may take the test. Results should be of significance in advising the student regarding continuance of the study.

Norms.—Individual scores may be compared with norms for high school students who have had one, two, three or four years of Latin in high school. Norms are also provided for college students who have had three or four years of Latin.

Reliability.—Individual results are consistent.

Test	Coefficient	Sigma of distribution
Reading..........................	.82	15.70
Vocabulary......................	.88	12.13
Grammar........................	.92	15.50
Total score.....................	.93	35.12

Validity.—The test may be considered a valid instrument.

Publisher and Cost.—Cooperative Test Service, 500 West 116th Street, New York. Price, each test $0.05, less discount for quantities.

References.—*Tables of Norms and Reliability Coefficients.* Cooperative Test Service.

E. HISTORY AND SOCIAL STUDIES

1. **Cooperative American History Test,** by H. R. Anderson and E. F. Lindquist.

Description.—Ninety minutes are required for the three parts of this test, which measures the student's knowledge of facts and relationships in the field of American history. Part I, calling for multiple-choice responses, covers historical personages and terms and geographical terms. Part II tests knowledge of dates and events and Part III measures historical judgment by means of the multiple-choice technique. New forms are provided each year.

Designed For.—Students who have had a high school course in American history may be given this test.

Norms.—Comparisons are possible with norms derived from scores made by eleventh- and twelfth-grade students in different parts of the country.

Percentile	Score
100	160
75	75
50	55
25	40
1	14

Reliability.—The test yields consistent results. The corrected odd-even coefficient is .9153 (26.29 sigma of distribution).

Validity.—The individual test items were carefully prepared and checked by test makers and history teachers in order to include only those items which seemed to them of value in determining amount of information in the field of American history.

Publisher and Cost.—Cooperative Test Service, 500 West 116th Street, New York. Price, each test $0.05, less discount for quantities.

References.—E. F. LINDQUIST, "The Form of the American History Examination of the Cooperative Test Service," *The Educational Record*, October, 1931.

2. Cooperative Modern European History Test, by H. R. Anderson and E. F. Lindquist.

Description.—The purpose of this test is to measure achievement in modern European history which is offered as a one-year course in high school. Ninety minutes are necessary for the three parts, which require a knowledge of historical personages, terms and events and historical judgment. Comparable forms are provided each year.

Designed For.—This test may be given to students who have had a course in world or European history in high school.

Norms.—Scores may be compared with national norms for high school students who have had a year's course in modern European history.

Percentile	Score
100	133
75	51
50	34
25	21
1	3

Reliability.—Consistent results may be expected. The corrected odd-even coefficient is .9311 (25.92 sigma of distribution).

Validity.—The test provides a valid measure of achievement in this subject-matter field.

3. Cooperative World History Test, by H. R. Anderson and E. F. Lindquist.

Description.—The purpose of this test is to measure the amount of material which the student has retained from high school world history courses. Ninety minutes are required for the test, which measures the student's knowledge of historical personages and events and historical judgment. New and comparable forms are published each year.

Designed For.—Students who have had a course in world history in high school, or equivalent, may take the test.

Norms.—National norms for all four years of high school and the first two years of college are available for interpretation of individual scores.

END-OF-YEAR NORMS BY SCHOOL GRADES
(1935 form)

Percentile	9	10	11–12	Entering college freshmen
100	95	120	135	120
75	29	43	57	69
50	18	29	42	50
25	11	19	29	33
1	1	2	10	11

Reliability.—The test measures achievement in world history reliably. The corrected odd-even coefficient is .93 (26.40 sigma of distribution).

Validity.—The items were carefully constructed in order to include only those most diagnostic in determining the degree of the student's familiarity with the field.

Aside from this assurance of the test's validity, we have some indication that this type of achievement is related to success in courses which are offered in the arts course in college. According to an unpublished study made at the University of Minnesota by E. G. Williamson on over 600 freshmen, the relationship between these test results and honor-point ratio for the first quarter in residence was as high as that between English achievement test results and honor-point ratio. The relationship was actually somewhat higher than that existing between the College Ability Test and grades. The following coefficients for arts college freshmen were found:

    Average first-quarter grade............ .31 for 827 students
    Average social science grade........... .40 for 595 students
    Average history grade................. .43 for 351 students
    Average economics grade.............. .27 for 284 students
    Average political science grade......... .50 for 153 students
    Average sociology grade............... .24 for 182 students

Publisher and Cost.—Cooperative Test Service, 500 West 116th Street, New York. Price, each test $0.05, less discount on quantities.

References.—*Tables of Norms and Reliability Coefficients*, Cooperative Test Service.

4. Cooperative Contemporary Affairs Test, by A. C. Eurich, E. C. Wilson, G. Hill and collaborators.

Description.—The test is "intended to measure the extent to which students keep abreast of significant current affairs in the fields of art, literature, government, international relations, politics, economics, religion, etc."

The test of two parts is 25 pages in length and requires 2 hours of working time.

Part I deals with public affairs. The student is expected to recognize the particular positions or contributions of national and international political and public personalities, persons prominent in sports and scientists. One section is devoted to current terms appearing in periodicals. Another section tests information regarding national and international events in political, economic and social fields. There is one section which requires an understanding and interpretation of prominent political, social and economic problems and policies of the United States and foreign governments. Part II measures aesthetic interests. Section 1 tests the ability to recognize personalities in current literature, drama, art and music. Section 2 involves the ability to recognize certain current terms of significance in the aesthetic fields. Section 3 tests familiarity with current books, plays, musical compositions and works of art, their authors and contents.

Comparable forms enable the counselor to measure growth of the individual's interest in, and knowledge of, contemporary affairs.

Designed For.—The test may be applied to persons of upper high school, college, or adult levels for whom a measure of knowledge of current affairs is desirable. Its use is especially recommended for students considering the professions of law or journalism as these students make, on the average, outstandingly high scores on this test.

Norms.—Adequate norms are available for college freshmen and sophomores and norms for juniors and seniors have also been provided for a smaller number of cases. Great differences are apparent in different college communities and for this reason it is desirable for local norms to be computed.

END-OF-YEAR NORMS BY YEARS OF STUDY
(1935 form)

Percentile	10	11	12	Entering college freshmen	College freshmen	College sophomores	College juniors	College seniors
100	200	250	330	225	340	365	310	350
75	82	95	112	113	134	146	158	170
50	60	72	87	85	98	108	120	126
25	43	51	69	59	68	78	88	83
1	15	20	30	17	12	25	14	15

It appears that course work in current affairs has a decided influence upon the average test score. The average score for a group of University of Minnesota General College students who had taken a course in contemporary affairs was significantly

Number	Professional goal group	Median percentile
82	Journalism	75
107	Law	66
149	Medicine	58
57	Ministry	55
...	Teaching	54
49	Engineering	46

higher than the average for arts college freshmen, sophomores, juniors and seniors who had not had the advantage of that course.

The figures in the table at the bottom of page 151 indicate the great differences among professional goal groups.

Reliability.—The length of the test alone attests to its reliability, which is reported as $+.97$ for the corrected odd-even correlation on over 300 students (59.60 sigma of distribution).

Validity.—Because of the nature of the test and the lack of any outside criterion, which is itself a valid indication of knowledge and interpretation of contemporary affairs, the validity rests upon its construction, the validity of the individual items themselves, and the extent to which group differences are disclosed. In constructing the test, the current periodical literature was analyzed to determine the subject-matter content and to include a proportional representation in the different fields of interest. For the 1934 provisional form, the research workers launched upon the ambitious project of summarizing and classifying all articles, 9908 in all, appearing in 25 representative magazines between January 1, 1933, and March 1, 1934. The following classification was the result, and formed the basis of proportional representation in the scale:

Foreign affairs	24 per cent
Arts	21 per cent
Economics	19 per cent
Social affairs	16 per cent
Political events	15 per cent
Scientific events	5 per cent
Geography	2 per cent

After this analysis, 1000 test items were constructed and submitted for review to sixteen University of Minnesota faculty members representing varied fields of interest. They were then tried and revised.

An unpublished study made at the University of Minnesota on 827 freshman men and women found a correlation of $+.34$ between test scores and honor-point ratios in all courses for the first quarter in residence.

An advantage of the test is that it acts as a decided incentive to increased reading alertness and interest. A low score need not be discouraging to a student, as the counselor may point out the fact that the test measures information which can be acquired by application.

The indications are that there is some relation between amount of intelligence and knowledge of current affairs. This relation is higher where there is no formal training in contemporary affairs offered. In a situation where interest in current events is stimulated, such knowledge is more a factor of increased learning opportunities than of the native intelligence of the student. The following coefficients were found for Arts College freshmen:

  Average social science grade............42 for 595 students
  Average history grade..................43 for 351 students
  Average economics grade...............28 for 284 students
  Average political science grade.........56 for 153 students
  Average sociology grade...............34 for 182 students

Publisher and Cost.—Cooperative Test Service, 500 West 116th Street, New York. Price, each test $0.06, less discount for quantities.

References.—Report by the Committee on Educational Testing of the American Council on Education, "The 1934 College Sophomore Testing Program," *The Educational Record*, October, 1934 and 1935. See also, other reports in the same journal in October of each year.

F. GENERAL CULTURE

1. Cooperative General Culture Test, by E. F. Lindquist, H. R. Anderson, C. W. Hart, J. Tiffin, A. Learned, J. Storck and others.

Description.—By measuring the individual's information over a wide range of subject matter, sampling the field of ancient, medieval and modern history, social studies, foreign literature and fine arts, makers of this test have attempted to obtain some quantitative measure for what they have termed "general culture."

The length of the test alone is quite formidable, covering 36 pages and requiring 3 hours of working time. Part I samples the fields of history from ancient to contemporary times and social studies, men and their contributions, terms and their meanings, geographical locations and their significances are matched by the examinee. Historical events are placed in order of their chronological sequence and a number of multiple-choice items call for information on current and historical facts in the fields of social studies, politics and science.

Part II samples the field of foreign literature, the examinee being asked to match men and their contributions, book titles and their contents, Biblical and literary characters and their literary source, geographical locations and their significance, etc.

Part III consists of questions in the fine arts, music, art and drama. Terms and meanings are matched, artists and their contributions, etc.

A new and comparable form is provided each year.

Designed For.—The test has been used most extensively with college sophomores, but it may be administered to students in any year in college, since norms are available. Other adults taking the test may be compared with these college groups. The test results are probably of greatest vocational value for students considering professions in which a cultural background is essential, such as journalism, the ministry and law.

Norms.—National norms are provided for students in each of the college years. It is advisable to construct local norms, since there are such great differences among students in different colleges with respect to scores achieved on this test. These differences should be borne in mind when interpreting the individual's score. The student's score should be compared with those of students in his own competing group, as well as with scores of students in the larger national group reported by the Test Service.

END-OF-YEAR NORMS BY YEARS OF COLLEGE STUDY FOR TOTAL SCORES[1]
(1935 form)

Percentile	Freshmen	Sophomores	Juniors	Seniors
100	470	595	570	570
75	177	210	229	255
50	122	151	163	183
25	81	103	113	124
1	24	27	29	38

[1] More complete norms for separate sections of the test are published by the Cooperative Test Service.

The following data (interpreted in terms of national percentile values, and approximated from a chart in the Report of the Committee on Educational Testing, "The 1935 College Sophomore Testing Program," *The Educational Record*, October, 1935) show the percentile scores for the college population made by the average student in the following groups of college sophomores of different professional ambitions:

Number	Group	Average percentile
71	Journalism	71
253	Ministry	70
346	Law	64
...	Teaching	54
609	Medicine	52
171	Engineering	38

Whether or not "general culture" is more essential for success in journalism, the ministry or law than it is in engineering and medicine, we cannot tell. These facts are of some significance, however, with their implication that, on the average, students with higher scores in "general culture" are more apt to be interested in careers in the linguistic than in the technical professions.

Reliability.—The coefficients of reliability for the individual tests, as well as for the test as a whole, are sufficiently high to meet the criterion which has been set up for tests when used with individuals.

Test	Coefficient	Sigma of distribution
History and social studies..........	.94	32.52
Foreign literature................	.97	34.03
Fine arts.......................	.96	34.54
Total score.....................	.98	88.70

Validity.—Since the test itself represents one of the first attempts to secure a quantitative measurement of "general culture," it has seemed impossible to find a more adequate measure of the trait with which to check the validity of the test. As yet, there have been no attempts to discover relationships between test scores and ratings of general culture. We shall have to look elsewhere for some measure of the test's validity. In the first place, only those items were selected which seemed to be a measure of "culture" in the opinions of the test makers and other competent judges. Individual items were then, in a sense, validated. They were ranked according to the percentage of persons in the experimental trials who were able to answer them correctly. The criterion of acceptance of any item was that it must differentiate persons in the highest from those in the lowest quartiles. Thus the test contains items of known difficulty which are responded to more correctly by persons who make the higher scores. There is enough correlation (.53) between the test and average college grade for two years to indicate that it is measuring "general scholarship," in so far as college grades are a satisfactory criterion. There seems to be no sex difference as far as achievement on this test is concerned.

Very complete data, in terms of differentiation of groups of students, are given in reports of the Cooperative Test Service.

Publisher and Cost.—Cooperative Test Service, 500 West 116th Street, New York. Price, each test $0.10, less discount for quantities.

References.—Report of the Committee on Educational Testing, "The College Sophomore Testing Program," *The Educational Record*, October, 1933, 1934 and 1935. See, also, other reports appearing in the same journal in October of each year.

CHAPTER VI
VOCATIONAL ACHIEVEMENT TESTS

There are very few well-standardized achievement tests for vocational education courses. The scarcity of good tests in this field is partly accounted for by the fact that the shop courses themselves are not so standard from school to school as are the regular academic courses. There are wide variations in the types of courses offered, the amount of time devoted to the different courses, and their grade placement. This situation has not been stimulating to the standardization of achievement tests on a national basis. Since the tests must be validated in terms of course content, items which might be suitable in one school system would be invalid in another. Norms developed from pupils in widely divergent school systems would have very little meaning under these circumstances.

This situation, however, should not discourage efforts to produce standardized measurements in this field. In fact, such instruments will themselves probably tend to decrease undesirable variation in curriculum content. But it will probably be necessary to construct local norms rather than national norms for tests in this field.

Another factor that is responsible for lack of progress in this field is the fact that research specialists in university departments of psychology and educational psychology are themselves academically trained and "academically minded." This bias in outlook leads them to direct their research efforts toward problems in the traditional school subjects. It is to be hoped that an increasing number of such research specialists will recognize the importance of occupational adjustment problems and will attack measurement problems in this area.

Some of the vocational achievement tests which have been developed have aimed to measure information as well as performance. A few tests appear to be sufficiently well standardized to warrant use, but many are to be criticized on a number of points. The construction of the tests and test items has not been done with sufficient care. Objectives of courses have not been outlined and items selected to sample these objectives. The items often are not based upon a careful and detailed analysis of the work. In most cases they are not validated from the standpoint of the test as a whole. The reliabilities, when reported at all, tend to be too low for use with individuals, but in some cases they are satisfactory for the comparison of classes. Norms are often in terms of median achievement of a small number of pupils who have probably received a special type of training. These general norms are not very useful, but they are improved when the norm group is described in terms of the amount of time spent in training. In some tests the scoring is rather subjective and involved.

A. SHOP COURSES

No attempt will be made here to describe in detail any of the tests in this field. The Fischer Mechanical Drawing Tests might be sufficiently reliable for use in comparing the achievement of classes, but the coefficient of +.79 reported, would not warrant its use with individuals. No information on reliability and validity is furnished in the Manual for the Castle Mechanical Drawing Tests. The Newkirk and Stoddard Home Mechanics Test appears fairly adequate from the standpoint of reliability, but the general norms given in terms of median achievement of subjects who have had different backgrounds of training are not very useful. The Nash-Van Duzee Achievement Tests in Woodwork and Mechanical Drawing appear to be superior to some of the other tests, especially because of the fact that the percentile norms are based on groups with known amounts of instruction. The performance part of the woodwork test, however, possesses a reliability which is too low for individual comparisons.

Persons interested in developing achievement tests in this field will be aided by consulting the volume on Minnesota Mechanical Abilities Tests which describes the construction of information tests as well as performance tests that can be used in measuring achievement in shop courses.

B. HOME ECONOMICS TESTS

The situation with respect to standardized measurement devices in the field of home economics is similar to that in the field of shop courses. Well-standardized, reliable and valid tests are few in number. Those which have been developed do not compare in quality with measuring devices found in other academic fields.

1. **Engle-Stenquist Home Economics Test,** 1931, by E. M. Engle and J. L. Stenquist.

Description.—The three tests in this series are printed in separate folders and are as follows: Foods and Cookery, Clothing and Textiles, and Household Management. One hour is allowed for each test. Two equivalent forms are provided. Each test contains four parts which are differentiated on the basis of the type of objective question used. Part I consists of multiple-choice questions, Part II of true-false, Part III of matching and Part IV of brief answer.

The foods and cookery test measures information on nutrition, and the selection, preparation and serving of foods. The clothing and textiles test measures a knowledge of textiles, and the selection, planning and construction of clothing. The household management test deals with budgeting, family relationships and the furnishing of the house.

Designed For.—The purpose of the tests is to measure information in the three aspects of the field of home economics which are covered at the junior high school level. Results of this test may be used to compare the achievement of individuals and classes after a period of training, to measure growth, to classify students for instructional purposes, and to analyze the aspects of the subject matter of home economics in which the students are strong or weak.

Norms.—Age and grade as well as percentile norms are provided for both forms of all three tests. The norms are based on from 10,000 to 15,000 girls in the Baltimore public schools. Percentile ranks are given for pupils in 5B, 6B, 7B, 8B, and 8A. This makes it possible to compare an individual's score with others in her own grade. These norms are not reproduced here, since they are readily available in the test manual.

Reliability.—The authors report test-retest reliability coefficients for different groups of pupils at different grade levels. Their results, which follow, indicate that the separate tests yield consistent results within a single grade level.

Grade	Reliability coefficient	Number of cases
Foods and cookery		
5	.93	117
6	.94	110
7	.93	110
8	.92	110
Clothing and textiles		
5	.93	149
6	.96	115
7	.94	110
8	.94	110
Household management		
6	.85	115
7	.91	103
8	.96	125

Validity.—The authors' claim for the test's validity rests upon the nature of the items selected, as well as its correlation with teachers' grades. The items included are those which are common to the best textbooks and courses of study. They have also been approved by curriculum experts. The validity coefficients obtained for different groups of 100 cases at different grade levels are reproduced from the test manual. They were obtained by correlating scores obtained on this test with scores obtained on teachers' objective classroom tests. These coefficients are surprisingly high.

Grade	Test	Correlation
6	Foods and cookery	.52
6	Clothing and textiles	.81
5	Foods and cookery	.98
5	Clothing and textiles	.90

Publisher and Cost.—World Book Company, Yonkers-on-Hudson, New York. Price, 25 of any one test for $1 net.

References.—E. M. ENGLE and J. L. STENQUIST, *Engle-Stenquist Home Economics Test. Manual of Directions*, Yonkers-on-Hudson, New York: World Book Company, 1931.

2. Unit Scales of Attainment in Foods and Household Management, 1933, by Ethel B. Reeve and Clara M. Brown.

Description.—There are two equivalent forms, each containing two scales, for this test of achievement in the field of cooking and household management. Questions are of the single-choice and completion types. Each form requires only about one school period in which to complete it.

Designed For.—Students in junior high schools who have had the type of training called for may be given this test. It is devised for the purpose of measuring gain in achievement during the course of study and differences among pupils in the achievement measured.

Norms.—The raw scores for both scales are converted into C-scores and averaged to obtain the final C-score. The C-score units are comparable over the entire range of scores. In this way, it is possible to determine the absolute accomplishment of the pupil, since the C-score represents the level of difficulty which the pupil can reach and get half of the items right.

Reliability.—The probable error of the final C-score on each form is 1.8 points, indicating that there is a fifty-fifty chance that the student's "true" score varies within 1.8 C-score points from her obtained score. This degree of reliability compares favorably with other tests of this same length in other subject-matter fields.

Validity.—The test's claim for validity rests upon the items included and the extent to which these items sample the field.

Publisher and Cost.—Educational Test Bureau, Minneapolis, Minnesota. Prices: 25 copies of either form for $0.75; sample set, $0.20.

References.—E. B. REEVE and C. M. BROWN, *Unit Scales of Attainment in Foods and Household Management. Directions for Administering and Scoring*, Minneapolis, Minnesota: Educational Test Bureau, Inc., 1933.

3. The Minnesota House Design and House Furnishing Test, 1936, by Clara M. Brown and Muriel F. Puhr.

Description.—There are two equivalent forms of this test, each requiring about half an hour of time and measuring ability to recognize good design and management in houses and house furnishings. Accompanying the test there is a series of three paired pictures of houses and interiors concerning which the examinee is asked to make certain judgments. She is asked to indicate whether or not certain statements regarding design and arrangement apply to the pictures of exteriors, living rooms and bedrooms. She is also asked to indicate agreement or disagreement with certain statements concerning ways in which the houses or rooms might be improved.

Designed For.—While this is most appropriate for students in high school who have had the advantage of a course in house design and house furnishing, the authors suggest that it may also be given at the junior high school and college levels, although it is too easy for most advanced students.

Norms.—At the present time norms are being compiled by the test authors, and tentative ones may be secured from them at the University Farm, St. Paul, Minnesota.

Reliability.—The reliability coefficients for either form have been reported by the authors to be .90 for a high school group and .87 for a college group. While indication is given of the variability of the group, these coefficients appear to substantiate the claim for the test's ability to yield consistent results for individuals at the secondary and college levels.

Validity.—Claim is made for the test's validity on several counts. In the first place, test items were passed upon by competent persons in the field as involving the principles of harmony, proportion, balance, rhythm, etc. Furthermore, items were included if they discriminated between different grade levels of students. In addition, one group of high school students which was below the average of high school groups in intelligence, but which had had better than average instruction in related art, scored above the high school average and equalled the college norm.

Publisher and Cost.—University of Minnesota Press, Minneapolis, Minnesota. Prices: $2 per hundred; photographs, 25 for $1; sample set, $0.35.

References.—C. M. Brown and M. F. Puhr, *The Examiner's Manual for the Minnesota House Design and House Furnishing Test*, Minneapolis, Minnesota: University of Minnesota Press, 1936; C. M. Brown, *Syllabus for Educational Measurement, Part A*, Minneapolis, Minnesota: University of Minnesota Division of Home Economics, 1936.

C. TYPEWRITING AND STENOGRAPHY

1. **Blackstone Stenographic Proficiency Tests (Typing)** 1923, by E. G. Blackstone.

Description.—The first test of this series measures proficiency in typing. There are five forms of equivalent and carefully constructed business letters which make it possible to measure progress without repeating the same material. Three minutes are allowed for the test and the score is determined by taking into account the number of strokes completed and the errors made.

Designed For.—The test is appropriate for students of varied amounts of training in typing.

Norms.—The Manual of Directions contains norms established for 2188 students who have had various amounts of training. The median scores of these groups with different amounts of practice are given.

Reliability.—The author reports a reliability of +.93 for 105 students with 20 months of instruction. The students repeated the test by taking a second form. The probable error of the score is 5.8 points. The test may be considered sufficiently reliable for use with individuals.

Validity.—There is a significant differentiation on this test between mean scores obtained from students with different amounts of training in typing.

  Publisher and Cost.—World Book Company, Yonkers-on-Hudson, New York. Prices: 25 of each form for $1; sample set, $0.10.
  References.—E. G. BLACKSTONE, *Manual of Directions, Blackstone Stenographic Proficiency Tests*, Yonkers-on-Hudson, New York: World Book Company, 1923.

2. **Blackstone Stenographic Proficiency Tests (Stenography Test)** 1932, by E. G. Blackstone and Mary McLaughlin.

Description.—There are two forms of the stenography test, each containing seven parts: (1) English, (2) syllabification, (3) office practice, (4) alphabetizing, (5) abbreviations, (6) business organization, (7) transcription.

The transcription test consists of two letters dictated at a standard rate. Twelve minutes are allowed for transcription and the remaining tests require about 35 minutes. Details for scoring are provided.

Designed For.—The test may be administered to students with varying amounts of training in stenography.

Norms.—Mean scores on the total test and on each subtest are provided for 1000 students with various amounts of training and for successful stenographers on the job.

Reliability.—The author reports a reliability coefficient of $+.88 \pm .02$ for the two forms given to 1000 high school students.

Validity.—When efficiency ratings for 37 stenographers were correlated with test scores, the coefficient was found to be $+.62 \pm .06$. For 49 additional stenographers a coefficient of $+.79 \pm .03$ was obtained. The validity indices may be regarded as satisfactory, in view of the variety of factors other than ability that are likely to enter into efficiency ratings.

> **Publisher and Cost.**—World Book Company, Yonkers-on-Hudson, New York. Prices, 25 of each form for $1.20; sample set, $0.20.
>
> **References.**—E. G. BLACKSTONE, *Manual of Directions. Blackstone Stenographic Proficiency Tests,* Yonkers-on-Hudson, New York: World Book Company, 1923.

3. Stenogauge, 1923, by E. J. Benge.

Description.—The purpose of this test is to "gauge" the stenographer's ability to take dictation, to transcribe a letter rapidly and accurately and to spell. The test consists of a standard letter of several hundred words which is dictated at a rate as rapid as the individual can take. The letter is then typed out and the time and errors are recorded. A list of spelling words, one-half of which are misspelled, are checked for errors. The individual's score consists of the sum of the words dictated per minute, the words transcribed per minute, the percentage of words correctly transcribed and the percentage of words spelled correctly.

Individual testing is desirable. The time required for the examinee is about 15 minutes and for the examiner about 7 minutes.

Designed For.—The test may be administered to persons who claim some skill in typing and shorthand. Although it is most appropriate for stenographers, it may be used for typists by having them copy the letter.

Norms.—Percentile norms based on over 500 stenographers are provided in the test manual. Percentile norms for typists are also included.

Reliability.—No published information.

Validity.—The author reports a follow-up study of 24 stenographers who were employed, from among 145 applicants of one concern, partially on the basis of Stenogauge test scores. They were rated from one to ten by "a competent rater" and it was found that the three applicants who were rated lowest had received the lowest test scores. The test separated the failures from the successful workers but did not separate the "excellent" from the "average" workers. There was a rank order correlation of +.44 between test scores and success ratings.

When 17 stenographers in another concern were rated by six executives, the correlation of test scores and combined ratings was +.89. There is some evidence here that a high score on this test is associated with success on the job.

Publisher and Cost.—Stenogauge Agency, 3136 North 24th Street, Philadelphia, Pennsylvania; also distributed by Psychological Corporation, 522 Fifth Ave., New York. Prices: one set—containing instructions, norms, and 10 blanks for $3; additional blanks, each, $0.05.

References.—E. J. BENGE, "Gauging Stenographic Ability," *Administration*, February, 1923, 156–163; M. FREYD, "Selection of Typists and Stenographers," *Journal of Personnel Research*, 1926–1927, 5: 490–510; H. E. GARRETT and M. R. SCHNECK, *Psychological Tests, Methods, and Results*, pp. 173–174, New York: Harper & Brothers, 1933.

D. BOOKKEEPING

1. Elwell-Fowlkes Bookkeeping Test, 1928, by F. H. Elwell and J. G. Fowlkes.

Description.—According to the authors, "These bookkeeping tests are designed to furnish a reliable, valid and comparable measure of achievement in bookkeeping for use in high schools and business colleges." There are two tests, each consisting of two nearly equivalent forms, *A* and *B*. The first test covers subject matter included in the standard curriculum of first semester bookkeeping and the second measures achievement in second semester bookkeeping. There are nine parts, covering the main fields in bookkeeping: General theory, journalizing, classification, adjusting entries and closing the ledger, and statements. The questions are objective true-false, multiple-choice, and completion types. The time required for administration is about one hour.

Designed For.—Test 1 is designed for high school and business college students who have completed the first semester in bookkeeping and Test 2 is for second semester students.

One of its purposes is to aid in advising students regarding continuing and specializing in bookkeeping. The authors suggest that those in the upper 5 per cent may be encouraged to major in bookkeeping, other things being equal. The student, who evidences by this test that his achievement is below average, may be advised against taking more advanced courses.

This objective test may be used to supplement or supplant the regular course examination. It should also prove valuable in the assignment of pupils to beginning courses where it is difficult to ascertain the student's achievement because of transfer from another school, or for other reasons. Especially in borderline cases, this test might be administered to ascertain whether the pupil has sufficient command of the subject matter to advance.

Norms.—The author has supplied percentile norms for the two forms of both tests, based upon about 250 students each. Abbreviated norms taken from his table are given below:

Percentile	Test 1 Form *A*	Test 1 Form *B*	Test 2 Form *A*	Test 2 Form *B*
90	94	93	91	88
75	86	87	84	79
50	79	79	71	68
25	67	67	57	55
10	59	52	50	43

Reliability.—For a group of 256 students in first-semester bookkeeping the coefficient of reliability between Form *A* and Form *B* was $+.82$. For Test 2, which was given to 226 second-semester students, the form versus form correlation was $+.87$. Since two forms are available, it is advisable to administer both forms to increase the reliance which can be placed upon any one individual's score.

Validity.—The fact that the items have been very carefully selected by subject-matter and test experts to represent a comprehensive list of facts covered in the curriculum attests to the instrument's validity. Further evidence of validity has been its tryout and favorable acceptance by teachers of bookkeeping courses.

Publisher and Cost.—World Book Company, Yonkers-on-Hudson, New York. Price, when purchased in packages of 25, $0.052 per test.
References.—F. H. ELWELL and J. G. FOWLKES, *Elwell-Fowlkes Bookkeeping Test. Manual of Directions*, Yonkers-on-Hudson, New York: World Book Company, 1929. L. A. THOMPSON, *Interview Aids and Trade Questions*, New York: Harper & Brothers, 1936.

E. TRADE TESTS

1. Interview Aids and Trade Questions, 1936, by L. A. Thompson, Jr., D. C. Lawrence and A. Allardyce.

Description.—The above authors have published, in *Interview Aids and Trade Questions for Employment Offices*, 131 different oral trade tests. The number of questions in each different test is in the neighborhood of twenty. The general form is similar to those developed for use in the army and many of the questions from the army tests have been retained, while others have been revised and brought up to date to agree with present practices. Some entirely new tests have been constructed.

The questions and the answers are presented orally while the examiner records the answers verbatim and scores the responses. The total score is interpreted by reference to norms which give a decile rating, which may in turn be interpreted as "expert," "journeyman," "apprentice" or "novice."

In constructing the trade questions the following rules, laid down by the Trade Test Division of the Committee on Classification of Personnel in the Army, were used:

1. Each question within each trade group must be applicable to the trade.
2. The question must represent a principle of action which is based upon sound trade practice and custom.
3. It must be suitable for use in any geographical location.
4. It must differentiate between the various levels of trade ability in such a way that: (*a*) no novices can obtain high scores; and (*b*) apprentices within the occupation must have lower scores than journeymen, and so far as possible, experts should be able to answer the questions in a distinctly superior manner to the journeymen.

5. The questions must not yield a wide variety of correct answers.
6. Questions must not contain colloquial terms or require colloquial terms as answers.
7. Questions must be free from ambiguity.
8. They must be simple to administer.
9. Catch questions must not be used.

The above rules are quoted in full because they apply in the construction of informal new-type subject-matter tests, as well as for standardized achievement tests. In fact, the trade-test technique itself has contributed directly to the development of educational achievement tests.

Designed For.—The purpose of these trade questions is to supplement other information regarding an individual's trade status and proficiency. They are of especial assistance to the employment interviewer faced with the need for determining an individual's qualifications and correctly classifying him for employment.

They may be of some value to the school counselor in determining the trade knowledge of the pupil who has had some trade training or experience and who is leaving school to seek employment. Such information should be transmitted to the placement interviewer, together with other pertinent school records.

Norms.—For each trade test there is furnished a rating table by which scores may be transmuted into decile ratings. These, in turn, may be interpreted in terms of degree of trade knowledge. The individual may be assigned a position on the scale from "expert" to "novice."

The authors point out the necessity for a liberal interpretation of test scores. A great many other factors should supplement the test data before a rigid assignment is made to any one trade classification.

Reliability.—No figures on the consistency of any of the tests are reported by the authors.

Validity.—Although the authors advise against a ready acceptance of test scores as perfectly valid indices of the individual's trade knowledge and skill, their manner of construction indicates that they are superior to less objective procedures.

In gathering together the individual items, persons known to be experts were consulted, as well as current trade journals and other sources of information. In some cases, items were included which were shown to differentiate between persons making high scores on the test as a whole and those making low scores.

Publisher and Cost.—Harper & Brothers, New York. Price, $2.50.

Reference.—L. A. THOMPSON, JR., and Associates, *Interview Aids and Trade Questions for Employment Offices*, New York: Harper & Brothers, 1936.

CHAPTER VII

PERSONALITY TESTS AND QUESTIONNAIRES

In discussing tests of scholastic aptitude and achievement we were dealing with a field of human measurement which has been most fruitful. Years of careful experimentation and statistical analysis have produced a body of systematized knowledge, as well as a definite methodology. Moreover the significance or validity of the traits measured has been fairly well established, so that today the counselor has available extensive knowledge of the meaning of the scores of many tests of aptitude and achievement. A counselor not only can diagnose these traits with reasonable accuracy, but he also can use the test results with a fair degree of assurance in making a prognosis of educational and occupational adjustment.

However, diagnosis of personality traits is more complicated. The history of research in this field is much shorter, less extensive and less fruitful. Nevertheless, the problem of constructing reliable personality tests has apparently reached a fairly satisfactory stage and we now have available a number of tests which have odd-even and test-retest reliability coefficients of fairly high magnitude, although these coefficients are, in general, lower than those for tests of intelligence and achievement. But progress has been impeded, if not blocked, by failure to develop an adequate methodology for determining validity.

The usual method of determining the validity of an intelligence test is to correlate its scores with another measure of intelligence. This so-called "outside criterion" may be another, standardized and accepted, *test* of intelligence; or *judgments* of intelligence made by teachers, employers or other persons who have had opportunity to observe the persons tested.[1] This use of an outside

---

[1] MAY, M. A., and HUGH HARTSHORNE, "Objective Methods of Measuring Character," *Ped. Sem.*, 1925, 32: 45–67; see also D. G. PATERSON, et al., *Minnesota Mechanical Ability Tests*, p. 586, Minneapolis: University of Minnesota Press, 1930.

criterion as a check on validity, or measure of it, has, unfortunately, introduced certain serious errors which depress our coefficients of validity. That *judgments* of abilities and achievement are shot through and through with errors is a well-established fact and needs no supporting review of the literature. But if we cannot validate a test by correlating it with a judgment criterion which is low in reliability and validity, then how shall we determine validity of our tests?

Such circuitous reasoning has led a great many statistical psychologists and test makers into the defensible position of arguing for the *self-validation* of tests.[2] If a test measures a trait reliably then, *ipso facto*, it is measuring that trait validly. In this methodology, then, a test is validated by making a rigorous item analysis to make certain that only items which contribute to, or correlate optimally with, the total score, are included. The next step involves determination of the maximum validity possible, assuming a perfect criterion which is itself another measure of the trait, afforded by a *statistical* or *mathematical* validation and not by correlation with an *outside* criterion.

Another school of test makers continue to determine validity by correlating tests with outside criteria, but with full awareness of the limited coefficients attainable when criteria are faulty. These psychologists recognize that validity coefficients of .60 or .70 are really extremely high in view of the faulty criteria used and that coefficients of .80 and higher are unattainable at the present time.

One more significant point may be drawn from other fields of test construction. Validity has come to mean not only, does a test measure what it is supposed to measure, but also, what is the significance of the trait measured? That is, a good deal of trial-and-error search is made to discover with what a reliable test will correlate. In other words, test makers correlate tests with many things to discover what is being measured, this procedure eventually leading to a definition of the meaning of a test in terms of the things with which it correlates. In regard to tests of intelligence, this empirical search has led to the knowledge that what the tests measure is found, used or

[2] The statistical basis for this point of view is presented in M. A. May, H. Hartshorne and F. K. Shuttleworth's *Studies in the Organization of Character*, pp. 454–456, New York: The Macmillan Company, 1930.

involved in getting grades in academic school subjects and in succeeding in certain types of occupations. By way of briefly elaborating the last point, we may point out that it was discovered in analyzing test scores of white recruits in the World War that occupations may be arranged in a hierarchy according to the level of intelligence possessed by men in such occupations.

Aptitude and achievement tests, then, are validated by discovering the outside criteria with which they are correlated. We have at hand in our social order two judgment criteria, teachers' classifications of pupils and employers' classifications of employees. These outside criteria simplify the task of validating tests of intelligence and achievement.

On the other hand, when we turn to tests of personality we discover that nowhere in our social order are people sharply classified as to types and amounts of personality traits. The commitment of persons to insane institutions is, of course, an exception to this statement, but such persons cannot always be used as criterion groups, because of difficulties in eliciting responses to test questions. To return to our point, if we had in society some sifting out and classification of persons on the basis of personality traits, then more rapid progress in this field might result. At the present time test makers search diligently for such outside criteria with but meager results.

We have made this lengthy preface to a presentation of personality tests in order that the reader will better understand the nature of such tests, will be sensitive to the technical problems involved in test construction, and will not carry over from previous chapters a rigid interpretation of validity indices. These data should be interpreted, not only in terms of what is desirable, but also in terms of what is possible with the present methodology. Parenthetically, such an attitude should be acquired by those mathematical purists who complain because our validity coefficients of intelligence tests are less than 1.00, utterly ignoring the errors of teachers' grades.

As stated at the beginning of this chapter, progress has been made in constructing personality tests with fairly high reliability, but high validity is more difficult to achieve. Moreover, what to do with test scores, what interpretations to make, and what prognoses to record are questions that can be answered only tentatively at the present time. Our statistical analyses and clinical uses of personality tests are only now beginning to yield promising results.

A final word of orientation. There are no right or wrong answers to tests of personality, such as there are in tests of intelligence. All test scores are "high" or "low," "favorable" or "unfavorable," relative to the scores of other persons. All scores are *relative* to a defined criterion group. If an individual has a test score similar to that made by members of a defined group, then he may be said to resemble members of that group. In the case of some tests, this is tantamount to prognosticating that he will prove to be, or is adjusted or maladjusted, since he resembles persons selected as being adjusted or maladjusted. In the case of Strong's interest test a student who gets a score similar to that made by the criterion group of successful accountants may be diagnosed, *other things being favorable*, as a potential good risk for training and employment in that field. With respect to diagnosis and prognosis, therefore, personality tests may be used in much the same way as are other tests, even though the rightness and wrongness of test questions are not the same. But it should be repeated that we know less of the significance of scores of personality tests; that is, we know less of what a student with a given personality test score can and will do, than is true of scores of other types of tests.

The coefficients of correlation between personality tests and school grades are so low as to indicate negligible relationships. This means that such tests cannot be used for predictions of scholarship in the way intelligence tests are used. In other words, personality tests must be used in diagnosing and counseling with respect to emotional and attitudinal problems. Clinical experience indicates that such problems may have a bearing on achievement, but the relationship is not direct. It is evident, therefore, that personality tests should be used to diagnose emotional maladjustments, which, in turn, may or may not be associated with scholastic problems. In other words, the school counselor will not confine his use of these tools to problems of educational guidance alone.

With this introduction, we turn now to a presentation of a number of personality tests. In this review we shall not include any of the so-called "character" tests, since most, if not all, of them have been developed as instruments for research or survey purposes. At the present time such tests have not been used sufficiently in clinical and counseling practice to evaluate their usefulness, at least such clinical use has not been reported in the literature of psychology and guidance.

A. INTEREST INVENTORIES

1. Interest Questionnaire for High School Boys, by O. K. Garretson and P. M. Symonds.

Description.—This questionnaire contains 234 items covering such topics as occupations, school subjects, activities, things to own, magazines, prominent men in different fields of endeavor, qualities most admired in people and activities of parents. Each item has three possible answers, *L* (like), *I* (indifferent) and *D* (dislike). Most students fill out the questionnaire in 30 minutes. It may be given individually or to groups.

The questionnaires of 460 pupils with average marks above the average of their classes were subjected to item analysis to determine which items differentiated between boys enrolled in the academic curriculum, the commercial course or the technical course of study. Item scoring weights derived from the item analysis were then used to score the questionnaires of 300 new pupils.

Designed For.—This interest inventory, yielding three interest scores, is designed for use with boys in Junior High School. Biserial *r* between the total scores and enrollment or non-enrollment in the technical curriculum was .87; for the commercial curriculum the *r* was .73; and the coefficient for the academic curriculum was .56.

Norms.—A score of 235 on any of the three keys indicates "neutral" (or indeterminate) interests; a score above 235 indicates definite preferences, and a score below 235 indicates the absence of preferences for a particular type of curriculum.

Reliability.—The corrected odd-even coefficient for 75 pupils (25 from each of the three curricula) was .95 for the technical key; .93 for the commercial key; and .86 for the academic key.

Validity.—One important indication of validity is revealed by the biserial coefficients reported above. The three keys do indicate a high degree of accuracy in the differentiation of groups of pupils enrolled in these different curricula. The authors, using an arbitrary critical score on each of the three keys, found that 80.5 per cent of the pupils with technical inclinations, 75.5 per cent of those with commercial preferences and 73.6 per cent of those with academic interests were placed or located in the proper curriculum by the interest inventory.

The correlation between the technical key and school marks, however, was only .29; between the commercial key and marks the coefficient was .03; and between the academic key and school marks, .15. There is, therefore, little relationship between curricular preferences and achievement in those curricula. Thus, this seems to indicate that achievement in any curriculum is dependent upon intelligence and special abilities and not upon measured interests. Presumably, the interest test measures the type or kind of interests a boy possesses without any guarantee that the boy will be able to succeed in the field of his special interest. In spite of low correlations between interest and ability, it is obvious that the interest test has important guidance value, since it helps to identify the type of work the boy will find congenial. Ability tests will then help to identify the *level* within a field that will permit success.

The relationship between technical and commercial interests is indicated by coefficients of −.74, −.71, and −.69 for three different schools. The coefficients between technical and academic interests are −.62, −.57, and −.50. The corresponding relationship between academic and commercial interests is indicated by the coefficients of +.21, +.04, and −.02.

Publisher and Cost.—Bureau of Publications, Teachers College, Columbia University, New York. Price, $3 per hundred.

References.—O. K. GARRETSON, "Relationships between Expressed Preferences and Curricular Abilities of Ninth Grade Boys," *Contributions to Education*, 396, New York: Teachers College, Columbia University, 1930; P. M. SYMONDS, *Tests and Interest Questionnaires in the Guidance of High School Boys*, New York: Bureau of Publications, Teachers College, Columbia University, 1930.

2. Vocational Interest Blank for Men, 1927, by E. K. Strong, Jr.

Description.—The blank is an eight-page leaflet listing 420 items covering occupations, amusements, school subjects, activities, peculiarities of people and estimates of present abilities and characteristics. The individual indicates whether he likes, is indifferent to or dislikes each item. Most men complete the blank in half an hour, but longer time is allowed if needed.

Scoring is complicated and expensive. The tests may be scored at Stanford University, the Columbia University Statistical Bureau and the University of Minnesota Testing Bureau. The blank may be scored for fewer than the total number of occupations for which scoring keys have been prepared. The intercorrelations between certain of the occupational scoring keys are high, making it possible to obtain a rating in one occupation which will be characteristic of a group. For example, the physicist interest pattern is typical of the science group; the life insurance, of the selling group; the minister and the personnel manager, of the social service group; and the accountant, of the business group. The C.P.A. key, however, seems to be in a class by itself. The lawyer, journalist and advertiser scales are quite similar.

Designed For.—This test indicates in general the occupational field in which an individual is most likely to find satisfaction, provided, of course, that he has the requisite aptitudes. It affords a means for comparing an individual with successful persons in a given occupational field, on the basis of a wide variety of likes and dislikes. The author of the test has pointed out that it is an attempt to measure "the sum total of all interests that bear in any way upon an occupational career."

Although high scores cannot be taken as indications of ability in the occupation, yet they do measure interest, which is one important aspect of occupational adjustment. In at least one of the occupations, life insurance selling, however, Strong has shown that there is a high positive correlation between measured interests and success.[3] It appears that this key, in a sense, is a measure of social intelligence, which in turn is the ability necessary for success in this vocation. On the whole, though, the man who resembles successful men in his occupation in regard to this complex pattern of interests will not necessarily be particularly successful. He will, however, have greater chances for satisfaction in that occupational field than if he were totally unlike his co-workers with respect to these measured interests.

The applicability of the blank is limited at the lower range of the age scale. Use of the test probably should be restricted to age levels above 18, and preferably to men above 20 years of age.

[3] STRONG, E. K., JR., "Relation of Interest to Ability in Terms of Life Insurance Scores and Sales Production," *Psychol. Bull.*, 1934, 31: 594.

Since the test was not standardized on occupational groups of women, no basis for interpretation of women's scores is possible.

Results are useful in the case of those men students who want confirmation of their vocational choice, as well as those who are entirely undecided about a field of work for which to prepare. It may be used as a check against the student's claimed vocational interests, which are often founded upon very superficial bases. Such claimed interests are more likely to be based upon some chance factor in the environment, such as the well-meant but often inappropriate advice of parents and friends.

Norms.—Weighted scores for each item have been based upon differential responses made by criterion groups composed of successful persons in the occupation. The number of persons in each criterion group varied from 60 in the advertiser group to 382 engineers representing the four engineering societies. The fact that differential scoring keys were possible tends to prove the truth of the old adage, "Birds of a feather flock together."

The occupations for which the blank may be scored are the following:

I. Science Group
    Architect
    Chemist
    Dentist
    Engineer
    Farmer
    Mathematician
    Physician
    Physicist
    Psychologist
II. Linguistic Group
    a. Advertiser
       Journalist (newspaper editor)
       Lawyer
    b. Life insurance salesman
       Real estate salesman

III. Social Service Group
    a. Minister
       Teacher
       Musician
    b. Personnel manager
       City school superintendent
       Y.M.C.A. physical director
       Y.M.C.A. general secretary
       Y.M.C.A. boy's secretary
       Boy Scout Master
IV. Business Group
    Accountant
    Office clerk
    Purchasing agent
    Vacuum cleaner salesman

V. Miscellaneous
    Certified Public Accountant
    Artist
    Masculinity—Femininity

A rating of A indicates that the individual has responded to the items in the same way as three-fourths of the criterion group. B indicates that the individual is similar in interests to one-fourth of the successful men in the occupation. C indicates that the individual's pattern of interest resembles only 2 per cent or less of those successfully engaged in the occupation.

In the case of men less than 25 years of age, there is a tendency for some scores to be lower than a subsequent score will be when interests become more matured. For this reason, a small percentage of C's will later become B's and about one-fourth of the B's will become A's. The reverse, however, is true of some keys.

Crawford and Burnham[4] have demonstrated that with the exception of the journalist and Boy Scout Master keys, the scores on the various occupational keys are significantly different from those obtained by chance. This is further indication that the test measures likes and dislikes which are far from being random guesses.

Reliability.—Two methods were used to determine the reliability of the various scoring keys. Strong reports an average reliability coefficient of about +.85 (corrected). Retests of high school juniors and college freshmen after a year's interval showed that the results are more reliable in the case of the older students because of a greater relative instability of interests at the lower age levels.

Validity.—Responses made by persons in different occupational groups are so different that they constitute rather distinct patterns of likes and dislikes to which responses of other men may be compared. For example, 75 per cent of the criterion group of engineers made certain typical responses. Only 15 per cent of the persons in other groups made similar responses, and these persons were engaged in scientific fields closely allied to engineering.

Not only do the results differentiate between persons engaged in contrasting occupations, but they distinguish between persons with different occupational choices. Whereas 63 per cent of a group of non-law seniors rated C as lawyer, only 15 per cent of the law majors rated C and none of this latter group was planning to enter law.

A follow-up study made by Strong of seniors at Stanford shows that upper-class students tend to continue for at least two

[4] CRAWFORD, A. B., and P. S. BURNHAM, "The Vocational Interests and Personality Test Scores of a Pair of Dice," *J. of Educ. Psychol.*, 1935, 26: 508–512.

years with occupational plans in line with their tested interests. After a two-year period, 67 per cent were still planning to enter or were engaged in work in line with their first or second highest rating on the test. On the basis of chance alone only 11 per cent would be so engaged.[5]

A significant fact about these occupational interest ratings is that they are not influenced to any great extent by actual experience in the occupations and are often found even when students have not had any experience in a given occupation. This test is, therefore, measuring a pattern of interests which precedes specific occupational experience. This important point should be explained to students when they are given advice based upon the results of this test. Thus it is possible to compare an inexperienced man's ratings with criterion groups composed of persons who have been engaged in the particular field of work. Under-class, as well as upper-class, engineering students and engineering graduate students have patterns similar to successfully engaged engineers. Apparently the test is tapping fundamental basic interests which constitute factors directing the individual towards the engineering field rather than interests resulting from experience in the field.[6]

Research indicates that the fundamental pattern of interests which the individual possesses is stable. But his attention may be directed toward different constellations of these interests at various times, resulting in an apparent instability of pattern. This is an instability in the identification of interest pattern, rather than in the pattern itself. A shift in claimed interest from engineering to law, for example, may represent only a shift of emphasis from one set of the whole array of fundamental interests to another. Essentially, however, the basic patterns are stable.

This fact suggests that these interest patterns are a surprisingly permanent aspect of the personality equipment of the individual. Thurstone and Strong have shown that the total array of occu-

[5] This and results included herein are from Strong's manual (see reference).
[6] DVORAK, B. J., "The Adjustment of Pre-Medical Freshmen to the University: A Study in Vocational Guidance," M.A. Thesis in file in the University of Minnesota Library, Minneapolis, 1930. ROSENSTEIN, I., "The Vocational Interest of Freshmen Engineers and a Development of a Short Method for Scoring the Strong Vocational Interest Test," M.A. Thesis in file in the University of Minnesota Library, Minneapolis, 1930.

pational interest patterns may be boiled down to a small number of basic patterns, such as interest in science, in language, in people and in business.

The greatest change in pattern of interests comes in the early years, for the most part prior to 25 years of age. Changes occurring after 25 years of age are only as great as the differences in interest between the various engineering groups, which Strong has shown are so small that separate scoring keys for the several branches of engineering could not be made. Differences between occupational groups far outweigh differences in interest due to age alone.

A most important question arises from the use of the Interest Blank with high school and college students. Are interests, as measured by this test, stable enough during later adolescence to serve as a basis for vocational counseling? This problem has been investigated by Strong and by Berman, Darley and Paterson. As stated above, Strong found that there were very slight changes of interest between successive 10-year intervals from 25 to 55 years of age. But there were marked changes in measured interests from the age of 15 to 25 years. From this study Strong has developed an interest-maturity key by means of which a counselor may determine the extent to which a student has "the interests of 55-year-old men as compared with those of 15-year-old boys." Thus a counselor may judge whether a student's interests are "adolescent" and hence unfocused as yet.

But the Minnesota study indicates that Strong's interest maturity scale actually measures not only maturity but also whether a student's interests are similar to those of men in the major professions or merely to those of men in occupations on a lower level. The suggestion is made that the name be changed to an "age occupational level index."[7]

From the foregoing discussion it is clear that use of the test with high school youngsters should be tentative. Considerable weight may be attached to A ratings obtained at an early age, but the fact that a 16-year-old boy receives only C ratings should

[7] BERMAN, I. R., J. G. DARLEY, and D. G. PATERSON, "Vocational Interest Scales, An Analysis of Three Questionnaires in Relation to Occupational Classification and Employment Status," *Bulletins of the University of Minnesota Employment Stabilization Research Institute*, 1934, III, No. 5: 19–23.

be discounted. The verdict in such a case should be, "The test has little significance as yet for your situation. Better take the test again at a later age." Of course, when such a boy waits until he is 20 or so and still receives only C ratings, there is every likelihood that he will continue into adult life without developing any crystallized vocational interest patterns for the particular occupations in which he received C ratings.

Publisher and Cost.—Stanford University Press, Stanford, California. Prices: 25 for $2; 100 for $6; 500 or more at $5 per hundred.
References.—E. K. STRONG, JR., *Manual for Vocational Interest Blank*, Stanford University Press, 1933. E. K. STRONG, JR., *Change of Interests with Age*, Stanford University Press, 1931.

3. Vocational Interest Blank for Women, 1935, by E. K. Strong, Jr.

Description.—The purpose of this inventory is to ascertain the extent to which a woman's interests resemble the interests of women who are representative of various occupational and professional groups. A high score does not assure success in the particular occupation, but rather indicates that, as far as interests are concerned, the woman tested resembles the average woman in the occupation. The blank is similar to the blank for men and contains 410 items covering lists of occupations, amusements, school subjects, etc., to which the person responds in a way to indicate degree of interest. All of these responses are then compared with those made by the average woman engaged in each occupation which has been studied so far. No time limit is required, but the usual time needed is about half an hour.

Designed For.—The following norms are available:

Lawyer
Librarian
Nurse
Physician
Teacher of English in high school
Teacher of mathematics and physical sciences in high school
Teacher of social sciences in high school
Teacher (in general) in high school
Artist

Author
Dentist
Life insurance saleswoman
Office worker, including bookkeeper, accountant, office manager, purchasing agent, etc.
Social worker
Stenographer-secretary
Y.W.C.A. general secretary
Masculinity—Femininity

The blank should be particularly applicable to women college students considering any of the above occupations. Since tested interests occasionally are quite different from claimed interests and often yield indications of unsuspected, though fundamental, patterns of characteristics, it is advisable to administer this blank, even though the individual's vocational choices are not included in the available scoring keys. One should always keep in mind, however, the limitation of the test, since the scoring keys cover only a few of the large range of occupational opportunities open to women. Because of certain changes with age, present interpretations of test results do not apply to girls below 15 years of age; ordinarily, the use of the test should be restricted to those 17 years of age and over. Students should consider as possible fields of endeavor occupations in which they rate A or B+; and enter upon occupations in which they rate B− or C only when they are definitely assured that their other assets are sufficiently strong to counteract the fact that they do not resemble in interests persons engaged in the occupation.

The blank may be found useful in making educational choices, since students can select courses in line with interest ratings to discover the types of work that will elicit maximum enthusiasm. In this way, final choice of a specific course of training can be made with increased assurance of subsequent satisfaction.

Norms.—At least 150 and in most cases several hundred women, employed for at least three years and representative of the occupations listed above, constitute the criterion groups. An A or B+ score indicates that the individual has interests which are typical of a large percentage of these women. A C rating indicates that, as far as interests are concerned, she is quite unlike most of the women in the occupation.

Reliability.—The test yields fairly reliable results upon repetition. Strong reports corrected odd-even reliability coefficients ranging from .74 for the scale for life insurance saleswoman to .94 for the author scale.

Validity.—Research indicates that this test actually differentiates women in the criterion groups engaged in the occupations listed above. It also differentiates women engaged in the occupation from women not so engaged. Women physicians are decidedly different in interests so measured from married women in general.

Publisher and Cost.—Stanford University Press, Stanford, California. Prices: 25 for $2; 100 for $6; 500 or more at $5 per hundred.

References.—E. K. STRONG, JR., *Manual for Vocational Interest Blank for Women*, Stanford University Press, 1935.

B. PERSONALITY, ADJUSTMENT AND ATTITUDE INVENTORIES

Inventories listed in this section range from attempts to measure such personality traits as "feelings of inferiority" and "schizoid characteristics" on the one hand and attitudes toward the school situation or toward controversial issues, such as evolution and prohibition, on the other. Counselors will find one or more of these measuring instruments of value, especially if they are supplemented by other techniques in a comprehensive guidance program.

A word of caution in regard to all such measures may be in order. As mentioned before, the role of conscious and unconscious motivation must be taken into consideration in the interpretation of such pencil-and-paper tests (as well as in interview situations, teachers' reports, etc.). We refer to the fact that the expression of symptoms may be markedly affected by motivation. One of the clearest instances is reported by Hollingworth.[8] The Woodworth Psychoneurotic Inventory, similar to the emotional adjustment items in the Bell Adjustment Inventory, was given to psychoneurotic soldiers who were patients in an army hospital. Scores on the inventory obtained before and after the armistice were compared. The hysteria patients, before the armistice, obtained a median score of 36 symptoms, whereas the median score dropped to 1 when the test was taken after the armistice. Hollingworth believed that the change in symptom scores was due to a change in motivation. Before

[8] HOLLINGWORTH, H. L., *The Psychology of Functional Neuroses*, pp. 117–150, New York: D. Appleton-Century Company, Inc., 1920.

the armistice, presumably, there was an unconscious desire to appear mentally ill in order to escape from duty in the front-line trenches, whereas after the armistice there was a desire to appear well in order to return to "home and mother" as soon as possible. Such motivation may operate without the subject himself being aware of its presence. This principle should be clearly recognized by the guidance counselor. A student may "cover up" symptoms and hence the measurement will be ineffective; or the student may "exaggerate" symptoms in order to gain the solicitous attention of the counselor. Hence, it is essential to establish an effective rapport between examiner and student and to persuade the student to take an objective attitude toward himself and his problems when answering items in these inventories.

1. The School Inventory, by Hugh M. Bell.

Description.—The School Inventory consists of 76 questions concerned with a pupil's attitudes toward school life. Each question in the test is answered by marking "Yes," "No," or "?." Usually fifteen minutes is ample time to complete the blank. It can be given to groups or to individuals. Special attention must be given to the problem of securing rapport so that students will give frank and honest answers.

Pupils who make low scores tend to be well adjusted to the school situation. They say they like their teachers and their classmates. They feel that the school is run systematically and fairly. Students who make high scores, on the other hand, tend to be poorly adapted to the school. They say they dislike their teachers and they believe the principal is unfair. They are likely to want to withdraw from school.

Designed For.—The test is primarily suitable for use with high school students who have attended a particular school for at least three months. If the test is used to survey the whole school population, it will help to identify those students in need of special counseling and to determine the underlying causes of dissatisfaction as a basis for readjustment work with the individual.

Norms.—The following tentative norms based upon the responses of 391 high school boys and girls are available:

Type of School Adjustment	Score Range
Excellent	0– 3
Good	4–12
Average	13–30
Unsatisfactory	31–39
Very unsatisfactory	above 39

Reliability.—The corrected odd-even coefficient for 242 high school students was found to be +.94.

Validity.—The original test of 114 items was given to 254 students and the critical ratio between the upper and lower 15 per cent in total score was computed. Nondifferentiating items were discarded.

Teachers were then asked to identify "poorly" and "well" adjusted pupils. There were 71 in the "well" and 59 in the "poorly" adjusted groups. The former group obtained a mean score of 14.82 (S.D. 10.95) whereas the mean score for the latter group was 32.25 (S.D. 16.45). The critical ratio of the difference between the means was 6.97, indicating that, on the average, the two groups were significantly different in their responses to the inventory.

The author reports that, in one high school of over 1000 students, student members of the scholastic honorary society had a mean score of 16, in contrast to a mean score of 50 for a group of failing students.

Publisher and Cost.—Stanford University Press, Stanford, California, 1936. Prices: 25 for $1.50; 50 for $2.75; 100 for $5; 500 for $20; 1000 for $35.

References.—H. M. BELL, *Manual for the School Inventory*, Stanford University Press, 1936.

2. The Adjustment Inventory, 1934, by Hugh M. Bell.

Description.—This inventory consists of 140 questions dealing with behavior in the areas of home, health, social and emotional adjustments. The student evaluates his own behavior by checking or encircling "Yes," "No," or "?" after each question. The Inventory may be given to individuals or to groups of students; in the latter case, the examiner should read aloud a prepared statement of the general purpose of the test, why it is being given and how students can arrange to discuss the results with a counselor. In all cases, rapport must be established with students to insure that frank and honest answers are given to all of the questions. Not more than 30 to 40 minutes are required to answer all of the questions. The test is scored by means of a stencil giving the weight of an item for home, health, social or emotional adjustment. For each adjustment area a low score indicates satisfactory adjustment, whereas a high score indicates maladjustment. The specific meaning of the scores for these adjustment areas may be listed as follows:

Home Adjustment.—Low scores indicate that the student feels satisfied with his home situation. High scores indicate dissatisfaction with, and unhappiness in, family relationships.

Health Adjustment.—Low scores indicate denial of symptoms of poor health. High scores indicate the need for physical examination by a physician.

Social Adjustment.—Low scores indicate an aggressive and dominant attitude in social relationships. High scores indicate submissiveness and timidity in social contacts.

Emotional Adjustment.—Low scores indicate emotional balance, freedom from worries, fears and marked fluctuations in mood. High scores indicate emotional instability that may be sufficiently pronounced to require psychiatric treatment.

Although the fourth adjustment area is designated by the term "emotional," it is clear that emotional responses are involved to some degree in the other three areas of adjustment. The following intercorrelations based upon tests given to 197 students reveal this fact:

Emotional vs. health	.53
Emotional vs. social	.47
Emotional vs. home	.38
Home vs. health	.43
Social vs. health	.24
Social vs. home	.04

Even with intercorrelations as high as these, it is apparent that different aspects of behavior are being measured with social adjustments and home adjustments being highly independent of each other.

Designed For.—The test was standardized on high school and college students, both men and women. The Inventory may be used as a means of identifying those students who need to see a counselor and would profit from discussing with him their evaluation of their own behavior. It may be given as a part of a test battery administered to all students at the beginning of the school year or to students at the time they seek an interview with a counselor. In the first case, the total scores may be used as indications of counseling needs on the part of certain students who should be *invited* to see the counselor.

Norms.—The following norms are available for interpreting the scores:

Adjustment areas	High school score range Men (161)	High school score range Women (190)	Description	College score range Men (171)	College score range Women (243)
Home	0–1 2–4 5–9 10–16 Above 16	0–2 3–5 6–13 14–20 Above 20	Excellent Good Average Unsatisfactory Very unsatisfactory	0–1 2–4 5–9 10–16 Above 16	0–1 2–4 5–9 10–15 Above 15
Health	0–1 2–4 5–9 10–15 Above 15	0–1 2–4 5–11 12–16 Above 16	Excellent Good Average Unsatisfactory Very unsatisfactory	0–1 2–4 5–11 12–16 Above 16	0–1 2–4 5–9 10–15 Above 15
Social	0–4 5–9 10–20 21–26 Above 26	0–4 5–10 11–21 22–30 Above 30	Excellent Good Average Unsatisfactory Very unsatisfactory	0–3 4–7 8–17 18–25 Above 25	0–3 4–8 9–19 20–28 Above 28
Emotional	0–2 3–5 6–11 12–18 Above 18	0–3 4–8 9–18 19–24 Above 24	Excellent Good Average Unsatisfactory Very unsatisfactory	0–2 3–5 6–13 14–19 Above 19	0–3 4–7 8–15 16–21 Above 21
Total score	0–12 13–24 25–44 45–60 Above 60	0–15 16–31 32–57 58–74 Above 74	Excellent Good Average Unsatisfactory Very unsatisfactory	0–9 10–22 23–41 42–60 Above 60	0–12 13–24 25–47 48–65 Above 65

Reliability.—The corrected odd-even reliability coefficients given below were computed by Bell for the tests of 258 college freshmen and juniors:

Home adjustment	.89
Health adjustment	.80
Social adjustment	.89
Emotional adjustment	.85
Total score	.93

Turney and Fee[9] report the following results of correlating the scores on the Adjustment Inventory given twice, at an interval of 6 months, to 78 high school students:

Home adjustment	.85
Health adjustment	.74
Social adjustment	.83
Emotional adjustment	.79
Total score	.82

Validity.—Five methods of construction, standardization and validation were used by the author to select the final 140 questions from an original list of 411 questions. First, questions were included which differentiated between the upper and lower 15 per cent of the distribution of scores for each category. Second, only items which were checked by at least 25 per cent of the maladjusted group were retained. Third, items which were misunderstood by students (as indicated by penciled-in question marks) were eliminated. Fourth, the various items were used over a period of 2 years in personal interviews with 400 college students to make certain that they were eliciting the proper responses. Fifth, the section total scores were used to differentiate "well-adjusted" and "poorly adjusted" students in each area, as selected by high school and college counselors and administrators independently of the test results. The critical ratios of the differences between the mean scores obtained by these extreme groups are as follows:

Home adjustment	7.02
Health adjustment	6.58
Social adjustment	5.52
Emotional adjustment	5.32

[9] TURNEY, A. H., and MARY FEE, "An Attempt to Use the Bell Adjustment Inventory for High School Guidance," *School Rev.*, 1936, 44: 193–198.

Bell reports the following correlation of sections of the Inventory with other personality tests:

Personality tests	Group	Corrected coefficient
Allport vs. social adjustment............	46 men	.72
Allport vs. social adjustment............	50 women	.81
Thurstone Schedule vs. emotional adjustment.............................	96 men and women	.93
Thurstone Schedule vs. total score......	96 men and women	.94
Bernreuter B4-D ("Social Dominance") vs. social adjustment................	39 men and women	.90

Publisher and Cost.—Stanford University Press, Stanford, California, 1934. Prices: 25 for $1.75; 50 for $3; 100 for $5.50; 500 for $25; 1000 for $40.

References.—H. M. BELL, *Manual for the Adjustment Inventory*, Stanford University Press, 1934; H. M. BELL, *The Theory and Practice of Student Counseling*, Stanford University Press, 1935.

3. The Minnesota Inventories of Social Attitudes, by E. G. Williamson and J. G. Darley, 1937.

Description.—Form *P*, *Inventory of Social Preferences*, includes questions measuring preferences of a student with reference to the extent and type of social relationships desired. It measures these preferences on a continuum extending from a desire to restrict one's social relationships to a very few contacts, to the opposite extreme of the desire to experience relatively unrestricted social contacts. The latter extreme of the continuum is characteristic of those persons who "like people in general."

Form *B*, *Inventory of Social Behavior*, includes questions which sample estimates of a student's own behavior and his feelings in social situations.

Each item has the following five possible answers, which are printed on the test: almost always; frequently; occasionally; rarely; almost never. Not more than 15 to 20 minutes are required to answer all questions on either form.

The tests were given to 500 college men and to 500 college women. Each item or question was then analyzed in terms of the extent to which it differentiated between the highest one-third of the group in total score and the lowest one-third. These item differentials were usually high, ranging from 1.93 to 20.92 for Form *P*, and from 1.56 to 19.27 for Form *B*. About half the items yielded differentials greater than 10.00 in value; only five were below 3.00.

Each form is scored by giving a weight to the student's answer, these weights being printed on the test itself. No scoring stencil is required.

Designed For.—These two forms are to be used with college students. It is obvious that tests of this type are as necessary in the field of social adjustment as are mental tests in dealing with problems of scholastic adjustment.

SOCIAL PREFERENCE SCORES BY CLASS AND SEX

Class	Men Number	Men Mean	Men Standard deviation	Women Number	Women Mean	Women Standard deviation
Freshmen	378	129.60	22.21	245	145.12	18.62
Sophomores	427	129.01	22.35	244	141.52	22.21
Juniors	284	129.09	22.13	181	139.37	20.36
Seniors	223	129.40	21.27	165	137.36	20.92
Graduate students	88	120.91	23.09	45	128.56	20.13
Total	1400	128.61	22.14	880	140.63	20.95

SOCIAL BEHAVIOR SCORES BY CLASS AND SEX

Class	Men Number	Men Mean	Men Standard deviation	Women Number	Women Mean	Women Standard deviation
Freshmen	378	133.41	22.17	245	136.10	21.74
Sophomores	427	133.67	22.38	244	131.23	23.46
Juniors	284	135.60	22.75	181	132.57	22.39
Seniors	223	136.44	24.20	165	132.64	22.80
Graduate students	88	132.84	24.47	45	127.00	26.13
Total	1400	134.38	22.87	880	132.90	22.94

The *Inventories* may be used in the following ways:
1. In school or class surveys, to identify students needing personal and social guidance.
2. To check teachers' observations and judgments of social inadequacy.
3. In counseling, to provide leads for locating, diagnosing, and treating problems of emotional and social relationships.
4. In research, to determine the relationships with other personality tests and to make factor analyses of test items and total scores.
5. To compare groups, classes, sexes and colleges with regard to the social characteristics of students.

Norms.—The two forms of the Inventory were given to 2280 students in the University of Minnesota (1400 men and 880 women). The table on page 190 gives, for each test, the mean scores and sigmas of the distributions of students classified by sex and college classes:[10]

Abbreviated norms, derived from the test scores of the same 2280 college men and women are as follows:

	Raw score on Form *P*	Raw score on Form *B*
Highest score	190	200
Q_3 (75th percentile)	149	149
Median	135	135
Q_1 (25th percentile)	118	118
Lowest score	80	80

Reliability.—The corrected odd-even reliability of each form was computed separately for 500 men and 500 women and is given below:

Forms	Men	Women
Form *P*—social preferences	+.90	+.91
Form *B*—social behavior	+.92	+.91

[10] WILLIAMSON, E. G., and J. G. DARLEY, "The Measurement of Social Attitudes of College Students, I. Standardization of Tests and Results of a Survey," *J. of Soc. Psychol.*, 1937, 8: 219–229.

Intercorrelations.—The correlation of Form P with B for 1400 college men was $+.47$ and for 880 college women was $+.44$. The correlation of Form P with the American Council on Education Psychological Examination, 1935 form, is $+.16$ for men and $-.11$ for women. The corresponding correlations for Form B and the same intelligence test are $+.23$ and $-.10$. The correlation of Form P with first quarter college grades is $-.10$ for men and $-.04$ for women. The corresponding coefficients for Form B are $+.06$ and $+.03$.[11] Evidently both forms measure factors unrelated to academic intelligence and achievement and, therefore, should be used in research and guidance activities which are not dependent upon or directed toward the criterion of scholarship.

Validity.[12]—The two forms were validated in the following ways:

1. *"Well" versus "Poorly" Adjusted Students.*—From a sampling of 2280 anonymous questionnaires filled out by college students, 200 "well" adjusted and 200 "poorly" adjusted students were selected for study. The selection was made on the basis of the number and type of organized and informal social activities in which these students participated and found enjoyment, the amount of money and time devoted to social activities; the number of acquaintances made in college; and recorded expressions of the student's satisfaction or dissatisfaction with his own social life.

The following critical ratios (D/σ Diff) were found for the differences between the mean scores of the two groups on the two forms:

	Critical ratios	
Forms	"Well" vs. "poorly" adjusted men	"Well" vs. "poorly" adjusted women
Form P—social preferences	9.69	6.21
Form B—social behavior...	8.94	9.60

[11] From an unpublished study by E. G. Williamson, based on the test scores of 827 college freshmen.

[12] WILLIAMSON, E. G., and J. G. DARLEY, "The Measurement of Social Attitudes of College Students, II. Validation of Two Attitude Tests," *J. of Soc. Psychol.*, 1937, 8: 231–242.

2. *Fraternity versus Non-fraternity Students.*—Since members of fraternities are usually the more socially inclined members of the student body the two forms were applied to determine to what extent they differentiated students affiliated with fraternities from those not affiliated. The following critical ratios were found between the group means for men and women on the two forms of the Inventory:

| | Critical ratios ||
Forms	Fraternity vs. unaffiliated men	Sorority vs. unaffiliated women
Form P—social preferences	6.56	2.53
Form B—social behavior	4.76	2.56

3. *Additional Indications of Validity.*—Other indices of validity are reported elsewhere by the authors. Some of the indices may be summarized briefly as follows. The critical ratio for men on Form P between those spending less than $5 per college quarter on social activities and those spending over $25 was 7.72; the ratio for women was 4.86. The corresponding ratios for Form B were 7.96 and 3.77. The critical ratio for students on Form P, classified by reports on an increase versus a decrease in amount of college social activities, was 3.07 for men and 3.83 for women. The corresponding ratios for Form B were 1.52 and 1.41.

Publisher and Cost.—The Psychological Corporation, 522 Fifth Ave., New York, 1937. Prices: 1 to 100 copies of either test for $0.05 each; 100 to 500 for $0.045 each; over 500 for $0.04 each.

References.—E. G. WILLIAMSON and J. G. DARLEY, *Manual for the Minnesota Inventories of Social Attitudes*, Psychological Corporation, 1937; E. G. WILLIAMSON and J. G. DARLEY, "The Measurement of Social Attitudes of College Students, I. Standardization of Two Tests and Results of a Survey," *J. of Soc. Psychol.*, 1937, 8: 219–229; E. G. WILLIAMSON and J. G. DARLEY, "The Measurement of Social Attitudes of College Students, II. Validation of Two Attitude Tests," *J. of Soc. Psychol.*, 1937, 8: 231–242.

4. **Minnesota Scale for the Survey of Opinions,** 1936, by E. A. Rundquist and R. F. Sletto.

Description.—This scale of 132 items, each with five expressions of degree of agreement, is designed to measure attitudes and opinions indicative of morale, feelings of inferiority, family relationships and adjustment, respect for and enforcement of law, economic conservatism, the value of education and general adjustment. Between 30 and 40 minutes are required to answer all of the questions. Each of the first six traits or attitudes is measured by 22 different items arranged in serial order. General adjustment is measured separately by means of 16 items included among the items comprising the six scales. Each of the seven scores is found by using a special tabulation sheet (equivalent to a stencil for each scale) which identifies the items for each scale. The weights for the answers to each item are printed on the test itself.

Designed For.—The scale was standardized on 1000 young people, 500 of each sex. Included in the standardization group were 400 college students, 200 high school seniors and 400 young employed or unemployed persons registered in adult education classes in high schools. Counselors may identify students who are atypical and who may need special counseling concerning attitudes. These scores are indicative of actual or potential maladjustments. The scale may also be used for surveys of students and adults or for research studies.

Norms.—The following norms were derived from the raw scores of 827 arts college freshmen of 1935 in the University of Minnesota.[13]

	Morale	Inferiority	Family	Law	Economic conservatism	Education	General adjustment
75th percentile...	47	56	47	49	56	39	32
Median..........	52	63	52	54	62	45	36
25th percentile...	57	69	58	59	68	49	39

[13] From an unpublished study by E. G. Williamson. The authors of the test arranged scores so that a higher score indicated a greater amount of the trait. In the norms given here, the scores have been reversed, in line with the usual practice of indicating the "favorable" end of the distribution by a high percentile rank. Therefore, a high percentile rank indicates a "favorable" attitude and a low percentile indicates an "unfavorable" or "undesirable" attitude.

Reliability.—The corrected odd-even reliability coefficients for the standardization group are as follows:

Traits	500 men	500 women
Morale	.79	.81
Inferiority	.78	.82
Family	.83	.88
Law	.84	.82
Economic conservatism	.85	.82
Education	.82	.83

The following test-retest coefficients are reported by the authors for the time interval of two months:

Traits	70 men	75 women
Morale	.72	.61
Inferiority	.81	.77
Family	.83	.78
Law	.78	.78
Economic conservatism	.86	.82
Education	.84	.85

These coefficients indicate that too much dependence should not be placed upon some of the single scales. The reliability of these scales could probably be improved by increasing the number of items.

Validity.—The authors of the scale have determined its validity by means of (1) statistical item analysis and (2) by comparing the scores, on each separate scale, of various groups classified as to certainty of maintaining or obtaining employment; overageness or retardation in school; amount of previous education; occupation of parent; home conditions, including residence of students in their home, separation or divorce of parents, and unemployment of father and mother; employment status of the standardization group; and other variables.

Additional Data.—For a small group of students, the authors report the percentages of identical responses on all scales, and the percentage of shifts of more than one position (on a five-step response pattern) in test and retest of the same students. Data are also presented showing the stability of the quartiles for test and retest and showing the coefficients of correlation for individual items of each scale.

The intercorrelations between the scores on the different scales vary from +.08 to +.53. In general, there is a low positive correlation between the scales, those between the morale scales and the others being the highest for both men and women.

Negligible correlations exist between scores on the seven scales and college grades or intelligence as measured by the Psychological Examination of the American Council on Education as shown in the following table:[14]

Traits	454 college freshman men		373 college freshman women	
	Grades	A.C.E. test	Grades	A.C.E. test
Morale	.09	.10	−.005	.04
Inferiority	−.04	.04	−.05	.04
Family	.10	−.05	−.05	−.14
Law	.06	.02	−.09	−.11
Economic conservatism	−.05	.03	−.14	−.01
Education	.12	.02	.08	.05
General adjustment	.08	.09	−.02	.03

Publisher and Cost.—University of Minnesota Press, Minneapolis, Minnesota. Prices: single copy for $0.10; 25 for $1.50; $5 per hundred.

References.—E. A. RUNDQUIST and R. F. SLETTO, *Personality in the Depression, A Study in the Measurement of Attitudes,* Minneapolis: University of Minnesota Press, 1936.

5. Personality Sketches, 1936, by J. B. Maller.

Description.—The Personality Sketches consist of 100 cards, on each of which is printed one test question. The subjects sort the cards into two boxes, one labeled, "Yes, I am the same," and the other, "No, I am different." Form A consists of questions on personal adjustment (neurotic tendencies). Form B measures social adjustment (delinquency tendencies). The test is administered individually without time limit; 10 minutes for both forms is adequate for high school pupils.

[14] From an unpublished study by E. G. Williamson.

Designed For.—The test is suitable for pupils in grades five through twelve, and is used to diagnose mild forms of maladjustment.

Norms.—The author provides tentative norms for both forms for a group of 302 sixth-grade pupils.

Reliability.—The odd-even reliability of the total score (Form A plus Form B) was $+.91$ for 190 sixth-grade children. It is obvious that both forms should be given.

Validity.—Each item was correlated (biserial r) with the total score of the preliminary form and only items with an r of .40 or more were retained. The author summarizes evidence of external validation as follows:

1. The critical ratio exceeds 3.5 for the difference in mean scores of 302 sixth-grade pupils and 188 probation school pupils of the same age.

2. A similar ratio was found for normal adults and psychiatric patients.

The author concludes that "the clinician will find the responses to the individual items much more significant than the total score." The differentiating value of each item of the test was computed for the following groups:

Delinquent *vs.* nondelinquent Negro boys

Delinquent *vs.* normal boys

Young inmates in a prison *vs.* normals

Problem boys in a probation school *vs.* normal boys of the same age

Children rated "very social" by teachers *vs.* those rated "very asocial" by teachers

Publisher and Cost.—The Psychological Corporation, 522 Fifth Ave., New York. Price, $1.75 per set of cards and box.

References.—J. B. MALLER, *Personality Sketches, Manual of Directions*, 1936, published by the Psychological Corporation, 522 Fifth Ave., New York; C. LANDIS, J. ZUBIN and S. E. KATZ, "Empirical Evaluation of Three Personality Adjustment Inventories," *J. of Educ. Psychol.*, May, 1935.

6. Humm-Wadsworth Temperament Scale, 1934, by Doncaster G. Humm and Guy W. Wadsworth, Jr.

Description.—The authors define their purpose in developing this test as follows: "To analyze temperamental mechanisms which underlie the characteristic reactions of a person to his environment and to other people; . . . the effect upon behavior of emotionality, self-interest, harmony or disharmony with environment and similar factors."[15]

The scale consists of 318 questions, each designed to permit the measurement (analysis) of traits (components) of temperament and to permit the identification (diagnosis) of the components which appear to predominate in the temperamental make-up of a given subject. Rosanoff's theory of personality provides the basis of the scale and the diagnosis of individuals according to the following components: (1) "normal"; (2) hysteroid; (3)

Profile scores	Raw scores						
	Normal	Hysteroid	Cycloid manic	Cycloid depressed	Schizoid autistic	Schizoid paranoid	Epileptoid
Strong:							
+3	55–..	72–..	42–..	66–..	66–..	38–..	52–..
+2	46–54	56–71	35–41	56–65	59–67	32–37	44–51
+1	40–45	51–55	29–34	44–55	46–58	30–31	37–43
Borderline:							
0	35–42	38–50	22–28	34–43	38–45	24–29	29–36
Weak:							
–1	30–34	30–37	20–21	25–33	28–37	22–23	24–28
–2	23–29	20–29	13–19	15–24	20–27	13–21	16–23
–3	0–22	0–19	0–12	0–14	0–19	0–12	0–15

cycloid (a) manic phase, (b) depressed phase; (4) schizoid (a) autistic phase, (b) paranoid phase; (5) epileptoid. There are, therefore, seven scores derived for each individual. The scores are classified for each type as "strong" (+1 to +3), "borderline" (0), or "weak" (–1 to –3) with the range of total scores for each group being provided in the authors' manual.

Designed For.—The test should be used with adults (including college students over 18 years of age) with I.Q.'s over 90.

This scale may be used by counselors with professional training in abnormal psychology to identify the temperament components of an individual. It is to be expected that an individual will have more than one component. After identifying these components, a counselor should seek the assistance of psychiatrists

[15] Humm, D. G., and G. W. Wadsworth, Jr., "The Humm-Wadsworth Temperament Scale," Preliminary Report, *Personnel J.*, 1934, 12: 314–323.

in checking the results of testing and in treating the subject should the test scores indicate the probability of mental pathology.

No time limit is set but subjects usually require from 30 to 90 minutes; the average time required is 55 minutes. The answers are written by the subject and the test may be given individually or to a group of subjects.

Norms.—The table on page 198 shows norms for this test.

Reliability.—The split-half corrected reliability coefficients (presumably for the standardizing group of 436 subjects) are of the following magnitudes:

Normal	.82
Hysteroid	.85
Cycloid manic	.73
Schizoid autistic	.88
Schizoid paranoid	.70
Epileptoid	.75

These reliability coefficients fail to meet the usual standards for individual diagnosis, hence interpretations of obtained test scores must be made with larger reservations.

Validity.—The total scores of the scale were validated for the standardizing group of 436 cases by correlation with case studies and clinical records. The coefficient of validity, with biased scales eliminated, was .999. With a second group of subjects the validity coefficient was .81; with biased scales eliminated, this coefficient becomes .98. Most psychologists would be inclined to question the objectivity of a validation method which produces validity coefficients of +.98 to +.999.

Out of some 2000 test questions devised by the authors, 450 were tried out on 436 subjects of known temperamental characteristics. Hysteroid subjects were selected from criminals in a state prison. Cycloid, schizoid and epileptoid subjects were selected from inmates of state hospitals for the insane. Some cases of epilepsy came from homes for indigents or were private patients. "Normal" subjects were selected from "company employees and other individuals, actually adjusted to employment or other pursuits, and whose case studies revealed no evidence of psychopathic tendencies. . . . "[16]

Each item in the scale was validated by the following method:

[16] HUMM, D. G., and G. W. WADSWORTH, JR., "The Humm-Wadsworth Temperament Scale," *Amer. J. of Psychiatry*, 1935, 92: 163–200.

These questions were arranged according to the component each represented. A distribution of scores made in each component by subjects whose mental examinations evidenced a strong degree of that component was compared with a contrasting distribution of scores made by subjects in whom the component was found to be weak or virtually absent.[17]

The total scores of the standardizing group were used in similar manner to differentiate subgroups with known components.

The authors, noting the tendency of some subjects to answer with too many "yes" or "no" responses, have devised a correction. If the number of "no" responses falls between 138 and 196, the scale has been "acceptably taken." If the number is less than 138, the subject is given a colored pencil and told to circle the "yes's" concerning which he is doubtful; these are then counted as "no" responses. If the count is above 196, then a similar procedure is followed for marking the doubtful "no's" which are then counted as "yes" responses.

The senior author of this scale has generously supplied us with the following correlations (corrected for rectilinearity) computed on 1012 unselected cases:

Subject tested	I.Q.	Age
Normal	.19	.25
Hysteroid	−.47	−.21
Cycloid manic	.08	−.11
Cycloid depressed	.04	−.10
Schizoid autistic	−.05	−.10
Schizoid paranoid	−.09	−.19
Epileptoid	−.33	.15

Publisher and Cost.—Published by Doncaster G. Humm, 157½ North Kenmore Ave., Los Angeles, California. Prices: 25 for $2.50; specimen set for $0.50; report of research for $0.50. Also distributed by the Psychological Corporation.

References.—D. G. HUMM and G. W. WADSWORTH, JR., "The Humm-Wadsworth Temperament Scale," Preliminary Report, *Personnel J.*, 1934, 12: 314–323; D. G. HUMM and G. W. WADSWORTH, JR., "The Humm-Wadsworth Temperament Scale," *Amer. J. of Psychiatry*, 1935, 92: 163–200; D. G. HUMM and G. W. WADSWORTH, JR., "The Humm-Wadsworth

[17] HUMM, D. G., and G. W. WADSWORTH, JR., "The Humm-Wadsworth Temperament Scale," *Personnel J.*, 1934, 12: 314–323.

Temperament Scale," *Manual of Directions*, 2d ed., published by Doncaster G. Humm, 157½ North Kenmore Ave., Los Angeles, California, 1934.

7. Specific Attitude Scales, by L. L. Thurstone and Associates.

Thurstone and his associates have constructed a large number of attitude tests using a psychophysical method of item analysis and scale construction. These scales have high reliability, despite the small number of items.

Not more than 15 or 20 minutes are required of students to check the answers. Each item of these tests has been scaled and located by statistical methods on an attitude continuum of eleven steps. The final score is the scale value of the mid-question checked by the student. This is in contrast to most of the other tests described in this chapter, in which all questions receive equal weight and are summed to get a total score, which is transmuted into sigma or percentile units.

The following scales are available for measuring attitudes toward:

The Church	Evolution	The Bible
War	Treatment of criminals	Capital punishment
The Negro	Patriotism	The Chinese
Prohibition	The Constitution	The Germans
Communism	Birth control	Sunday observance
Censorship	God	The Law

Counselors will have frequent occasion to utilize this type of measurement. Students contemplating the ministry as a vocation, for example, might well be persuaded to take several of the Thurstone scales to provide a clue as to the nature and type of theological training that would be appropriate. Students who exhibit an adjustment problem in the religious area, such as religious conflict, might be asked to take several of the scales as a point of departure in identifying more accurately present attitudes. Situations in which attitudes toward other races and nationalities is an important factor might be handled far more intelligently by counselor and student if accurate knowledge of the relevant attitudes is available. Counselors will also find the scales of value in dealing with group situations in the school as a means of measuring the effects on student attitudes of particular courses, programs, etc., inside and outside of the school. In short, the availability of these scales opens up a new approach to student personnel problems falling in the area of social psychology and social control.

Publisher and Cost.—University of Chicago Press, Chicago, Illinois. The price varies with the scales.

References.—L. L. THURSTONE and E. J. CHAVE, *The Measurement of Attitudes*, Chicago: University of Chicago Press, 1929. Also, see Annual Subject Index in *Psychological Abstracts* for specific references.

8. Generalized Attitude Scales, 1934, by H. H. Remmers and Associates.

H. H. Remmers and his associates[18] have developed a new type of attitude test upon the principle of generalized statements which may be used to measure attitudes toward a variety of situations within a given attitude continuum. For example, a test composed of such items as "Is the most admirable of institutions," may be used to measure attitudes (upon separate administration of the test) toward any college or class of a university, any student activity, etc., etc. Scales have been constructed to measure (1) attitude toward any institution; (2) attitudes toward defined groups (*e.g.*, racial groups); (3) attitude toward any homemaking activity; (4) attitude toward any practice (*e.g.*, Sunday observance, drinking, petting, methods of discipline, etc.); (5) attitude toward any occupation; (6) attitude toward any school subject; (7) attitude toward teaching; (8) attitude toward any teacher; (9) attitude toward any existing or proposed social action; and (10) attitude toward any dramatic production, etc. Two equivalent forms were constructed for each scale.

Each of the scales has been constructed by means of the Thurstone technique, in which each item receives a scale value between 1 and 11. A student's score on the test is, therefore, a position or point on the scale of 11 points; this score is found by identifying the mid-scale value of all items checked by the student.

The use of these generalized attitude scales is greatly simplified in comparison with the Thurstone scales so far as scoring is concerned, because the statements are arranged in order of their scale values. Not only does this arrangement make it easier to locate the mid-scale value, but it also permits the scoring clerk

[18] "Studies in Higher Education XXVI," directed and edited by H. H. Remmers, *Bull. of Purdue University*, 1934, Vol. 35, No. 4.

to note more readily consistency or inconsistency of a given student's attitude. Not only is the scoring simplified, but the time for taking one of these attitude tests is minimal—not more than 2 or 3 minutes being required.

The generalized attitude scale toward any occupation or vocation will be of especial interest to the vocational counselor. Examples of favorable statements are: "I'd rather work at this occupation than eat," "This is the ideal vocation for a lifework." Examples of neutral statements are: "This job is all right when no others are available," or "I enjoy only parts of this work." Examples of unfavorable statements are: "This is the worst occupation in the country," "I would refuse this work even if I were starving." In all there are 45 statements in Form A and an equal number in Form B.

The reliabilities of the attitude scores for this scale vary somewhat according to the specific occupation being rated. Correlations between forms A and B for four vocations are reported to be: $+.76$ for the ministry; $+.79$ for homemaking; $+.84$ for high school teaching; and $+.85$ for engineering. The corrected reliabilities for forms A and B together range from $+.87$ to $+.92$. A total of 429 college sophomores in agriculture, home economics, engineering, science, pharmacy, and industrial education were used as subjects. Reliabilities for this same scale when used with high school students also vary in accordance with the particular occupations being measured, but in general they are lower ($+.47$ to $+.77$). This fact suggests that the attitudes of high school youngsters toward any particular occupation are far less crystallized and systematized than are the attitudes of college sophomores who have already selected their vocations.

As one would expect, there is a high degree of specificity of attitude toward different occupations. The correlation between attitudes toward the ministry and toward engineering approximates zero. The same is true for homemaking and high school teaching and for engineering and high school teaching. There is a slight positive correlation (from $+.37$ to $+.46$), however, between ministry and high school teaching. These results suggest that attitude patterns will emerge as these scales are used with various groups.

Engineering students exhibit a most favorable attitude toward engineering as a vocation (mean score $8.31 \pm .05$), whereas these same students exhibit a somewhat negative attitude toward the ministry as a vocation (mean score 4.58 ± .09). In fact the difference is so marked that the most favorable attitude toward the ministry is only slightly above the least favorable attitude toward engineering.

In general, Remmers and his research associates have shown that these generalized attitude scales are reliable and valid measuring instruments that will be helpful in surveys of student populations, in measuring vocational attitudes in courses in occupations, and in educational, vocational and social counseling.

Publisher and Cost.—All of the generalized attitudes are copyrighted by Purdue Research Foundation under the directorship of Mr. G. Stanley Meikle. Permission to reproduce these scales should be obtained from Director Meikle.

References.—H. H. REMMERS, *et al.*, "Studies in Attitudes," *Bull. of Purdue University*, 1934, Vol. 35, No. 4, pp. 1–112; H. H. REMMERS, *et al.*, "Further Studies in Attitudes, Series II," *Bull. of Purdue University*, 1936, Vol. 37, No. 4, pp. 1–298.

CHAPTER VIII

SPECIAL APTITUDE TESTS

Actually, the "special aptitude" tests described in this chapter have characteristics in common with other types of tests already described. They are not pure measures of "special" aptitude since they also measure the "general" trait of academic intelligence. Likewise, they are no more measures of special "aptitude" than some of the so-called "achievement" tests which clearly are designed to determine the degree to which the individual has retained information once learned. They deserve the label only on the ground that their purpose is the measuring of some element of an ability which is related to subsequent success but which has not yet been subjected to extensive formal training.

No claim is made for completeness in listing and describing such tests. There are other promising tests which might have been included here. For example, the Seashore Motor Skills Unit is one which should at least be mentioned. Its cost, however, would prohibit its use in many school guidance projects. The additional fact that industrial operations requiring these particular special abilities have not yet been located limits its practical usefulness at the present time. The O'Rourke and Detroit mechanical tests and the Lewerenz art test, along with a number of others, have been omitted, although for some purposes these tests may be better than some of the tests chosen for treatment.

The inclusion of a given test does not prove that it is a model instrument. Some are included in lieu of better measures and others appear to have potentialities for practical application, provided additional research is completed. The discussion should aid the counselor in selecting those which may best serve his purpose. It goes without saying that the counselor should interpret the results with caution and insight into their limitations.

A. CLERICAL APTITUDE TESTS

1. Minnesota Vocational Test for Clerical Workers, 1931, by Dorothy M. Andrew and Donald G. Paterson.

Description.—The short form of this test consists of two parts, a number-checking test, and a name-checking test. Each part contains 200 paired items, one-half of which are exactly the same and the other half of which are different. The speed and accuracy with which the individual can detect the differences in the series of paired numbers and paired names are measured directly. The test requires 15 minutes of working time. Both the number- and name-checking tests should be administered, since in some persons these two abilities are relatively discrete. Usually individuals obtain similar percentile ratings for the two parts, however, because of the rather high relationship between them. The correlation between number checking and name checking was found to be $+.77$ for 63 sophomore college students.

Designed For.—The test may be administered to men and women of all ages, although at the present date norms have been published only for adult groups. Age and grade norms for students in the junior and senior high schools are now being compiled. That will extend the usefulness of this guidance tool to include the ages in which evidence regarding the aptitudes for commercial training is most needed. These test results should be used to supplement other information regarding the individual who is considering entrance upon clerical training. Clerical success should not be predicted by this information alone, but when used as a part of the clinical picture it will be of definite value in guiding away from clerical training those individuals whose chances for profiting from this type of experience are limited. Persons considering clerical work of any kind or related types of occupations involving clerical detail should be given the test, preferably in combination with a measure of general intelligence, interests, and personality inventories. When only one test can be resorted to, the authors advise the use of the name-checking test, since this measures general intelligence to some extent also.

Employers interested in the clerical potentialities, as well as the present accomplishments of applicants, would find the clerical scores enlightening.

Norms.—Percentile norms are now available for men and women representing an occupationally unselected group, as well

NORMS FOR MEN IN CLERICAL OCCUPATIONS

Number tested	Groups	Mean score Numbers	Mean score Names	Median percentile Numbers	Median percentile Names
29	Accountants and bookkeepers..	144	127	97	93
17	Bank tellers..................	137	134	95	95
44	General clerical workers........	134	131	94	94
31	Minor bank officials...........	125.6	118.9	91	88
30	Routine clerical workers........	124	118	91	88
27	Miscellaneous minor executives.	116.1	120.9	87	90
59–60	Life insurance salesmen........	108.7	107.7	81	80
86–85	Retail salesmen................	108.6	101.1	81	74
18	Draftsmen.....................	107.8	97.8	80	72
23	Shipping & stock clerks........	104	102	77	76
171	Manual training teachers.......	102.8	97.2	75	71
124	Policemen.....................	94	86.1	66	58
101	Garage mechanics..............	85.6	.....	54	..
59–36	Ornamental iron workers.......	80.2	78.9	51	47
118	Casual laborers................	61.9	.....	24	..

NORMS FOR WOMEN IN CLERICAL OCCUPATIONS

Number tested	Groups	Mean score Numbers	Mean score Names	Median percentile Numbers	Median percentile Names
21	Office machine operators.......	149	134	86	72
181	Stenographers—typists.........	147	158	85	90
60	General clerical workers........	139	147	80	84
24	Routine clerical workers........	133	134	76	73
317	Nurses........................	117	124	60	64
137	Retail saleswomen.............	108.6	103	48	41

as for men and women representative of the clerical population and special clerical occupations. Because of sex differences, an individual's test scores should be referred to his particular sex norm, unless he is competing with workers of the opposite sex, in which case it is desirable to use those percentiles also in the interpretation.

Complete norms may be found in the test manual and in the Employment Institute Bulletins listed in the references. A sample of the norms given in the table on page 207 is included to indicate the differences between men and women, between gainfully occupied persons in general and those in clerical work, and between persons engaged in different types of clerical work. These differentiations substantiate the claim for the validity of the test.

Reliability.—The consistency of this clerical aptitude test compares well with some of the best intelligence tests. The reliability for the short form taken as a whole test for 138 employed clerical workers was +.90, and when 48 University of Minnesota business students were retested with the same test the correlation was +.85. The corrected split-half coefficient of reliability for the number-checking test was +.85 and for the name-checking test, +.89.

Validity.—A number of indications of the test's ability to measure that which it claims to measure may be pointed out. The differential occupational ratings, samples of which are found above in the discussion on norms, provide evidence not only that the test differentiates the clerical from the general population but that different occupational groups in the clerical field form a hierarchy with respect to average clerical test scores.

When clerical scores were related to supervisors' ratings of employed clerical workers, there was some indication that the test could be used to predict efficiency on the job, but the true relationship is obscured by the unreliability of the ratings. The correlations obtained for different groups numbering from 22 to 97 ranged from +.28 to +.42.

It appears that success in commercial courses, as rated by teachers, may be predicted better by this test than success on the job. When a group of over 100 vocational high school students were rated by their teachers, the correlation with test scores was +.58. The correlation between intelligence test scores and the ratings for this same group was +.43, showing that the clerical test alone would have given a better prediction of success in the training course than the intelligence test. When both are used, however, the correlation rises to +.66, showing the value of combining test evidence in building up a clinical picture of the student before training suggestions are given.

In a group of 167 university accounting students only one student with a percentile score below 41 on the number-checking test and no students with a percentile score below 51 on the name-checking test received an A or B grade in the course.

Additional confidence in the test's validity is furnished by the fact that it correlates to the extent of +.71 with "The Scott Company Test for File Clerks." We feel that the Minnesota test is superior to the Scott Company test, which is more influenced by the factor of verbal intelligence. The correlation with intelligence is only +.23 for different homogeneous groups of students and employed clerks. For very heterogeneous groups, however, this relationship rises to +.47 for number checking and +.65 for name checking.

The description, clerical aptitude, is not a misnomer, for, as the authors point out, there is a small negative relationship between abilities measured by this test and age and years of clerical training, and a very slight relationship with amount of clerical experience. Retests after 5 months of commercial training showed that training itself does not improve test scores.

Publisher and Cost.—The Psychological Corporation, 522 Fifth Ave., New York. Prices: $3 per hundred, including manual and key; sample set for $0.25.

References.—D. M. ANDREW, "An Analysis of the Minnesota Vocational Test for Clerical Workers," Ph.D. Thesis, University of Minnesota 1935; D. M. ANDREW and D. G. PATERSON, "Measured Characteristics of Clerical Workers," *Bulletins of the Employment Stabilization Research Institute*, 1934, Vol. III, No. 1, Minneapolis: University of Minnesota Press; D. M. ANDREW and D. G. PATERSON, "Minnesota Vocational Test for Clerical Workers," *Test Manual*, The Psychological Corporation, 1933; MILLICENT POND, "What Is New in Employment Testing?" *Personnel J.*, 1932, 11: 10–16.

2. **Other clerical aptitude tests** (O'Connor, O'Rourke, Thurstone) are on the market and will be found useful in counseling and research. The best single reference to a discussion of clerical aptitudes is W. V. Bingham's *Aptitudes and Aptitude Testing*, Chapter XII, The Field of Clerical Occupations, and Appendix V, Tests of Clerical Aptitudes.

B. ART TALENT TESTS

1. Art Judgment Test, 1929, by N. C. Meier and C. E. Seashore.

Description.—The most significant index to art talent, aesthetic judgment or "the capacity for perceiving quality in aesthetic situations relatively apart from formal training" is revealed according to the originators, by the responses which the individual makes to these test items. It is not measuring creative ability, but rather, art appreciation. It is likewise not measuring other capacities and skills which together constitute that complex called "art talent." The authors contend, however, that the test is measuring "art judgment," which is the most important single factor in this galaxy, and that it is indispensable to one considering art as a career, more to be desired than initial ability to handle the brush or the art tools with skill. The authors state that scores made on this test will enable counselors to obtain a quantitative basis for predicting the extent to which persons may expect to progress in art.

The equipment consists of a booklet of 250 pictures, arranged in pairs, which differ in one respect. These differences are pointed out on the test blank on which the examinee indicates his preference for one of the two representations. The score is the number of correct choices, no time limit being set, although an hour is usually adequate.

The correct choices represent the recognized works of old masters. Items selected were considered to be of artistic repute and to conform with some recognized art principle in the judgment of competent critics. Incorrect choices are deliberate attempts to modify the accepted work in some detail and with a view toward decreasing its artistic merits.

Designed For.—The possible usefulness of a reliable and valid measure of art judgment for educational and vocational guidance is apparent. The authors claim that persons ranking in the upper quartile "should, other things being equal, find almost certain success in an art career." They suggest that corroborating evidence should be used for those in the lowest quartile and that they "should reconsider before going farther in art." This corroborating evidence should probably not be limited to persons receiving low test scores. In fact, suggestions regarding further art training or art work as a vocation should never be based upon this one source of information. Whenever possible, samples of a student's art work should be submitted to competent art critics for judgment as to artistic potentialities.

Persons considering occupations not directly in the well-recognized art field, such as advertising, commercial photography, costume illustration, department store buying, interior decoration, etc., should also profit from this test.

Norms.—Percentile norms are furnished by the authors for large groups of students of the seventh and eighth grades, ninth and tenth grades, and eleventh and twelfth grades. In interpreting an adult's score, the norms for senior high school students may be used. Median scores made by different groups are presented below. The fact that these different groups are differentiated on the average is indicative of the test's validity.

Number	Group	Median score
360	Eighth-grade pupils	66
233	Tenth-grade pupils	72
169	Twelfth-grade pupils	76
264	Art students	82
35	Art faculty	87

Reliability.—Too much reliance should not be placed upon this test, since it does not furnish with all cases so consistent results as are desirable. The table on page 212 shows reliability coefficients obtained by different investigators.

Validity.—There appears to be a definite relationship between art judgment as revealed by scores and educational attainment. The norms show that the average score increases in the upper grades. Art students and faculty are differentiated, on the average, from non-art students. Non-art faculty persons are inferior when compared with art faculty.

Low scores are very rarely made by persons of recognized artistic ability. The fact that some young persons with no art training obtain scores as high as gifted art students indicates that the test is measuring a "natural capacity" apart from learning.

The test is measuring something other than general academic intelligence. All degrees of art judgment are present in persons of low, average and high general intelligence. Figures reported in different investigations show the small amount of overlapping between the traits measured by the test and intelligence tests. The correlations reported in six different studies range from −.14 to +.28.

The manner in which the test items were selected is to some extent evidence of their validity. In order to be included, they must have been accepted by 25 art experts and by 60 to 90 per cent of 1081 subjects. In addition, these works of masters have all stood the test of time.

The authors believe that the test is measuring "natural

Investigators	Subjects	Coefficient method
Meier	69 undergraduates	+.71 Retest
Meier	100 non-advanced art students	+.71 Spearman-Brown
Meier	77 Minneapolis Central H.S. art students	+.85 Spearman-Brown
Hevner	100 college students	+.66 Spearman-Brown
Carroll and Eurich	135 college students	+.78 Spearman-Brown
Carroll and Eurich	49 art majors	+.61 Retest—1 yr.
Carroll and Eurich	103 non-art students	+.69 Retest—1 yr.
Leighton	art students	+.79 Retest at end of course
Leighton	non-art students	+.65 Retest
Farnsworth and Misumi	212 Stanford non-art students	+.59 Odd-even

capacity" rather than an acquired ability. The range of scores in any group homogeneous with respect to art training is always large, although the average for the group as a whole may differ quite substantially from that of another group. One study shows a very slight increase in scores obtained by art majors after a year of art training.

Correlations between scores and ratings of art talent made by teachers are not high, but this may be a reflection upon the ratings, as well as upon the validity of the test. Carroll reports a correlation of +.40 ± .06 between instructors' ratings and Meier-Seashore art scores and a correlation of +.15 between the same instructors' ratings and McAdory art-test scores.

Brigham and Findlay report a correlation of +.46 between art grades and test scores of 50 students.

Wallis reports a correlation of +.37 between the Meier Seashore and McAdory art tests, indicating that the two tests are not measuring the same "art judgment."

Sex differences, as revealed by this particular measure, are quite striking, women scoring on the average significantly higher than men, according to a study made by Eurich and Carroll.

Publisher and Cost.—Bureau of Educational Research and Service, University of Iowa, Iowa City. Prices: Test booklets for $0.90 each; manual for $0.10; record sheets, $2 per hundred.

References.—N. C. MEIER and C. E. SEASHORE, *The Meier-Seashore Art Judgment Test Examiner's Manual*, Iowa City: Bureau of Educational Research and Service, 1930; H. A. CARROLL, "What do the Meier-Seashore and the McAdory Art Tests Measure?" *J. of Educ. Res.*, 1933, 26: 661–665; H. A. CARROLL and A. C. EURICH, "Abstract Intelligence and Art Appreciation," *J. of Educ. Psychol.*, 1932, 23: 214–220; A. C. EURICH and H. A. CARROLL, "Group Differences in Art Judgment," *School and Soc.*, 1931, 34: 204; P. R. FARNSWORTH and I. MISUMI, "Notes on the Meier-Seashore Art Judgment Test," *J. of Appl. Psychol.*, 1931, 15: 418–420; N. C. MEIER, "Can Art Talent Be Discovered by Test Devices?" *Annual Report*, Western Arts Association, 1927, Cincinnati, 1928; N. C. MEIER, "A Measure of Art Talent," *Psychological Monographs*, 1928, 39; MADELINE KINTNER, *The Measurement of Artistic Abilities*, New York: The Psychological Corporation, February, 1933.

2. The McAdory Art Test, 1929, by Margaret (McAdory) Siceloff.

Description.—The originator of this scale attempted to devise a method for determining the individual's "good taste" in the field of visual perception. This measure is secured by determining the extent to which the individual approaches the opinions of art experts on the relative merits of a series of plates involving various subjects and art elements. It is a measure of art judgment and not creative ability.

The test material consists of a book containing 72 plates in black and white or in color with four representations for each plate. The art subjects used include textiles, clothing, furniture, architecture, painting, etc. In most cases, the four different representations of each plate involve variations in line, dark and light or color, the correct order of ranking having been established by a large group of art experts.

About an hour is required for the individual to consider all the plates and his score is the number of correct judgment rankings, made on a sheet prepared for this purpose.

Designed For.—Norms are available for age groups from 10 years to the adult level and from the third through the twelfth grade. When further art training is being considered, this objective rating of art judgment should furnish supplementary evidence as to the advisability of such training.

Norms.—Tentative norms for different groups have been established and the following table, prepared by the test designer, is reproduced here, since it indicates the rather marked differences between averages of dissimilar groups.

	Men	Women
The score attainable by mere chance..................	68	68
The ability of an average 10-year old child in the New York City schools.................................	103	114
The ability of the average first-year high school pupil in the New York City schools.........................	135	156
The ability of the average adult in New York City......	145	160
The ability of the average first-year student in an art school..	173	179
The ability of college graduates engaged in teaching.....	162	180
The ability exceeded by only 1 per cent or fewer of the adult population...................................	202	220

The sex difference in this trait is noticeable in the above table, the average for women exceeding that for men in all groups.

Reliability.—Different figures have been presented regarding the test's reliability and these figures vary somewhat according to the group tested and the method used. The reliability coefficients are not all high. A score for a given person might be considerably changed if the test were to be repeated after a time interval of a few months. On the other hand, this test appears to be more reliable than some other measures of art judgment and equals in reliability certain other recognized character and aptitude tests. In view of the less reliable subjective methods for determining this rather intangible quality, as well as the lack of other reliable and objective measures, one is justified in the judicious use of this device to supplement other data. Results obtained in some of the studies of the test's reliability are given in the table on page 215.

Validity.—An attempt was made to include only those items approved by "competent critics" in the art field. At least 64 per cent of the group of 100 judges, made up of art producers, teachers, critics, buyers and competent lay critics, was required to approve the ranking of each item before it was accepted. Included items also differentiate between persons scoring high and those scoring low on the entire test.

The differences in averages between groups is some evidence of the validity of the measure. Age differences are apparent, but there is a wide range of scores within a given age. Groups which would logically be expected to test high confirm one's

Investigators	Subjects	Correlation
Carroll and Eurich.....	100 college students	+.82—corrected by Spearman-Brown formula
McAdory.............	100 unselected adults	+.93—split-half
McAdory.............	100 art students (not advanced)	+.81—odd-even
McAdory.............	101 art school students	+.73—retest after one week
McAdory.............	95 art school students	+.63—retest after 2 months
McAdory.............	47 college students	+.59—retest after 1 year
McAdory.............	100 sixth-grade pupils	+.80
Leighton.............	60 art students	+.50—retest after course

expectation. Art experts rate highest. The fact that some untrained persons score much above others trained in art leads one to suppose that the scale is based upon a native trait rather than one which is acquired through training alone.

It cannot be said that the test measures general intelligence to any extent. Carroll and Eurich report a correlation of +.10 between the McAdory test and Miller Analogies for 203 subjects. They found a correlation of +.24 with another intelligence test for 88 art students. Bright and dull children are not so sharply differentiated on the basis of art judgment as they are on intelligence. A very dull child is occasionally found to possess outstanding talent in this field.

Correlations between these objective results and instructors' ratings of talent of college art majors are low. Carroll reports a correlation of +.15 for 94 students. Since instructors' opinions are unreliable and the group judged is homogeneous, those results may not be so devastating as they appear.

Whatever the test measures, it seems to be quite different from that which the Meier-Seashore test measures, since the correlation between these two tests is surprisingly low. Carroll reports a correlation of +.27 between the McAdory and Meier-Seashore tests for 111 subjects and Wallis has found a correlation of +.37. The conclusion one must draw from these data is that "art judgment" is dependent to a great extent upon the content of the art judgment test and that both tests should be given whenever possible.

Evidence indicates that, whatever the test measures, it is little affected by art training. Groups differing in amount of art training do not differ markedly in test results and there are wide variations in scores within a group homogeneous in respect to amount of art instruction.

Publisher and Cost.—Bureau of Publications, Teachers College, Columbia University, New York. Prices: Test book for $15; record sheets, 25 for $0.40.

References.—MARGARET MCADORY, "The Construction and Validation of an Art Test," New York: Bureau of Publications, *Teachers College, Contr. to Education*, 383, 1929; MRS. MARGARET (MCADORY) SICELOFF, *Validity and Standardization of the McAdory Art Test*, New York: Bureau of Publications, Teachers College, Columbia University, 1933; H. A. CARROLL and A. C. EURICH, "Intelligence and Art Appreciation," *J. of Educ. Psychol.*, 1932, 23: 214–220.

C. MUSICAL ABILITY TESTS

1. Measures of Musical Talent, 1919, by C. E. Seashore.

Description.—According to Seashore, musical talent is not a single trait but is composed of a hierarchy of traits. This particular test measures only a few basic sensory capacities, which are a part of that complex we call musical talent. In order to obtain a more complete indication of the individual's ability, it would be necessary to measure musical memory and imagination, musical intellect and feeling and capacity to produce musical tones with skill. Although we lack objective means of measuring some of these other factors, it is possible with Seashore's records to obtain a reliable indication of the capacity for pitch and tonal memory at least. These two tests meet the criteria for reliability and validity and we suggest that only these two of the six tests be given, especially when time is limited. The other tests in the battery do not measure so reliably or validly what they are supposed to measure: that is, the individual's sensitivity for intensity, time, consonance and rhythm.

Each test is recorded on a double-disk phonograph record which is played to the subjects, who indicate on prepared blanks their reactions to the paired stimuli. For example, in the pitch test, there are a number of paired sounds for each of which the subject indicates whether the second sound is higher or lower in pitch than the one first presented.

The intercorrelation between these tests is low so that we are justified in expecting that they are measuring different capacities with little overlapping.

The administration of this test is an important factor in securing reliable results and requires a trained examiner. About an hour should be allowed for the full battery.

Designed For.—The test may be administered to persons from the first grade upward. It is especially significant for those considering music as a career or avocation.

Norms.—In his original 1919 Manual, Seashore gives percentile norms for the different tests for large numbers of fifth graders, eighth graders and adults. Larson, in 1927, tested additional cases in these three groups and combined the scores with Seashore's to make a new set of norms on a larger sampling. Either set of norms may be used, since they are similar, but the 1927 norms are preferable, since they include more cases.

Reference to these tables shows that there is a slight correlation between age and scores on these measures and it is for this reason that the interpretations differ slightly for children and adults. Seashore explains that these age differences are due to factors other than differences in "innate capacity." Older persons are capable of more sustained attention and interest and such factors as these cause the differences in performance.

A very much abbreviated table of norms for the pitch and tonal memory tests from Larson's monograph is presented in the table on page 218 for illustrative purposes, but the complete tables of Seashore or Larson should be consulted for interpretation of an individual's score.

Norms for Pitch

Percentile	Per cent right		
	Grade 5	Grade 8	Adult
99	89	91	93
75	77	83	86
50	67	78	81
25	57	67	75
1	43	46	50

Norms for Tonal Memory

Percentile	Per cent right		
	Grade 5	Grade 8	Adult
99	90	95	98
75	65	74	84
50	50	63	74
25	39	51	61
1	23	30	36

Reliability.—A number of investigators have been concerned with measuring the reliability of this scale and it would be impractical to list here all the results obtained. The references may be consulted for the detailed information.

There is considerable disagreement among investigators as to the adequacy of the tests from the point of view of their reliability. When low reliabilities are reported, however, one cannot always interpret this to mean that the tests themselves are constructed in such a way as to yield inconsistent results with individuals. One source of unreliability may be in the conditions of administration. The subjects are apt to become bored and inattentive unless special precautions are made to maintain a high degree of attention and effort. An experienced and skillful test administrator is an important factor in procuring reliable results.

Despite the varying coefficients reported in different studies, there is remarkable agreement in the rank of the six tests when arranged in order of decreasing reliability. With very few exceptions, the tests of tonal memory, pitch, and intensity have the highest coefficients and the tests for time, consonance and rhythm are lower.

For information regarding absolute reliability figures, we must depend upon those studies which seem to have controlled the extraneous factors affecting the consistency of the individual's behavior.

Drake has found Spearman-Brown coefficients of +.86 for tonal memory, +.84 for pitch and +.88 for intensity for an unselected group of school children.

R. C. Larson's study of reliability seems to be among the best. She has retested large groups of fifth-, sixth-, seventh-, and eighth-grade students and adults at the same and at different sittings, and has presented data which indicate that the tonal memory and pitch tests are sufficiently reliable at all these levels to use for purposes of individual diagnosis. The intensity and time tests, especially with adults, do not meet the criterion for use with individuals. The tests of consonance and rhythm are entirely inadequate for individual measurement.

Validity.—When Seashore first described these scales, he pointed out the fact that they were only slightly related to measures of academic capacity and his statements have since been confirmed by others. According to data presented by Larson, the average of the various correlations between intelligence test scores and scores on the six Seashore tests taken individually for fifth, sixth, seventh, and eighth grades was +.23. The range of coefficients between intelligence and the different music tests varied between .00 and +.43.

The fact that scores on these scales are unaffected by musical training, as Seashore pointed out, also attests to their validity. Corroborating evidence has since been produced at the University of Iowa School of Music. On the basis of retests given to a fairly large number of students after they had been studying music for periods of one, two and three years, it was shown that the average gains made on all six tests, after the regular music courses, were so slight as to be insignificant. Similar results have been obtained by Stanton at the Eastman School of Music.

Despite the fact that scores do not increase with practice, there are significant differences in scores obtained by first-class musicians, semiprofessional musicians and amateur musicians, when they are compared with beginning music students and nonmusicians, as Stanton has shown. Evidently, the test is measuring something which persons possess who have achieved success in the field of music and this "something" is a native capacity which musical training does not improve. This makes it possible to compare scores of untrained individuals seeking guidance with scores obtained by musicians.

There have been a number of studies of the value of these tests in predicting success in music. Here, again, the results are likely to be a function of the method employed, but in these studies also the tonal memory and pitch tests appear to be the most valid. Drake concludes on the basis of his study of validity that the tonal memory and pitch tests alone are satisfactory when test scores were compared with teachers' estimates and an examination in music. Brennen found the highest validity coefficients for tonal memory and rhythm when scores of 20 students were related to musical performance as rated by four judges. Brown found a correlation of +.41 between tonal memory and the average of two rankings of musical capacity which were made by the teacher.

Dr. Stanton of the Eastman School of Music has contributed important information regarding the test's validity. She has shown that there is a definite tendency for students rated by teachers as possessing great musical talent to be those who obtain high scores on the tests. Especially interesting are her findings in regard to length of residence in relation to scores. Of 2104 cases tested, 13 per cent of those receiving low ratings on the tests remained in the school for 3 years, while 64 per cent of those receiving high records remained. On the basis of such results, the faculty decided to use the tests as a partial basis for admission and sectioning.

Publisher and Cost.—C. H. Stoelting Company, 424 North Homan Ave., Chicago, Illinois; Psychological Corporation, 522 Fifth Ave., New York. Price, six double-disk records, manual and key, for $8.40.

References.—A. W. BROWN, "The Reliability and Validity of the Seashore Tests of Musical Talent," *J. of Appl. Psychol.*, 1928, 12: 418–475; R. M. DRAKE, "The Validity and Reliability of Tests of Musical Talent," *J. of Appl. Psychol.*, 1933, 17: 447–458; R. C. LARSON, "Studies on Seashore's Measures of Musical Aptitude," *University of Iowa Studies*, Vol. 2, No. 6; C. E. SEASHORE: *The Psychology of Musical Talent*, New York: Silver, Burdett & Company, 1919; C. E. SEASHORE: *Manual of Instruc-*

tions and Interpretations for Measures of Musical Talent, New York: Columbia Graphophone, 1919, 16 pp.; H. M. STANTON, "Seashore Measures of Musical Talent," *Psychol. Monog.*, 1928–1929, 39: 135–144; H. M. STANTON, "Measuring Musical Talent," *Personnel J.*, 1928, 7: 286–292.

2. Musical Memory Test, 1933, by R. M. Drake.

Description.—The test was designed to measure musical talent, apart from training. It consists of 24 original two-bar melodies of slightly increasing difficulty. Following each of these standard melodies there are from two to seven variations which differ from the standard by a change in key, in time or in notes. The procedure consists in playing each standard melody on the piano to a single examinee or a group and then playing the variations, requiring the examinees to note on their answer sheets whether the changes were in the key, time or notes.

The time required is about 45 minutes and the score is the total number of errors.

Designed For.—The test may be used as an aid in determining the desirability of further musical training for vocational or avocational purposes. It would be particularly applicable in those cases of young students where no other evidence of musical accomplishment is available. A wide range of difficulty is covered, making the test suitable to equally wide ranges of talent.

Norms.—Percentile scores for boys and for girls from ages 7 to 23 are included in the Manual of Directions.

Reliability.—This test appears to be one of the few measures of musical talent which yield consistent results. Drake reports a split-half reliability of $+.85$ for 100 unselected school children and $+.93$ for a group of 46 music students.

Validity.—According to the author, this is the "only musical test which produces consistently high and significant validity coefficients." He reports a validity of $+.67 \pm .054$ for 46 music school students of 9 to 16 years of age with varied amounts of music training. When age and training factors are discounted, this relationship of test scores and teachers' estimates of "innate musical capacity" drops to $+.50 \pm .075$. Further studies of the validity of this test should be undertaken by other investigators.

Publisher and Cost.—Distributed by Psychological Corporation, 522 Fifth Ave., New York. Prices: Examiner's books for $0.25 each; manual of directions for $0.25; answer sheets for $0.02 each; sample set for $0.75.

References.—R. M. DRAKE, "The Validity and Reliability of Tests of Musical Talent," *J. of Appl. Psychol.*, 1933, 17: 447–458; R. M. DRAKE, *Manual of Directions*, Public School Publishing Company, Bloomington, Illinois, 1934.

D. MECHANICAL ABILITY TESTS

1. **Minnesota Mechanical Assembly Test,** 1930, by D. G. Paterson, R. M. Elliott, L. D. Anderson, H. A. Toops and E. Heidbreder.

Description.—The apparatus consists of three boxes with several compartments each containing parts, which, when correctly assembled, form simple mechanical objects. It is a revision of the J. L. Stenquist Mechanical Assembly Test. Time limits have been established for each object, but this allotment is usually ample and the test actually measures the ability to recognize and assemble these devices, rather than speed of performance. A certain number of points is given for each perfect assemblage and partial credits are given when parts of an object are correctly assembled. When the full time allowed is needed, the complete test requires about an hour. It is inadvisable from the standpoint of reliability of measurement to use one or two of the boxes instead of the complete set of three, when the purpose is to determine an individual's performance.

Considerable training is required in order to score the items, but detailed directions are given in the examiner's manual.

Designed For.—This test was originally designed to measure the mechanical aptitude of boys of junior high school age. When applied to other groups, its significance becomes more problematical. For persons beyond the junior high school age, mechanical experience and training are factors which vary so markedly among individuals that it is difficult to determine whether an individual's score may be attributed to "aptitude" or to mere exposure to the type of mechanical contrivances contained in the assembly boxes. It is only for persons of similar mechanical training opportunities that differences in scores may be said to reveal native differences in "aptitude." For men of considerable mechanical experience the test is too easy. Thus, differences in aptitude among them are not adequately determined by the test.

Norms.—Percentile norms are furnished by the authors for boys at each year level from the age of 11 through 21 years.

Norms for boys and girls from the seventh grade through high school, men in the engineering college, and men and women in the arts college are also given in the original publication.

For university students, scores should be compared with those obtained for a standard occupational sampling of men and women for whom norms have been established. This procedure is not very satisfactory and renders only approximate indications of standing in this group.

Below are listed a number of occupational groups who have been given the assembly test. The percentile equivalents for the mean of each group are given.

Number	Groups	Median percentile
61	Ornamental iron workers	69
169	Manual training teachers	68
102	Garage mechanics	68
18	Draftsmen	65
69	Janitors	60
69	Men office clerks	55
29	Minor bank officials	55
31	Machine operators	50
42	Retail salesmen	48
124	Policemen	48
47	Life insurance salesmen	47
494	Occupationally unselected men	44
123	Casual laborers	18

Reliability.—Although the test is a very reliable measure for boys of junior high school age as indicated by a corrected coefficient of $+.94$, results with adults are not sufficiently consistent to be depended upon in individual cases, the corrected coefficient for 444 occupationally unselected men being $+.79$ and for 127 women, $+.68$. Only extremely high or low scores have much significance for adults due to this error. Furthermore, the test appears to be too easy for adult men and too difficult for adult women. Until further research is available, it probably should be administered to adults in occasional cases only, and then the results should be interpreted with care.

Validity.—The test's validity for boys in shop courses has been shown to be adequate. It may be considered a good measure of mechanical aptitude, useful in predicting success in shop courses, such as woodworking, machine shop, sheet metal and auto mechanics, when administered to the mechanically naïve young person.

Some indication of the test's validity for adults is shown in the differential occupational patterns obtained and presented in the discussion of norms above. Group averages for mechanical workers are definitely superior to those obtained for occupations not popularly considered to be dependent upon mechanical ability, but this superiority may be a result of differential experience, as well as native ability differences.

The test is very acceptable from the standpoint of its freedom from the measurement of general intelligence. For several different groups of men and women, representing both the unselected population and occupationally selected groups, the correlations between scores on this test and the Pressey educational test range from $+.10$ to $+.26$. This means that mechanical ability as measured by this test is only slightly related to academic intelligence. Students who do well in academic school subjects would not necessarily do well in shop courses. It is important to note also that the relationship is not a negative one, that is, boys with low academic capacity are not, therefore, more likely to be mechanically gifted. If this were true, the regrettable practice of transferring failing students to mechanical courses might be justifiable. The possession of low academic capacity does not guarantee the possession of high mechanical intelligence. In fact, it decreases the chances that the individual is gifted mechanically. The relationship, however, is so low as to make it advisable to administer a separate test of mechanical aptitude before making any prediction of what might be.

Publisher and Cost.—Marietta Apparatus Company, Marietta, Ohio. Price, the set of three boxes for $29.

References.—H. J. GREEN, I. R. BERMAN, D. G. PATERSON, and M. R. TRABUE, "A Manual of Selected Occupational Tests for Use in Public Employment Offices," *Bulletins of the Employment Stabilization Research Institute*, 1933, Vol. 2, No. 3, Minneapolis: University of Minnesota Press; D. G. PATERSON, R. M. ELLIOTT, L. D. ANDERSON, H. A. TOOPS, and E. HEIDBREDER, *Minnesota Mechanical Ability Tests*, Minneapolis: University of Minnesota Press, 1930; D. G. PATERSON, ed., "Research Studies in Individual Diagnosis," *Bulletins of the Employment Stabilization Research Institute*, 1934, Vol. 3, No. 4, Minneapolis: University of Minnesota Press;

B. J. DVORAK, "Differential Occupational Ability Patterns." *Bulletins of the Employment Stabilization Research Institute*, 1935, Vol. 3, No. 8, Minneapolis: University of Minnesota Press.

2. Minnesota Spatial Relations Tests, 1930, by D. G. Paterson, R. M. Elliott, L. D. Anderson, H. A. Toops and E. Heidbreder.

Description.—This test is a revision of Link's Spatial Relations test. The equipment consists of four boards with 58 odd-shaped cutouts. There are two sets of blocks, one for boards A and B and another for boards C and D. The blocks for each board are placed in a definite order before the examinee and he is instructed to place them in their proper places in the board as rapidly as possible. The score is the amount of time required to replace the blocks in the four boards. Thus, the test measures directly the speed with which one can discriminate odd sizes and shapes and indirectly "mechanical aptitude."

Designed For.—The test has proved to be a valid indicator of mechanical aptitude for junior high school boys in shop courses. Since it is of such a nature that mechanical training and experience do not affect the score, it may be adapted to older age groups for whom it also yields fairly valid results. It will probably be of greatest usefulness when applied to young students considering occupations generally regarded as requiring mechanical aptitude, such as auto mechanics, woodwork, sheet metal work, general mechanics, and handicrafts.

Norms.—The authors provide age norms for boys at each year level from year 11 to 21 and grade norms for boys and girls from grade seven through grade twelve. Norms are also given for men engineering students and men and women arts college students.

Scores may also be compared with adult norms established by the Employment Stabilization Research Institute on a group of men and women representing the normal age and occupational distribution for three cities in Minnesota.

Darley has reported evidence which indicates that by using board A as a practice trial and by considering as the score the total time to place the blocks in boards B, C and D, the test's reliability is increased. For this reason, revised norms based upon such scores for occupationally unselected populations of men and women are presented here:

Letter rating	Mid-sigma score	Percentile range	Spatial Relations Test: boards B, C, D (Score in seconds)	
			Men	Women
A	7.0+	93.4–100.0	0–621	0–619
B	6.0	69.2– 93.3	622–814	620–838
C	5.0	30.9– 69.1	815–1047	839–1037
D	4.0	6.7– 30.8	1048–1557	1038–1579
E	3.0–	0.0– 6.6	1558 and over	1580 and over

Below are listed a few groups for whom mean scores on boards A, B, C and D are available. These differences between averages add to the evidence of validity. It must be remembered that there is considerable spread of scores within each occupation, however.

Number	Group	Median percentile
102	Garage mechanics	85
170	Manual training teachers	75
62	Ornamental iron workers	69
113	Men office clerks	66
20	Draftsmen	59
29	Minor bank officials	59
84	Retail salesmen	55
47	Life insurance salesmen	55
489	Occupationally unselected men	50
26	Minor executives	46
69	Janitors	30
124	Policemen	27
33	Casual laborers	2

Reliability.—Reliability coefficients calculated for men and women and for boys and girls indicate that the test, when given in its entirety, is sufficiently reliable for use with individuals. The corrected coefficient for 100 junior high school boys was +.84 and for 482 adult men, unselected for occupation, it was +.91. For adult women occupationally unselected the correlation was +.89.

Validity.—For young boys the test is measuring something related to success in mechanical shop courses. Sufficient research at the higher age levels has not been done to warrant any very definite statement as to particular occupations for which the test is useful. The material presented above under the discussion of norms, however, is evidence that, on the average, men in different occupations make substantially different scores. One-half of the garage mechanics tested make scores which are better than 85 per cent of men in general. Manual training teachers and ornamental iron workers are also very high on the average. Unpublished research results secured by the Adjustment Service in New York City and by the Rehabilitation Division of the National Tuberculosis Association show that kindergarten and nursery school teachers and occupational therapists make unusually high scores in the tests. This information should be of value to the woman student who "does not know what to prepare for" and who makes a high score in this test.

Although academic intelligence is not an important element in the time scores for the test, it is being measured to some extent as evidenced by correlations of +.43 between the test and Pressey scores for 334 occupationally unselected men and +.36 for 131 women. The relationship appears to be about the same for homogeneous groups of mechanical workers and slightly lower for groups of clerks and junior high school boys.

Publisher and Cost.—Marietta Apparatus Company, Marietta, Ohio. Price, set of equipment for $34.

References.—(Same as for Mechanical Assembly.)

3. **Revised Minnesota Paper Form Board Test,** 1934, by R. Likert and W. H. Quasha.

Description.—As indicated in its title, this test is a revision of the earlier paper form board devised by the Minnesota investigators in their study of mechanical abilities. The earlier test was difficult to score and the scoring involved an undesirable element of subjectivity. This revision has overcome some of these limitations. It is included here because it appears to have important guidance values which may be developed with further use and experimentation. The revision simplifies the scoring by changing the items to the multiple-choice type. In each of the two comparable forms, the examinee is presented with 64 items, each consisting of a diagram of from 2 to 5 disarranged parts of a geometrical figure. In each item, there are 5 diagrams indicating how these parts might appear if fitted together. Only one of the 5 choices is correct. Four examples are given and the examinee is allowed to practice on the four samples before beginning the examination proper for which 20 minutes are allowed. The test presumably measures the same type of ability as is required in the test of spatial relations. It measures ability to visualize spatial patterns in two dimensions. The paper-and-pencil task involves more of the linguistic type of intelligence, however, than does the form board. This is disadvantageous when individuals with less than average intelligence are examined.

Designed For.—The original test was used for junior high school pupils, but with the norms which the present authors have furnished, the scores of examinees from 9 years and above may be compared. The authors have not as yet shown conclusively, however, that the scores for these older age groups have the same meaning as those for the younger groups on whom the test was originally standardized.

Norms.—The authors furnish percentile norms for a considerable number of groups, a few of which are condensed here.

Number	Groups	100th percentile	Q_3	Median	Q_1	5th percentile
344	Freshman engineering students..................	64	48	43	38	30
238	Senior engineering students	64	51	46	41	32
247	Liberal arts college freshmen....................	62	44	38	33	24
1288	High school seniors (male)..	62	45	39	33	22
173	Printers' apprentices.......	56	44	39	33	24
100	Adults (men and women)..	52	37	31	23	9

In addition to the above groups, norms are furnished for engineering students of different amounts of training, first-year vocational school students, elementary school boys and girls of different grades and ages, and men and women adults classified into two age categories.

Reliability.—The considerably lengthened revision yields more consistent results than did the short original form. The split-half reliability of the revision is about $+.92$ for one form as determined by averaging a number of corrected coefficients calculated upon different rather homogeneous groups. The range of the corrected coefficients for these groups is from $+.83$ to $+.98$ with the bulk of them exceeding $+.90$.

Validity.—A number of findings point to the probability that the test at least approaches its predecessor in validity. In the first place, it appears to be measuring about the same traits, as indicated by a corrected correlation of $+.89$ with the earlier device. The original form correlated to the extent of $+.65$ (uncorrected) with a quality-information criterion of mechanical ability which was developed by the Minnesota investigators.

The norms for different groups reveal differences in the expected direction. For example, engineering students score about 6 points higher on the average than do arts college students. Printers' apprentices make scores about 5 points higher than those for the general population of men from 16 to 25 years of age. There is considerable overlapping of scores between populations, however.

The authors report a correlation of $+.49$ obtained between scores made on the revised form and mechanical drawing grades for 174 students. The authors report a correlation of $+.40$ between the test and the Otis Self-Administering Examination for 77 students.

Publisher and Cost.—The Psychological Corporation, 522 Fifth Ave., New York. Prices: tests for $0.04 each; $3.50 per hundred.

References.—R. LIKERT, "A Multiple Choice Revision of the Minnesota Paper Form Board Test," *Psychol. Bull.*, 1934, 31: 674; R. LIKERT and W. H. QUASHA, *Revised Minnesota Paper Form Board Test. Manual of Directions*, The Psychological Corporation; D. G. PATERSON, R. M. ELLIOTT, L. D. ANDERSON, H. A. TOOPS and E. HEIDBREDER, *Minnesota Mechanical Ability Tests*, Minneapolis: University of Minnesota Press, 1930; W. H. QUASHA, "The Revised Minnesota Paper Form Board Test—An Experiment in Test Construction," M.A. *Thesis*, New York University, May, 1935.

4. Kent-Shakow Form Boards, 1928, by Grace Kent and D. Shakow.

Description.—The industrial model of the Kent-Shakow revision of the Worcester Form Board Series is a wooden frame

22 inches long by 10 inches wide with 5 recesses of slightly different shapes. There are 7 different sets of blocks with which the recesses may be filled, and each of the sets constitutes a different task for the examinee. Each task is presented 5 times because of the 5 recesses of slightly altered shape. For example, the first task (2S) involves fitting each of the 5 recesses with 2 blocks which are cut on the straight line and divided in the same way. For the second task (2D), the examinee fits each of the 5 recesses with a different set of blocks which are cut on the diagonal. The number of blocks in each recess is still 2 for this task. In the third task (3S) 3 straight-cut blocks are placed in each recess. In the fourth task, (3D) 3 diagonally cut blocks are required to fill each recess. Likewise, for the fifth task (4S), each recess requires 4 straight-cut blocks; for the sixth (4D), 4 diagonally cut blocks; for the seventh (4DD), 4 other diagonally cut blocks; and for the eighth (5D), 5 diagonally cut blocks.

For each task the set of blocks is arranged in a random order and the score is the time in seconds required to fill the 5 recesses. The individual is not required to proceed beyond the task in which a failure to place the blocks occurs, unless the task is one involving diagonal forms. In that case, the next higher test, involving straight-cut blocks is attempted. According to the procedure used in the Cincinnati Employment Center, where research with these boards is in progress, all examinees who take the test are given the first three simpler tasks and the first of the more complex tasks. The time required to complete these determines whether the next more complex task shall be administered. The time required for task six determines whether task seven shall be administered, and so on through the eighth task of the set.

Final ratings on the entire test are two: (1) the mean percentile on tasks 2D, 3S, and 4S giving a rating on the simple problems; the mean percentile on one, two, three or four of the more complex tasks (3D, 4D, 4DD, 5D) giving the rating on complicated problems.

Designed For.—Although originally designed to measure mental capacity and mechanical aptitudes of mental hospital patients, these form boards now appear to have some promise as measures of a type of manual or mechanical aptitude which is found in varying degrees in different occupational groups. At the present stage of research on this test, the concern is not so much with naming the trait which is being measured as with studying occupational differences. It is because of the promise of this test, as determined from research which is now being conducted at the Cincinnati Employment Center by Dr. Lorene Teegarden, rather than because of extensive published results, that they are described here. They plan to publish more findings regarding the test, its interpretation and age, sex, educational and occupational differences. The counselor alert for new techniques for determining in a reliable fashion differences between persons that may have important occupational implications, will find it worth while to keep in touch with the literature on this test and others which are being tried out in practical employment situations. In the meantime, it may be used provisionally for students leaving school to enter occupations involving a rather high degree of skill in manipulation, such as helpers to skilled workers, apprentices, wrappers and packers, factory machine operators, bench assemblers, laundry workers, etc.

Norms.—The only norms which are available are those established at the Cincinnati Employment Center. The norms, which they have established on a group of unemployed young adults, ranging from 16 to 25 years of age and applying for jobs involving the manipulation of materials, are abbreviated below for interpretive purposes. The schooling represented in this population varies from college to no schooling at all, and the group includes some college students applying for manual

ABBREVIATED GENERAL NORMS (IN SECONDS) FOR KENT-SHAKOW
(Based on 400 Males and 300 Females)

Per-cen-tile	Simple tasks						Complex tasks									
	2D		3S		4S		3D		4D		4DD		5D	
	M	F	M	F	M	F	M	F	M	F	M	F	M	F
95	18	19	38	41	56	60	72	80	176	185	130	162	300	288
75	27	28	56	55	77	79	119	128	314	342	210	241	630	628
50	33	34	72	71	100	101	168	209	535	642	423	905		
25	43	47	93	96	124	125	269	328						
5	73	86	172	191	206	235	508	660						

occupations for part-time or vacation jobs. Otherwise, the occupational experiences of those in the norm group include, for the main part, factory work, restaurant work, outdoor labor, domestic service, sales work, delivering of newspapers and similar work.

In addition to the general norms given in the table on page 231, occupational norms have been established at Cincinnati by testing unemployed workers classified by previous occupation. These norms are included here in abbreviated form.

OCCUPATIONAL NORMS FOR KENT-SHAKOW FORM BOARDS

Occupations	Number tested	Mean percentile ratings Simple tasks	Mean percentile ratings Complex tasks
Male:			
Helpers in skilled trades...............	82	63	68
Errand and delivery boys..............	42	63	60
Sales clerks in stores..................	118	57	59
Truck drivers and chauffeurs..........	75	55	62
General factory labor, hand processes...	52	55	57
Packers and wrappers.................	44	55	56
Waiters, bus boys, kitchen helpers, dishwashers.........................	62	42	45
Truck helpers and loaders.............	40	38	38
Female:			
Power machine operators..............	72	57	61
Packers (candy, glass, dishes, food, cakes).............................	20	55	60
Sales clerks in stores..................	73	54	58
Operators of factory machines.........	59	52	60
Factory assemblers....................	50	47	60
General factory, labor, hand processes..	111	43	53
Packers, labelers, sorters..............	86	50	41
Domestic workers.....................	207	43	45
Waitresses, restaurant.................	120	33	53
Laundry workers.....................	54	37	37

Reliability.—There has been no attempt to determine statistically or experimentally the reliability of this test.

Validity.—Evidence with respect to validity consists in differences disclosed when the test has been given to occupationally distinct groups. Differences, such as are presented in the Occupational Norms Table above, have been found. It is possible that these differences might have been even more significant had the groups tested been more homogeneous with respect to occupational experience and efficiency. The table of occupational norms includes unemployed persons who have had a paid job in the occupation for one month or more. It is obvious that so poor a criterion includes many individuals who are unemployed because of inefficiency in their previous work.

A study of the table of occupational norms will show that, in spite of the poor criterion, there is a considerable range, on the average, in the performance of different occupational groups.

Publisher and Cost.—C. H. Stoelting Company, 424 North Homan Ave. Chicago, Illinois. Price, $60 for industrial model. Recent information indicates sharp advance in price. These boards are also made on order by Mr. Sven G. Nilsson, 16 Maverick Rd., Worcester, Mass., for $45.

References.—G. H. KENT and D. SHAKOW, "A Graded Series of Form Boards," *Personnel J.*, 1928, 115–120; D. SHAKOW and G. H. KENT, "The Worcester Form Board Series," *Ped. Sem.*, 32: 599–611.

5. MacQuarrie Test for Mechanical Ability by T. W. MacQuarrie.

Description.—This is a paper-and-pencil test designed to measure aptitude for mechanical and manual types of work. There are seven parts, each preceded by a practice exercise. These are tests of tracing, tapping, dotting, copying, location, blocks and pursuit. They seem to measure eye-hand coordination, speed of movement and ability to deal with spatial relationships. The entire battery requires about half an hour.

Designed For.—The test may be found appropriate for junior and senior high school students for whom shop courses are being considered. This test should serve as a check on estimates of mechanical ability or other mechanical tests before students enter upon vocational training requiring this type of aptitude.

Norms.—An abbreviated form of the age norms supplied in the pamphlet of instructions follows:

Year	10	12	14	16	18	20
Mean raw score	26	44	53	60	65	68

Bingham's mean scores on the subtests secured by 124 toolmaker apprentices are as follows:

Subtests	1	2	3	4	5	6	7
Mean raw score	39	37	18	37	21	13	20

Reliability.—The author reports reliability coefficients on the subtests which range from +.72 to +.86, but the group used was not described. The whole test yielded a retest reliability of over +.90 when given to three groups numbering 35, 80, and 250 students.

Bingham reports a standard error of measurement of a person's total score of 5 points only. For the subtests the individual's "true" score is not quite so well estimated by the score which he actually obtains. The score on the total test may be considered to be a reliable measure.

Validity.—When test scores are compared with teachers' ratings of mechanical ability, there is a fair degree of relationship, as represented by a correlation of +.48. When actual performance on mechanical projects is compared with test scores, the relationship varies from +.32 to +.81, but the author does not describe in detail the criterion or the group.

Studies have been made to determine the extent to which the test is measuring verbal intelligence. The author points to two studies in which the correlations with group mental tests were +.20 and +.002 with a group of 60.

Pond has found the following relationships between this test and other measures:

Years of schooling	+.29
O'Connor Wiggly Block	+.34
Otis (Higher) Intelligence	+.38
Kent-Shakow	+.43

Bingham states that the test "provides only a rough indication of the degree to which a person has some of the aptitudes desired in mechanical or manual occupations." Other evidence should supplement the test scores whenever possible. Extensive use of the test in the practical counseling situation should await further research.

Publisher and Cost.—Research Service Company, 4529 South Van Buren Place, Los Angeles, California; The Psychological Corporation, 522 Fifth Ave., New York. Prices: tests, including directions, keys and norms, 25 copies for $1.50; sample set for $0.15.

References.—T. W. MacQuarrie, "A Mechanical Ability Test," *J. of Personnel Res.*, 1927, 5: 329–337; W. V. Bingham, "MacQuarrie Test for Mechanical Ability," *Occupations, the Vocational Guidance Magazine*, 1935, 14: 202–205.

E. DEXTERITY TESTS

1. Finger Dexterity Test, 1928, by Johnson O'Connor.

Description.—This apparatus consists of a metal plate in which 100 holes, each large enough to hold three small metal pins, are drilled. The individual picks up three pins at a time from the shallow tray attached to the plate, and places them in the holes as fast as he can. The score is a measure of the speed with which an individual can use his fingers in work requiring fine eye-hand coordination.

The time required for the test varies, but 15 minutes are usually ample.

Designed For.—Finger dexterity as measured by this test seems to be necessary in occupations requiring rapid hand work with small objects. It may be administered to girls seeking employment in machine, clock and instrument assembling, packing and office machine operating. Stenographers, typists and office clerks score much higher, on the average, than the norm for adult women. If this skill is not acquired on the job, the counselor should give some negative weight to a low score for a girl planning to enter clerical occupations. It probably has some meaning also for men planning to enter clerical occupations and drafting. Extremely poor performance on this test may be an indication that the individual will be too slow and awkward for many occupations in which nimble fingers are an asset.

Norms.—For adults, norms may be used which have been established by the Employment Stabilization Research Institute on a standard sample of men and women in Minnesota representing the normal age and occupational distribution. O'Connor also furnishes norms for men and women in *Born That Way*. The norms for women differ from those for men because of superior performance by women in this simple skill. Some work has been done at different plants in establishing norms for selected types of work. In the table on page 236 are listed mean scores for a number of different occupations. The indicated per cent of the general population who are excelled by the average person in the occupational group allows one to judge the approximate superiority of the group in question. It should be remembered, however, that there are wide variations within some of these occupational groups.

MEN

Number	Groups	Mean scores	Median percentile
17	Bank tellers..........................	243.0	80
113	Office clerks..........................	255.0	70
27	Accountants—bookkeepers.............	255.0	70
63	Retail salesmen.......................	255.4	70
21	Draftsmen............................	258.6	69
170	Manual training teachers...............	257.8	67
47	Life insurance salesmen................	261.1	66
23	Shipping—stock clerks.................	263.4	64
26	Miscellaneous minor executives.........	267.7	60
29	Minor bank executives.................	268.6	60
61	Ornamental iron workers...............	271.3	57
102	Garage mechanics.....................	278.4	51
124	Policemen............................	288.0	43
69	Janitors..............................	292.3	39
31	Machine operators....................	331.3	18
228	Casual laborers.......................	385.1	7

WOMEN

Number	Groups	Mean scores	Median percentile
180	Office clerks..........................	225.5	71
180	Stenographers—typists.................	230.4	65
21	Office machine operators...............	231.0	64
65	Retail saleswomen.....................	231.6	64
15	Food packers.........................	235.3	59
19	Butter packers........................	247.9	47
317	Graduate nurses......................	252.0	42
31	Butter wrappers (1 lb.)................	261.0	33

Reliability.—Sufficiently consistent results for use with individuals may be expected with this instrument. According to one study, the Spearman-Brown corrected reliability coefficient was +.93 for 475 men and +.90 for 215 women representing a normal occupational sampling from Minnesota.

Validity.—Investigation of the occupational significance of this test should be extended. The material included under the discussion of norms is merely suggestive.

For one study, 36 women applicants were interviewed, rated, tested and hired for factory assembly work. Of those whose scores were in the lowest quartile, 36 per cent terminated their employment before 8 months of service while only 6 per cent of those in the highest quartile left during the same time interval. Over 50 per cent of those who had been rated "A" by interviewers left the concern in this time. Other studies also have shown that the establishment of critical scores on this test for hiring purposes substantially decreases the number of failures and terminations.

Correlations between the Finger and Tweezer Dexterity tests reveal the fact that there is some element in common, although the relationship is not marked, as indicated by correlations of about +.56 for a large and heterogeneous group of men and +.33 for women.

Publisher and Cost.—J. O'Connor, Stevens Institute of Technology, Hoboken, New Jersey. Price, board for finger and tweezer tests with pins, for $20. The Department of Mechanical Engineering at the University of Minnesota, Minneapolis, will also supply the test on order.

References.—D. M. ANDREW and D. G. PATERSON, "Measured Characteristics of Clerical Workers," *Bulletins of the Employment Stabilization Research Institute*, 1934, Vol. 3, No. 1, Minneapolis: University of Minnesota Press; B. J. DVORAK, "Differential Occupational Ability Patterns," *Bulletins of the Employment Stabilization Research Institute*, 1935, Vol. 3, No. 8, Minneapolis: University of Minnesota Press; H. J. GREEN, I. R. BERMAN, D. G. PATERSON, and M. R. TRABUE, "A Manual of Selected Occupational Tests for Use in Public Employment Offices," *Bulletins of the Employment Stabilization Research Institute*, 1933, Vol. 2, No. 3, Minneapolis: University of Minnesota Press; MILDRED HINES and JOHNSON O'CONNOR, "A Measure of Finger Dexterity," *J. of Personnel Res.*, 1926, 4: 379–382; JOHNSON O'CONNOR, *Psychometrics*, Cambridge, Massachusetts: Harvard University Press, 1934; JOHNSON O'CONNOR, *Born That Way*, Baltimore: Williams & Wilkins Company, 1928; D. G. PATERSON, ed., "Research Studies in Individual Diagnosis," *Bulletins of the Employment Stabilization Research Institute*, 1934, Vol. 3, No. 4, Minneapolis: University of Minnesota Press.

2. Tweezer Dexterity Test, 1928, by Johnson O'Connor.

Description.—The apparatus for this test is the same as that for the finger dexterity test, except that the reverse of the metal board, in which are drilled 100 holes, each large enough to hold one small metal pin, is used. The tray holds the pins, which are picked up one at a time with a pair of tweezers and placed in the holes as fast as possible. The score is a measure of the skill and speed with which the person is able to manipulate a small tool in work requiring fine eye-hand coordination. Rarely is more than 10 minutes needed for administration.

Designed For.—Several occupations have been studied by O'Connor. He suggests that the test be given to persons planning to enter work requiring unusual steadiness of motor control and rapid eye-hand coordination in the use of fine tools. High scores in tool dexterity are necessary in the following occupations, according to O'Connor: Laboratory work in physiology, biology, botany and geology; surgery; dentistry; designing in engineering, drafting, and architecture; art work; dressmaking; watch and clock repairing and assembling; miniature instrument and spring assembling; jewel work; and machine and hand glass work.

According to O'Connor, a person with awkward fingers but with all other qualifications for an occupation calling for laboratory work should persevere with the laboratory work that is required, but plan to capitalize upon his other assets by entering some aspect of the field which does not involve the use of delicate laboratory apparatus.

For suggestions of other occupations for which the test may have some value, see the occupational norms presented below. Apparently some types of work requiring work with paper and pencil involve this type of manual skill. Occupations requiring larger body movements, such as heavy labor, janitor work, machine operating, shipping, and auto mechanics do not demand speed in making fine coordinations and in working with fine tools and articles.

Norms.—Norms for adults are furnished with the author's original presentation of the test. More recent ones based on a standard occupational sample of men and women in Minnesota are available in the manual of occupational tests which is cited in the reference. Scores for students in high school and college may be referred to these norms for interpretation.

The average scores made by a number of different occupational groups are listed in the table on page 239 showing the percentage of persons in the general population who are exceeded by the average person of the occupation.

Reliability.—Although no exact figures are available, there are substantial indications that this device yields results which are equally as consistent as those secured when the reverse of the board is used for measuring dexterity with the fingers.

MEN

Number	Groups	Mean scores	Median percentile
109	Office clerks............................	323.1	76
17	Bank tellers...........................	324.6	76
27	Accountants—bookkeepers...............	324.6	75
170	Manual training teachers.................	326.6	74
21	Draftsmen.............................	334.8	70
29	Minor bank officials.....................	336.9	68
62	Ornamental iron workers.................	341.3	65
46	Life insurance salesmen..................	345.2	62
43	Retail salesmen.........................	346.3	58
102	Garage mechanics.......................	352.2	56
23	Shipping—stock clerks...................	354.6	54
25	Miscl. minor executives..................	360.4	50
31	Machine operators......................	384.6	34
69	Janitors...............................	388.0	34
124	Policemen.............................	390.0	33
226	Casual laborers.........................	570.5	1

WOMEN

Number	Groups	Mean scores	Median percentile
178	Office clerks...........................	322.9	65
180	Stenographers—typists...................	333.0	57
317	Graduate nurses........................	334.0	55
19	Butter packers.........................	340.5	50
15	Food packers..........................	344.7	48
31	Butter wrappers (1 lb.).................	353.2	42

Validity.—The author claims that the test is sampling activities analogous to those employed by laboratory workers and persons who use fine instruments, such as physiologists, designing engineers, dentists, small-parts repairmen, jewelry and watch repairmen, etc.

Publisher and Cost.—Johnson O'Connor, Stevens Institute of Technology, Hoboken, New Jersey. Price, board for finger and tweezer tests, with pins for $20. The Department of Mechanical Engineering at the University of Minnesota, Minneapolis, will also supply the test on order.

References.—D. M. ANDREW and D. G. PATERSON, "Measured Characteristics of Clerical Workers," *Bulletins of the Employment Stabilization Research Institute,* 1934, Vol. 3, No. 1, Minneapolis: University of Minnesota Press; B. J. DVORAK, "Differential Occupational Ability Patterns," *Bulletins of the Employment Stabilization Research Institute,* 1935, Vol. 3, No. 8, Minneapolis: University of Minnesota Press; H. J. GREEN, I. R. BERMAN, D. G. PATERSON, and M. R. TRABUE, "A Manual of Selected Occupational Tests for Use in Public Employment Offices," *Bulletins of the Employment Stabilization Research Institute,* 1933, Vol. 2, No. 3, Minneapolis: University of Minnesota Press; JOHNSON O'CONNOR, *Born That Way,* Baltimore: Williams & Wilkins Company, 1928.

3. Minnesota Manual Dexterity Test, 1931, by W. A. Ziegler.

Description.—The apparatus for this test consists of a board measuring $39\frac{1}{2}$ inches by $10\frac{1}{4}$ inches (see references for exact dimensions). There are 4 rows of 58 round holes in the board. The blocks, which fit easily into these holes, are placed in a regular order beyond the board and the examinee is instructed to replace the blocks in the board in a specified manner and as quickly as possible. Four trials are allowed and the time for each recorded.

A second task, called the Turning Test, was devised, but directions and norms are not included in the manual. For this group of four trials the blocks are presented in their positions in the board. The examinee is instructed to start at one end of the board and to turn each block over by lifting with one hand and replacing with the other until all 58 blocks have been turned. The two parts measure speed of arm and hand movements in picking up and placing blocks in uniform holes. The entire test usually requires less than 10 minutes.

Designed For.—Although the test was originally used in connection with a minor study on the spatial relations test, subsequent work with factory wrappers and packers to whom the test was administered indicated its value as a possible technique for selecting workers for factory jobs calling for rapid hand coordination. It may be of some usefulness to the counselor who is dealing with high school students leaving school to enter semiskilled and unskilled jobs requiring the type of dexterity being measured by this device.

Norms.—Adult norms for the Placing Test for men and women separately are furnished in the Employment Institute Manual. Revised norms published in a later manual are reproduced here.

The score in this revision consists of the sum of the number of seconds taken in the second, third, and fourth trials. By using Trial 1 as a practice trial, the reliability of the results has been shown to be increased.

Letter rating	Mid-sigma score	Percentile range	Placing test (Score in seconds) Men	Placing test (Score in seconds) Women
A	7.0+	93.4–100.0	0–148	0–145
B	6.0	69.2– 93.3	149–167	146–161
C	5.0	30.9– 69.1	168–184	162–174
D	4.0	6.7– 30.8	185–219	175–197
E	3.0	0.0– 6.6	220 and over	198 and over

Mean scores made in the Placing Test by men and women in different occupations are given below:

Number	Groups	Mean score, in seconds	Median percentile
	Women		
18	Butter packers..........................	197.8	94
31	Butter wrappers (pound)...............	203.7	92
15	Food packers..........................	207.0	88
23	Butter wrappers (¼ pound)............	208.9	86
16	Butter "cartoners" (pound)............	210.0	85
164	Office clerks..........................	223.3	60
	Men		
66	Office clerks..........................	224.0	77
24	Minor bank officials...................	228.3	70
14	Other minor executives................	229.3	68
102	Garage mechanics.....................	236.6	55
382	Standard sample......................	240.4	50

Reliability.—Darley has shown that the test as a whole, and the Placing and Turning tests separately, are reliable for both men and women. The consistency of an individual's score is more stable, however, when the first trial is used as a fore-exercise practice trial. The coefficients, when corrected by the Spearman-Brown formula, are, for the most part, +.90 or above for groups representing a normal occupational sampling of urban population.

Validity.—The test's main claim for validity is that rather large differences in average scores have been found among different occupational groups. Persons in occupations calling for a high rate of speed in hand and arm movements have been found, on the average, to make strikingly higher scores than those in jobs not requiring such rapid coordination. According to Dvorak's study of the Placing Test, "100 per cent of the food packers, 100 per cent of the butter packers, 86.1 per cent of the wrappers of quarter pounds of butter, 92.9 per cent of the wrappers of one pound of butter, and 81.2 per cent of the butter cartoners reach or exceed the median of the standard sample of women." Furthermore, these workers are not differentiated from the general population by the O'Connor Finger and Tweezer Dexterity Tests. Further research is needed to determine whether the differences which are found are due to training on the job or to natural differences. It is conceivable that the slower moving persons have been eliminated from these semiskilled jobs, such as packing and wrapping.

Publisher and Cost.—Mechanical Engineering Department, University of Minnesota, Minneapolis, Minnesota. Price, $6.50 per set of original apparatus. Educational Test Bureau, 720 Washington Ave. S.E., Minneapolis, Minnesota. Price, $6.50 per set of apparatus. This apparatus is a slight revision of the original. The norms reported in the Institute bulletins were given for the original board.

References.—J. G. DARLEY, "The Reliability of the Tests in the Standard Battery," in "Research Studies in Individual Diagnosis," (D. G. Paterson, ed.) *Bulletins of the Employment Stabilization Research Institute*, 1934, Vol. 3, No. 4, Minneapolis: University of Minnesota Press; B. J. DVORAK, "Differential Occupational Ability Patterns," *Bulletins of the Employment Stabilization Research Institute*, 1935, Vol. 3, No. 8, Minneapolis: University of Minnesota Press; H. J. GREEN, I. R. BERMAN, D. G. PATERSON, and M. R. TRABUE, "A Manual of Selected Occupational Tests for Use in Public Employment Offices," *Bulletins of the Employment Stabilization Research Institute*, 1933, Vol. 2, No. 3, Minneapolis: University of Minnesota Press.

F. MISCELLANEOUS APTITUDE TESTS

1. Medical Aptitude Test, 1930, by F. A. Moss.

Description.—A new form of this test has been administered yearly to applicants in over 90 per cent of the medical schools in this country. The subtests are designed to measure the following abilities:

1. Comprehension and retention
2. Visual memory
3. Memory for content
4. Logical reasoning
5. Scientific vocabulary
6. Understanding of printed material

The time required for the test is less than an hour and a half. Considerable effort was put into the construction of the test in order to include only valid items. Preliminary forms were tried on persons of known ability and the items carefully constructed and submitted to a number of test and subject-matter experts before inclusion in the final form.

Designed For.—The use of this test has been restricted to medical colleges up to date for the testing of entering students, but it is possible that old forms may be made available to counselors desiring to advise students regarding plans for entering the medical profession.

Norms.—Percentile norms are issued by the committee concerned with the administration of this test.

Reliability.—No information is available.

Validity.—For a complete discussion of validity, the reader is referred to the articles cited below. In the secretary's report for 1935 a study was made of the relationship between test scores and subsequent success during interneship, as rated by superiors. Of those making a test score in the upper tenth of the 1000 graduating students studied, 43 per cent were rated as among the best internes which the hospital had had, while only 5 per cent were rated below average or poor.

Other studies indicate that the test predicts success during the medical training period also. Of the students tested in one year, 43 per cent of those scoring in the lowest tenth on the test had failed by their junior year, whereas only 2 per cent of those scoring in the upper tenth had failed. Moreover, the average grade of those low-scoring students who managed to pass was considerably lower than the average grade of those scoring high on the test.

The authors are clearly aware of the limitations of the test, and urge that it be used with other criteria such as premedical grades and personality ratings. Although this test has been shown to be the best single criterion of success in the medical school (a better criterion than premedical grades alone), prediction is improved when based upon more complete information regarding the individual.

If the test scores alone were to be used as a basis for selecting students, refusing to admit those in the lowest 10 per cent of the class would eliminate 25 per cent of the failures, 15 per cent of the mediocre students, 7 per cent of the fair students, and 3 per cent of the good students, according to one evaluator of this test.

Publisher and Cost.—Committee on Aptitude Tests for Medical Students, Association of American Medical Colleges. This test has been available only to members of the Association of American Medical Colleges for use in cooperative testing programs.

References.—A. M. CHESNEY, "Evaluation of the Medical Aptitude Test," *J. of the Assoc. of Amer. Medical Colleges*, 1936, 2: 15–32; F. A. Moss, "The Secretary's Report," *J. of the Assoc. of Amer. Medical Colleges*, September, 1931, May, 1932, January, 1933, March, 1934, June, 1935.

2. Aptitude Test for Nursing, 1931, by F. A. Moss and T. Hunt.

Description.—Less than an hour of time is required to administer this measure of aptitude for nursing. There are seven parts, dealing with scientific vocabulary, general information, understanding of printed material, visual memory, memory for content, comprehension and retention, and ability to understand and follow directions. The content of the various parts is concerned with material pertaining to the work of a nurse, but at the same time it does not assume previous training in that occupation. Some of the questions resemble those found in a general intelligence test and for this reason we should expect to find that at least part of what it is measuring is general capacity for work requiring abstract intelligence rather than a special capacity for nursing.

Designed For.—The test has been administered to students immediately before entrance to schools of nursing. It probably is not so suitable for young high school students considering nursing as a vocation because of the fact that they may not have had sufficient opportunity to gain the type of information called for.

Norms.—The test publishers supply percentile norms but, due to the wide variations in ability among different student groups, it is advisable for institutions to establish local norms for interpretive purposes.

Reliability.—No information on reliability has been published.

Validity.—According to an unpublished study made of private schools of nursing in Minnesota and cited in the references, the indications are that scores on the test are definitely related to achievement during the first year of work in the nursing school, as measured by teachers' grades and a comprehensive achievement test. The relationship is obscured in the correlation figures, however, as the authors point out, because of the unreliability and the low validity of these particular teachers' grades as criteria. When a measure of general intelligence and reliable achievement tests in English and general science are added to this test of nursing aptitude, prediction of achievement in first-year nursing courses would be considerably more substantial and higher than could be obtained from high school grades alone or from a measure of college aptitude. Harl Douglas, in an unpublished study at the University of Minnesota, found a correlation of $+.64$ between the Moss Test and first quarter grades in the School of Nursing. This coefficient becomes $+.72$ when high school grades are combined with the Moss Test.

Publisher and Cost.—Center for Psychological Service, Washington, D. C. The Psychological Corporation, 522 Fifth Ave., New York. Price, $12 per hundred.

References.—E. G. WILLIAMSON, R. D. STOVER, and C. B. FISS, "The Selection of Student Nurses," To appear in the *Journal of Applied Psychology*.

3. Law Aptitude Examination, 1927, by George D. Stoddard and M. L. Ferson.

Description.—After analyzing the abilities which seemed to be required in law, the devisers of this aptitude examination included in the four parts of the test, which requires about 65 minutes of time, items which presumably measure the following abilities:

1. Capacity for accurate recall
2. Comprehension and reasoning by analogy
3. Comprehension and reasoning by analysis
4. Skill in symbolic logic
5. Comprehension of difficult reading

In Part I the examinee is allowed 4 minutes to read a case. At the end of the examination he is tested for recall by a number of multiple-choice questions regarding this material.

In Part II a second case is given and, after reading it, the examinee is asked to answer true-false questions regarding it, to indicate the analogous points in a second hypothetical case, and to state whether certain facts in the original case were relevant or not in the hypothetical case.

Part III contains the only items which do not have a legalistic content. The examinee indicates whether the conclusions to given statements are true or false. The examinee's ability in symbolic logic is being measured.

In Part IV the examinee is asked to indicate, by reference to the material presented for reading, the marked selections which contain the answers to the questions. Comprehension in reading matter in the field of law is being measured.

The reading material in this test is largely drawn from legal documents, but training in law is not a prerequisite to taking the test. The content has more appeal to the prelaw student and appears to be getting at something in addition to general academic intelligence.

Designed For.—During the course of standardizing this examination it has been given to entering law students in many colleges in different parts of the country. It is to be used for this group of persons, for whom it was especially designed in an effort to improve the prediction of subsequent success in law school. It has not been generally available for counselors in high schools and universities who are concerned with the guidance of individual students expressing an interest in the law as a vocation.

Norms.—The most recent norms were issued by the publishers in 1935 and represent scores made by over 1000 law school applicants. Percentile norms are given for scores on the total test and the median, Q_1 and Q_3 scores are given for the separate parts of the test.

Reliability.—No figures have been published.

Validity.—This test is no exception to the rule that no one test alone can predict perfectly that which it purports to measure. As Crawford points out, however, it predicts better than any other single method and is especially useful for negative guidance purposes, to steer away from the law schools those whose chances for successful competition in the bar examinations are slight.

There is some indication that those scoring high will do better work in the law school than those scoring low. Some schools have gone so far as to set up critical scores on the basis of their experience with the examination. For a small number of students at Iowa, 52 per cent of the grades of students who were in the highest quartile on the test were A's and B's while only 9 per cent of the grades of students in the lowest quartile on the test were A's and B's. At that university the correlation between test score and first semester scholarship was +.55 for 100 entering students in law. Other investigators (Gaudet and Marryott) report a correlation of +.42 between law aptitude scores and freshman law grades. The authors of the test are of the opinion that this law aptitude examination is a better predictive device of subsequent scholarship in the law curriculum than a purely academic intelligence test would be, since the relationship between intelligence and scholarship would probably be less than the usual +.50 for the group of law school students who are relatively more homogeneous than the entire freshman class.

Although there are no figures available, it is quite probable that the abilities which are being measured by this test would overlap to a considerable extent those which are measured by the traditional academic intelligence test.

Publisher and Cost.—West Publishing Company, St. Paul, Minnesota. These examinations have been furnished to law schools without charge. A limited stock is now available and the publishers do not agree to continue to furnish free copies.

References.—A. B. Crawford, "Legal Aptitude Tests," *Illinois Law Rev.*, 1930, 24: 446–448; F. J. Gaudet, and F. J. Marryott, "Predictive Value of the Ferson-Stoddard Law Aptitude Examination," *Amer. Law School Rev.*, 1930, 7: 27–32; G. D. Stoddard, "Ferson and Stoddard Law Aptitude Examinations—Preliminary Report," *The Amer. Law School Rev.*, 1927, 6: 78–81.

4. Tests for Color Blindness, by Dr. S. Ishihara.

Description.—The series of 16 plates which constitute this test are mounted upon heavy black paper which is folded in such a way that the pages may be turned as in a book or removed from the cover and presented simultaneously. Each plate is a white cardboard, 4¾ inches square, upon which is printed a colored circle with a diameter of 3½ inches. The circle is not a solid color but is formed of many colored dots. These dots are arranged in such a way and are composed of colors in combinations such that they reveal by their design certain numbers to persons with normal color vision and different numbers to persons who are totally or partially color-blind. For example, one plate shows a red figure eight on a green background to the normal eye. This same plate, because of the introduction of orange dots on the left side of the figure, appears to the red-green blind individual to be a three.

The principles which Ishihara used in constructing these plates are that persons with red-green blindness are unable to distinguish the numbers which are printed in red or green on the brown, tan and gray backgrounds, but that they see blues, violets and yellows as brighter than they appear to the person with normal color vision. By arranging the colored dots in the background and in the numbers, Ishihara's plates reveal numbers to both the normal and the abnormal and the diagnosis of the difficulty and its particular variety may be made by the number which the subject reads. Ishihara has controlled the factor of intensity of colors in this test situation so that the numbers cannot be read on the basis of their intensity alone. It is this factor of intensity which makes it possible for the color-blind person to distinguish reds and greens, for example, in many practical life situations.

There are two kinds of color blindness, according to the inventor of the plates: total color blindness and red-green blindness. Few persons are totally color-blind, whereas about 8 per cent of men and less than one per cent of women are blind for reds or greens. The blindness is of varying degrees and in some cases complete. The red-blind person sees as colors only the blues and yellows of the spectrum and is unable to distinguish red from green. The green-blind person is unable to differentiate green from red.

Designed For.—According to the author, the test "is in use to test the sight of railway employees, candidates for the Navy, and others." To this list should be added all those persons who operate vehicles which are governed by the usual red and green traffic signals. Drivers of automobiles and airplane pilots should be subjected to the test. Ability to distinguish colors on the basis of their hues would seem to be necessary for success in many occupations where colors are employed.

Counselors should have this test on hand to administer to male students who might be entering types of work calling for the ability to distinguish colors. Since such a small percentage of women are color-blind, it is not so essential to test them unless one suspects this disability. The entire test requires only a few minutes to administer.

Norms.—The author includes with the discussion of the plates an "explanation" useful in interpreting responses made to each plate. The responses typical of the normal, red-green blind, and total color-blind are given. The diagnosis should be based upon a study of the number and type of errors made. Other authors cited in the references have presented tables showing the responses made by different color-blind subjects. The following results for men reported in the literature may be used as norms:

Investigators	Groups tested	Number tested	Number color-blind	Per cent color-blind
Von Planta, Miles, Haupt, Garth.......	European and American whites	5083	416	8.2
Miles and Craig.......	Drygoods salesmen	375	27	7.2
Copeland............	Unemployed nonunion painters	386	31	8.0
Copeland............	Unemployed union painters	232	9	3.9
Copeland............	Unemployed truck drivers	1076	72	6.7
Copeland............	Unemployed chauffeurs	104	6	6.0

Reliability.—No figures on the test's consistency are available in the literature, but an unpublished study conducted in the University of Minnesota Department of Psychology laboratory course indicated that the test-retest correlation is over $+.90$.

Validity.—The test's validity is an inherent feature of its construction. Men are separated on the basis of their responses to the items into two groups of approximately 8 and 92 out of every 100. If a check-up were made by asking the same subjects to compare color in an actual life situation, the two groups would undoubtedly be constituted of the same members on the basis of their responses, provided that, in the selection of colors in the check-up, the choice were made on the basis of hue alone and not intensity. In other words, the test sets up a standard and controlled situation comparable to the everyday situation, whereby an individual is judged as color-blind or not according to his ability to distinguish reds from greens, for example.

Further research is needed to determine the extent to which color blindness interferes with successful occupational adjustment. A recent report from the Cincinnati Employment Center (Copeland), as well as the report by Miles and Craig, suggests that color blindness may not be a bar to employment in occupations presumably requiring normal color vision. This suggestion arises from the fact that a rather large percentage (6 to 7 per cent) of salesmen of silk goods, and truck drivers and chauffeurs were found to be color-blind. To what degree these workers were handicapped in their work was not revealed, however. One may infer from Copeland's results on painters that freedom from color blindness may be a desirable trait, in view of the fact that color blindness among union painters was only one-half as prevalent as among nonunion painters.

Publisher and Cost.—C. H. Stoelting and Company, 424 North Homan Ave., Chicago, Illinois. Price, $7.50.

References.—J. H. CLARK, "The Ishihara Test for Color-blindness," *Amer. J. Physiol. Opt.*, 1924, 5: 269–276; S. ISHIHARA, *Tests for Color Blindness*, 5th ed., selling agent, C. H. Stoelting & Company, Chicago, Illinois; W. R. MILES, "One Hundred Cases of Color Blindness Detected with the Ishihara Test," *J. Gen. Psychol.*, 1929, 2: 535–543; W. R. MILES, and H. CRAIG, "Color Blindness in Dry Goods Salesmen," *Personnel J.*, 1931, 4: 437–449; H. A. COPELAND, "Occupational Differences in Color Blindness," *J. of Appl. Psychol.*, 1935, 19: 490–492.

5. Dynamicube Test of Power to Visualize, by Clair V. Mann.

Description.—A 60-minute test designed to measure power to visualize in terms of three-dimensional spatial relationships; to predict graduation from schools of engineering and architecture; and to test aptitude for college courses in mechanical drawing and descriptive geometry. This paper-and-pencil test, in 6 forms, consists of exercises or problems (each with 27 points) in the solution of which the student "thinks," "imagines" or manipulates *mentally* 27 imaginary cubes according to the author's directions. The student's answers to the problem are recorded on a prepared answer sheet.

Designed For.—The author standardized the test on 1222 freshman men in the Missouri School of Mines, Columbia, Yale and Iowa State universities; the test has also been used with junior and senior men in high schools.

In the references cited below, Dr. Mann describes in detail the use of this and other tests for sectioning engineering freshmen on the basis of aptitude and for giving individual guidance. In addition, a number of interesting and ingenious charts and record forms for summarizing students' test scores are described and reproduced.

Norms.—The following norms were established on 1222 freshman men in four engineering colleges.

Percentile	Total score
100	162
75	113
50	61
25	19
1	2

Reliability.—The odd-even correlation (corrected by Spearman-Brown formula) was .970 for 200 freshmen in an engineering college. This coefficient is so high as to indicate the need for verification with additional groups. The author's distribution of scores (used for computing the reliability coefficient) shows a concentration in the low and in the high ranks with very few in the middle range. This tendency to a bipolar distribution may explain the unusual coefficient of reliability.

Validity.—The test scores of 166 freshman men in an engineering college correlated $+.56$ with first semester grades in mechanical drawing; $+.59$ with first year scholarship; and $+.91$ with sectioning scores of the drawing classes.

Validity of this test is probably more accurately judged from the character of the test itself than from correlation with any criterion at present available. The test requires the subject to think intensively about objects and movements not concretely before him, and that is the object sought. If he can do that, in the manner the designing engineer does it, then the particular mental process used is not a matter of importance. Descriptive geometry is the one course in engineering that, more than any other, requires this manner of thinking. It is presumed that the test would be valid if the correlation between scores on it and grades in descriptive geometry were high. The correlations actually obtained are:

Dynamicube test and grades in descriptive geometry...... +.455 ± .050
Dynamicube test and final examination in descriptive geometry... +.301 ± .058

One weakness in the author's standardization of this and other tests of engineering ability is the failure to correlate scores with tests of intelligence and with standardized mathematics tests, and to combine old and new tests into a battery yielding a multiple correlation and multiple-regression weights. These steps are necessary in order to determine the extent to which new tests are measuring unique factors not measured by the other tests; that is, to determine the independent contribution of the new tests to the prediction of the validity criterion. This criticism applies to all of Mann's tests.

Publisher and Cost.—Missouri Educational Test Company, 3027 Locust Blvd., St. Louis, Missouri. Prices: $4 per one hundred; answer blanks at $1.25 per hundred.

References.—C. V. MANN, "Measurement of Engineering Students," *J. of Eng. Educ. Res.*, 1933, 1: 1–14; C. V. MANN, "Selecting and Guiding Engineering Students," *Civil Eng.*, 1936, 6: 581–584; C. V. MANN, "The Evaluation of Placement Examinations," *J. of Eng. Educ.*, N.S., 1928, 19: 288–300; C. V. MANN, "Objective Type Tests in Engineering Drawing and Descriptive Geometry," *J. of Eng. Educ.*, N.S., 1929, 19: 979–992; C. V. MANN, *Objective Type Tests in Engineering Education*, New York: McGraw-Hill Book Company, Inc., 1930; DAVID SEGEL, "Prediction of Success in College," *U.S. Office of Education Bull.* 1934, No. 15, p. 75, Government Printing Office, Washington, D.C.; C. V. MANN, "The Problem of Engineering Aptitude," paper presented at 40th annual "World's Fair" meeting of S.P.E.E., Chicago, June, 1933. Twelve-page mimeographed pamphlet.

6. Staticube Test of Power to Visualize, by Clair V. Mann.

Description.—A 90-minute test (6 forms) designed to measure visualizing aptitude required in college courses in mechanical drawing and descriptive geometry. A student is directed (by printed directions) to "imagine" or to visualize a large 15-inch cube subdivided into 125 smaller cubes, each measuring 3 inches on an edge and all numbered. The student is then asked to record on a prepared answer sheet his answers to problems involving the rearrangement of these smaller cubes.

Designed For.—The author standardized the test on freshman men in the Missouri School of Mines.

Norms.—The following norms were established on 500 freshman men in an engineering college:

Percentile	Total score
100	296
75	219
50	150
25	99
1	28

Reliability.—The odd-even reliability of the whole test was .91 for 129 freshman men in an engineering college.

Validity.—The question of validity is perhaps better determined by the nature of the test itself than by any criterion with which it may be correlated. It was intended to measure the ability to visualize which is involved in courses in descriptive geometry. The grades in descriptive geometry, of course, do not measure purely the power to visualize, so that no perfect correlation could be expected. In view of these circumstances, the following coefficient is considered high. The correlation between Staticube scores and term grades in descriptive geometry was .632 for 129 college freshmen.

Publisher and Cost.—Missouri Educational Test Company, 3027 Locust Blvd., St. Louis, Missouri. Prices: $4 per hundred; answer blanks at $1.25 per hundred.

References.—See references for the Mann Dynamicube Test of Power to Visualize.

7. Mutilated Cubes Test of Power to Visualize, by Clair V. Mann.

Description.—The test consists of 60 columns of drawings of mutilated cubes, or whole cubes cut one way or another and portions removed to more or less resemble die castings or small machine parts. At the top of each column is a direct top view of the mutilated cube; just below is a front view of the cube. The student is directed to judge which, if any, of 4 pictured objects is correctly represented by the top and front views printed just above the 4 pictured objects. The author says, "The test may be regarded also as an exercise in translation, converting from ideas expressed in pictorial form to those expressed in the conventional orthographic projectional form, and vice versa. Three-dimensional spatial imagination is required to turn the pictorial views mentally so as to permit of direct comparison with the orthographic views."

The time limit is 50 minutes for either Form A or B and 100 minutes for the two tests combined; the two forms are printed in the same booklet.

Designed For.—The test is appropriate for junior and senior high school pupils and college engineering freshmen. It was standardized on a large number of freshmen at Texas Technological College and Missouri School of Mines.

Norms.—The following norms were established on 301 freshman men in two engineering colleges.

Percentile	Total score
100	121
75	90
50	73
25	55
1	14

Reliability.—An odd-even coefficient of reliability (corrected by Spearman-Brown formula) of .90 was established on the scores of 150 freshmen in an engineering college.

Validity.—The correlation between scores on this test and grades in descriptive geometry is .43 for 131 cases. Like the other tests of visualization, validity can perhaps be as well based upon the nature of the test itself as upon correlation with grades in descriptive geometry.

Publisher and Cost.—Missouri Educational Test Company, 3027 Locust Blvd., St. Louis, Missouri. Prices: Test booklets for $0.15 each; answer blanks at $1.25 per hundred.

References.—See references for the Mann Dynamicube Test of Power to Visualize.

8. **Engineering Drawing Aptitude Placement Test,** by Clair V. Mann.

Description.—A 90-minute test designed to measure a student's aptitude for courses in engineering drawing and for general success in engineering colleges. The test consists of some 240 items which sample the student's knowledge of drawing instruments, plane geometry and geometric constructions. The test consists of text material in engineering drawing which the student reads and then answers questions based on this reading material.

Designed For.—The test is appropriate for high school junior and senior students and freshmen in colleges of engineering.

Norms.—The following norms were derived from the test scores of 2078 freshman men in a college of engineering.

Percentile	Total score
100	131
75	87
50	71
25	56
1	17

Reliability.—The odd-even coefficient (corrected by Spearman-Brown formula) was .91 for 220 freshmen in the Missouri School of Mines. The probable error of an individual score is 6.41.

Validity.—The author reports, "an average correlation coefficient between the drawing aptitude test scores and grades in engineering is .622 for 159 freshman men." When the final grade in drawing courses was a 200-question objective test, the coefficient of correlation with the aptitude test was .81. The aptitude test correlated .506 with grades in descriptive geometry. When a composite "drawing sectioning score" is made up, using one-half of the score on the drawing aptitude test and one-fourth of the score on the Dynamicube Test, the correlation between sectioning scores and grades in engineering drawing is raised from .622 to .760 (scores of 188 students, class of 1935, fall of 1931), which suggests the proper use of scores on these two tests.

The author reports the following results for the freshmen classes of 1931 and 1932 (a total of 190 students) in the Missouri School of Mines:

22 (21 per cent) of the upper half of the class, as so selected by the Drawing Aptitude Test, out of a total of 105 in that half, were failures so far as they went in their program. 63 (79 per cent) made passing grades. 80 per cent of all graduates come from this upper half of the class as selected by this test.

In the lower half of the class as so set up by the Drawing Aptitude Test, 62 (77.5 per cent) of the group were failures. 18 (22.5 per cent) were successes so far as they went. Only 10 per cent of this entire group graduated, and of these 75 per cent were above the lowest quarter of the class.

Armsby reports a correlation of .50 between the test scores of 1078 students at the Missouri School of Mines and a scholastic index of all grades received by these students during their entire residence in that school.

Publisher and Cost.—Missouri Educational Test Company, 3027 Locust Blvd., St. Louis, Missouri. Price, $15 per hundred.

References.—See references for the Mann Dynamicube Test of Power to Visualize; and H. H. ARMSBY, "A Ten-year Study of Iowa Placement Tests," *Bull. of the Amer. Assoc. of Collegiate Registrars*, July, 1937: 343–354.

CHAPTER IX

DIAGNOSIS AND TREATMENT OF EDUCATIONAL PROBLEMS

SELECTION OF CURRICULA AND COURSES

The selection of courses and curricula is the most frequently occurring type of problem in this general problem area. Perhaps the reason for this is that it does not constitute a single problem. The need for assistance in the selection of courses often reflects a fundamental indecision and lack of orientation as to educational and vocational destination. A student coming for registration advice often has a hazy picture of the direction in which he wishes to proceed and the goal he hopes to achieve. The counselor should avoid becoming a mere registration clerk. He should be on the lookout for those cases which involve the more complex problems he is equipped to handle. In such cases, he will want to proceed as he would with other cases of vocational and educational guidance; he will analyze the person's present status and developmental history, help to diagnose his problems, and map out a long-time plan of action for the student, besides helping him with the immediate problem of selecting courses.

Most high school students faced with the necessity for making a choice between a curriculum which will prepare them for college or one which leads to business or mechanical pursuits need this same type of analysis and treatment. Indeed, those who do not present questions regarding their selection of sequences may need this type of counseling as much as or more than those who apply for aid with their registration difficulties.

In dealing with problems of selection of courses, the counselor should recognize the value of courses as "tryout experiences." Such experiences may be of considerable help in formulating subsequent vocational decisions. For example, a high school student who is considering law as a choice should be encouraged to enroll in courses in history and social studies. Success in these courses, coupled with definite satisfaction in dealing with such course content, may be interpreted as evidence that law would be a good bet, other things being equal. Tryout in science courses should increase the pre-medic's prediction of his success in Medical School. Similar possibilities for early orientation and experience are abundant in the high school and junior college years. Orientation courses should be selected by students who continue to be in doubt in regard to future educational and vocational plans or who are likely to enter a vocation demanding an unusually broad background of information, such as journalism.

Should the student exhibit a definite vocational choice that cannot be met by any existing curriculum, it would be well to aid him to work out in detail a long-time program of courses which would yield adequate preparation. Every effort should be made to adjust the curricular requirements to meet the needs of the individual student. When there is a conflict between the needs of the student and the established curriculum, the curriculum should be adjusted and not the student. The recognition of differences in individuals and their needs should be considerable stimulus toward revitalizing the curriculum.

STUDY METHODS

As yet there exist few, if any, standardized techniques for the diagnosis of faulty study habits. Some work in this field has been done by A. C. Eurich in devising a check list of study methods used by college students.[1] C. G. Wrenn,[2] and P. M. Symonds[3] have also worked on the development of study-habit inventories. Counselors should be interested in putting some of these diagnostic devices to use or in conducting further experimentation with them.

One helpful device which has been used in the past is to urge students to describe in writing or orally just what particular

---

[1] EURICH, A. C., *The Reading Abilities of College Students*, pp. 1–108, Minneapolis: University of Minnesota Press, 1931. This includes Studiousness Rating Scale and Results.

[2] WRENN, C. G., *Study-habits Inventory*, Stanford, California: Stanford University Press, 1933. An inventory of thirty items, suitable for use in high school and college, giving percentile norms and scoring key.

[3] SYMONDS, P. M., "A Studiousness Questionnaire," *J. of Educ. Psychol.*, 1928. 19: 152–167.

difficulties they encounter in studying, if any. Professor Bird, at the University of Minnesota, contends that such a method is superior to check lists, which tend to suggest to students other difficulties which they may not actually experience. Below is presented his tabulation of study difficulties reported by students in essays which they were requested to write.[4] It serves to bring out the range and frequency of problems occurring most often among students in a "How to Study" class.

Study Difficulties Reported by 115 First-quarter Freshman Students and by 56 Second-quarter Freshman and Sophomore Students Enrolled in "How to Study" Classes

Kind of difficulty	First-quarter freshman students Number	First-quarter freshman students Per cent	Second-quarter freshman and sophomore students Number	Second-quarter freshman and sophomore students Per cent
Cannot concentrate; day-dreaming	94	81.6	47	84.0
Cannot make useful notes	46	40.0	19	34.0
Unable to find a motive for study; lack of interest in courses	42	36.5	17	30.4
Slow reader	29	25.2	15	26.8
Cannot study because of interruptions by other persons	28	24.4	10	17.9
Inability to plan activities so as not to interfere with study hours	28	24.4	6	10.7
Outside work too heavy to allow enough time for study	21	18.3	3	5.4
Procrastination—cannot start to study immediately	20	17.4	10	17.9
Cannot select important points in an assignment	19	16.5	11	19.6
Cannot allot time for the study of courses—neglect of some courses	8	7.0	20	35.7

The counselor should be able to locate some of these problems by means of questioning in the course of the interview. Any voluntary comments made should, of course, be noted and

[4] Bird, Charles, *Effective Study Habits*, p. 195, New York: D. Appleton-Century Company, Inc., 1931.

followed up with the purpose of locating causes as well as symptoms, if possible. Many students will complain that they "can't concentrate," for example, and in such cases it is important to determine the underlying conflicts or difficulties which are producing this frequently occurring symptom.

Another diagnostic device which is sometimes helpful is the daily time record which can be kept by the student for a given period. A sample of one such record sheet is included in Bird's *Effective Study Habits*. The counselor who persuades the student to use this device can often point out to the student specific ways in which time is being frittered away. On the basis of such "time-distribution records" the counselor can frequently help the student to budget his time more wisely. Sometimes the advice will be, "study less, but study more." In such cases, the counselor will point out the fact that increased total efficiency may result from planning shorter study periods during which the student may be able to work at a higher level of efficiency. Dawdling over books for long periods of time is a pernicious habit that some students seem to acquire.

Many persons need help in planning their daily programs and their study schedules. It is well to impress upon students the importance of "planned living." Especially for those who are entering upon college life with its fewer restrictions and greater demands upon the individual's own responsibility is it necessary that daily activities be planned. Students should be brought to realize that, as one grows older, time becomes a more and more precious asset. Even good students may be found who can appreciably increase their study efficiency by recording and analyzing actual time distribution. By budgeting hours the student is likely to secure more benefit from the assigned time.

By studying such a record of the actual distribution of the student's time, the counselor should be able to locate bad practices and to determine the amount of time spent in studying, as well as how it has been distributed. It becomes possible to show the student how his program compares with those of others. For example, in one high school, students were found to spend from $8\frac{1}{2}$ to $11\frac{1}{2}$ hours each week in preparation for their classwork; and in a typical university, from 21 to $26\frac{1}{2}$ hours per week were spent in outside study. The amount of time recommended by teachers for a normal program of college work is about 30 hours per week. Knowledge of these facts may help the student to plan and adhere to a reasonable program of study time.

Efforts should be made to build up habits of time planning, such as jotting down, each evening before retiring, the program for the next day. In a similar way, activities for the coming week should be anticipated and outlined. The student should also carry with him some mental image of the more remote activity schedules for the months and even years ahead. This type of planning and goal setting should result in more effective as well as more integrated and satisfying living.

It follows, of course, that this emphasis on planning could degenerate into a system of building air castles and day-dreaming about great achievements that will be tackled next week, or next month, or next year. Here again, the counselor must aid the student to avoid laying plans for the attainment of impossible goals. The student's planning must at all times be realistic and in line with reasonable expectations.

Reading tests and other achievement and aptitude examinations should be resorted to as a means for discovering difficulties with specific study skills. The findings may reveal the need for remedial treatment. On the other hand, when aptitudes are low, this condition should be understood and faced frankly. In such cases, one cannot expect, through the development of study methods, to have the student attain a level of achievement much beyond his capacity.

Back of the day-dreaming and procrastination which torment some students is often to be found a problem of motivation. Treatment of such problems varies with the individual and no general procedure may be adopted. Where efforts to motivate promise returns in the form of achievement and satisfaction, it is advisable. It is sometimes difficult, however, to determine the limits to which one should go in attempting to motivate students. Motivation of the positive kind is usually more productive of results in the case of students of high ability who are contenting themselves with mediocre work than with students of mediocre or low abilities. A good method in some cases is to point out the high relationship which exists between school achievement and subsequent business and professional success. Charts with data from experimental studies bring this out in a striking way to students.

The apparent lack of motivation in some cases may be due to drives which are spread out in too many diverse directions. The goals which are set up seem to require conflicting types of behavior patterns and the dissipation of effort in different channels. This type of situation results in disorganization, conflict and emotional disturbances which are found to affect the study habits of the individual. Counselors should aid such students to integrate their drives, develop goals and organize their purposes in such a way that their efforts may be mobilized towards achievement in a given direction.

One method for motivating students is to help them set up vocational goals. When one has such a purpose around which an appropriate program can be built, there are fewer chances for efforts' being dissipated for lack of motivation. It is essential that the vocational goal be an appropriate one, in line with the individual's aptitudes and interests, in order for them to become stimuli for increased effort.

Suggestions regarding the physical surroundings making for efficient study may be helpful. The student should learn to set aside some nook where he may retire for study purposes. This spot should be consecrated to study activity. When the same place is also used for non-study activities, such as reading for pleasure, visiting or resting, a conditioning process may set in which will later inhibit the student's tendencies to study. He will associate the place with these other non-study and, perhaps, pleasanter pursuits, and these associations will tend to lure him away from his more serious occupation.

A discussion of effective learning methods may be sufficient to aid some students whose study habits do not require individual attention over a longer time period. The recitation method should be stressed, since the act of reciting to oneself and answering questions on material read reduces the amount of time required for learning and the number of necessary readings to a striking extent. The student should learn to space his learning periods, rather than attempt to master all the details at one sitting. A more effective method is to go over the work several times with intervals of increased length. Lecture and reading notes should be reviewed very soon after they have been taken and then frequent reviews should be provided. Care should be taken to divide study periods into intervals of sufficient length to reach and maintain maximum efficiency. In some cases, where poor achievement cannot be remedied by suggestions made in a few short interviews, it is wise to persuade the student to enroll in a "How to Study" course. It is far more economical to organize "How to Study" courses and to individualize the work within such courses than it is for the counselor to attempt to undertake the work with individual students. The organization of such a course is a natural outgrowth of the counseling program. In such a course, effective study methods should be stressed and individual attention should be given the student to aid him in mastering the principles laid down. Instructions and practice in effective note taking should constitute one part of the program, in order that poor habits may be corrected early in the student's career. Most students can profit from such a program, provided their general academic ability is not too low and the desire to improve their habits is genuine.

The amount of space devoted to the topic of study habits in this chapter is primarily due to a conviction that the public school system has tended to neglect this important topic. Innumerable "bright" students seem to be able to survive elementary school and high school without acquiring efficient study habits. Their brightness seems to be their undoing, because it has enabled them to absorb enough from teacher-directed drills and classroom discussions to "get by" with passing marks. Counselors, who are alert to this situation, should see to it that this problem is attacked in a systematic and effective manner throughout the high school years.

THE NON-ACHIEVER AND THE SUPER-ACHIEVER

Discrepancies between aptitude and achievement may be discovered by means of objective test results and reliable measures of accomplishment. Whenever accomplishments are found to be far below expectations, or when accomplishments are found to be much greater than one would anticipate, there is likely to be found a well-developed or a potential problem of educational and emotional maladjustment.

Students with high academic capacities and poor achievement present some of the most difficult problems with which the counselor must deal. It is necessary to determine the causes for such poor achievement. Lack of motivation constitutes an important one. In many cases the student may actually be achieving in endeavors outside of the academic field. If energy is being expended upon other worth-while activities, such as are provided in the extra-curricular opportunities of the college, it may be unwise to urge the student to raise his academic achievement from C to A level. He may be deriving more benefit from his experience in debate, dramatics or work on publications than he could obtain from additional time spent in study. He may be discovering and exercising special talents which will be of advantage in his later occupational and leisure-time activities. Educational practice has tended to overlook the development of special traits of the individual in an effort to bring the classroom achievement up to a certain standard. This has resulted in a leveling which may not be desirable. Outstanding capacities should be developed, thus making for greater individual differences. Different occupations require different patterns of traits; hence, educational institutions should not turn out individuals in a common mold.

When the highly gifted student is doing failing work, the reason should be inquired into. When social activities are consuming too much time, efforts should be made to motivate the student toward higher academic achievement. Failure may be attributed to a lack of goal, and if such is the case, the problem resolves itself into one of aiding the individual to concentrate his activities toward achievement which will lead in the direction of a chosen goal.

Failure to achieve may be a symptom of underlying emotional maladjustments, family situations or social maladjustment. The important thing is to discover the cause before attempting to eliminate the symptom.

The student of poor ability who achieves beyond expectations is often not recognized as a problem, but may easily develop into one. Knowledge of college aptitude test records helps to locate such cases. Occasionally there may be someone who manages to make high grades with a very low scholastic aptitude test score. A retest is advisable in such cases, since emotional factors or environmental conditions may have combined to produce an unreliable result. Where the discrepancy is real, the student's time schedule should be carefully examined to make certain there is a balanced program of activities which will lead to satisfactory life adjustments. The student should be led to understand that there are other desirable ends to be achieved besides those of scholastic success and provision should be made for such opportunities.

POOR SCHOLASTIC APTITUDE

The determination of scholastic aptitude is a problem which has received considerable attention and, fortunately, there have been devised a number of techniques which are sufficiently reliable and valid for diagnostic and predictive purposes. In general, there are three devices which have proved most useful: teachers' grades, standardized general achievement test results and scholastic aptitude tests.

In the past, the emphasis has been upon using these devices to predict future scholastic accomplishment. The grades which a student makes in high school have usually yielded higher correlations with college scholarship than have entrance tests. Scholastic aptitude tests and academic achievement tests rank second in their ability to predict subsequent academic progress. When more than a single device can be used, a combination of high school grades, general achievement test scores and intelligence test results is very effective in picking out potential academic failures with a minimum of error.

Dean J. B. Johnston found that over a period of four years, only six students, or 4 per cent of 140 arts college freshmen, with college ability ratings in the *lowest quarter* of the distributions had managed to graduate from the arts college.[5] From this it is evident that college failure can be predicted from these results far better than it could have been predicted in the absence of such quantitative data.

It is not true, however, that failure can be expected of all students who stand poorly on a single test of scholastic aptitude and past scholarship. One study,[6] in which records of students of less than average college ability (less than 40th percentile) were

[5] JOHNSTON, J. B., and E. G. WILLIAMSON, "A Follow-up Study of Early Scholastic Predictions at the University of Minnesota," *School and Soc.*, 1934, 40: 1-8.

[6] BOARDMAN, C. W., and F. H. FINCH, "A Study of Case Histories of Students of Low College Ability Ratings," *Minnesota Studies in Articulation*, University of Minnesota Committee on Educational Research, Minneapolis, 1937, pp. 1-19.

followed up, indicated that one-fourth managed to graduate from some college. Subsequent vocational histories show that these students make a satisfactory and, in some cases, a superior vocational adjustment. The majority entered sales, clerical and miscellaneous occupations, including marriage. These are occupations that do not necessarily require high intellect or even college training. This study should be a warning to counselors to recognize that errors must necessarily inhere in predicting one variable from another when the relationship between the two is actually far from perfect. The chances for making correct predictions may be increased, but they do not reach certainty with the fallible data with which we deal. But exceptions to any general rule do not constitute evidence of lack of guidance values in existing predictive devices. It would be a mistake for counselors to accept this study as providing any warrant for the perpetuation of a "hitch-your-wagon-to-a-star" philosophy of education or for the further encouragement of students to plan their educational programs solely in terms of ambition, desire, hopes and irrational faith in higher education as the open sesame to success in life.

When the counselor has reason to suspect the reliability of a low test score, the student should be referred for a retest on another form of the test or on another measure of the trait. Even if the low test score is confirmed, the counselor may find that the student possesses some special aptitude. In such a case, the counselor's judgment of the student's ability to do college work may be modified. Generally, the more facts one can gather about the individual, the more accurate will be the estimate of his probable success.

The prediction of academic ability should be based on a clinical study of the case, involving objective measurements and subjective judgments in as many behavior areas as possible. This clinical study should be made in order that the counselor may aid in adjusting the opportunities to the needs of the individual. Too much emphasis has been placed in the past upon the mere prediction of accomplishment and too little effort has been expended toward assuring *adequate* accomplishment. Prediction implies a rigid, standardized and inflexible curriculum, with no means of adjusting to differences in needs, aptitudes and interests of students. The counselor should not be primarily concerned with attempting to predict what a given individual will do in a given set of standard conditions. His primary concern should be so to manipulate the conditions as to meet each student's needs. It surely is not a desideratum for prediction to be perfect and adjustment lacking, as in the case of predicting failure. The counselor should be concerned with effecting a maximum adjustment. Prediction then, becomes of secondary importance.

This means, of course, that the counselor should be alert to new ways for liberalizing the curriculum and adjusting it to fit the needs of students. At the secondary school level he should use his influence toward providing differential curricula, terminal courses, sectioning of classes and other means for giving opportunities to all his counselees who are retained in the school system through no desire of their own and who are entitled to educational offerings in proportion to their abilities to profit from them. Counselors in colleges should encourage similar moves to make the curriculum fit the students. Terminal courses at the end of the junior college are just as important as are preprofessional courses. Colleges and universities should direct their efforts toward providing profitable opportunities of a cultural and vocational nature to all their students with a genuine interest in learning, rather than merely in turning away a larger or smaller percentage because it "predicts" they won't be able to make the grade.

When it becomes necessary to counsel with the student of low aptitude who has chosen a goal out of all proportion to the probability of success the counselor must present the facts in as straightforward and yet as tactful a way as possible. Although the "Pollyanna" attitude is to be avoided, nothing is more despicable than tactless deflation of a person's ego. When necessary, the successful counselor manages to bring the student around to the point where he will see the advisability of substituting a new and more appropriate goal for a less appropriate one. It is, of course, inadvisable to use the term "intelligence" when pointing out deficiencies for the usual school setup. "Intelligence" connotes meanings to the student which are closely tied up with emotional attitudes. Fortunately, most intelligence tests are heavily weighted with vocabulary items and the student recognizes that vocabulary is something which can be improved with effort. He is not so apt to react emotionally when told that his "vocabulary" may be too low for a certain goal. He is more willing to accept low scores when it is pointed out that students with high scores are those who have read widely inside and outside of the school situation—those, in short, who are "bookishly inclined" or "academically minded." If he is desirous of improving his vocabulary, then specific suggestions should be given as to methods for improving his word knowledge.

Those individuals with limited "vocabularies" constitute such individual types that it is impossible here to make general suggestions as to treatment. When the school situation cannot be changed, the counselor may need to redirect efforts towards nonacademic training or experience. Some of these persons may possess other aptitudes, interests or ambitions along special lines, so that a careful selection of courses which will require a maximum of these special capacities and a minimum of "word knowledge" may yield the solution.

READING DISABILITIES

A survey of Stanford freshmen and transfer students[7] revealed that three major problems are: (1) standards of work; (2) inability to budget time; and (3) slow reading habits. One-third of the students checked this last item, indicating that this difficulty applied to them. Certainly, poor habits of reading are not restricted to Stanford students and yet counselors seldom recognize reading disabilities or suggest treatment. Undoubtedly, students themselves are apt to recognize such disabilities more readily than an outsider who does not have available objective reports of reading speed and comprehension. Some basis for the student's concern regarding these habits is afforded by results of reading tests indicating tremendous individual differences in both speed and comprehension of reading. It is not uncommon to find students in any college year who read more slowly than the average eighth-grade student. Such poor scores may underlie school failures in some cases, although, occasionally, good students also are found to be exceptionally slow readers.

[7] WRENN, C. G., and MILDRED GARRETT, "Adjusting Youth to College Life," *Occupations, the Vocational Guidance Magazine*, 1934, 12: 38–41.

The great improvements that have been effected by training hint that the cause may lie in mere inefficiency due to lack of effort or stimulation. Another cause of slow reading is the tendency to vocalize or to use inner speech. Reading with lip movements or calling up auditory images of words perceived requires more time and slows up speed and possibly comprehension.

A poor vocabulary is one of the chief causes of poor reading speed and comprehension. The student who does not readily recognize word and phrase meanings must fixate unfamiliar terms for a longer period. A poor vocabulary is usually a symptom of poor academic intelligence, but occasionally we find a student whose achievement and capacity in other fields indicate that the vocabulary has suffered, while development of specific traits has progressed normally. Such students should be motivated to improve their word knowledge, as this supplies them with the tools with which they may think and convey meaning to other persons. Extensive reading, with an intelligent use of the dictionary, is perhaps the most effective method. Motivation, as usual, is of prime importance.

Poor reading habits are readily diagnosed by objective measurement. Appropriate tests for speed and comprehension of reading should be resorted to whenever a reading difficulty is suspected. Norms established on students of various school levels enable comparisons which are interesting and stimulating to the student. In cases of more serious disabilities, photographs of movements of the eyes as they progress along the printed line may be helpful. Regressions and irregular fixations of the eyes are symptoms of poor reading. Some workers in this field claim, however, that the difficulty is not in the peripheral eye mechanism but rather in central factors involved in perception.

Improvement in reading speed is possible for most student readers, provided the incentive is sufficient.[8] One cannot predict the improvement which an individual will make, but it will usually range from 25 to 50 per cent, with extended daily practice and effort to remove the causes of the slow reading. Subvocal and actual articulation of words should be eliminated. An

---

[8] WRENN, C. G. and L. COLE, *How to Read Rapidly and Well. A Manual of Silent Reading*, pp. 1–16, Stanford, California: Stanford University Press, 1935. Price, $0.15. See also C. Bird, *op. cit.*

extended and long-time program for vocabulary improvement should follow and frequent progress checks be made to encourage the learner. Usually reading comprehension, as well as scholarship, shows a parallel improvement as speed of reading improves.

Where the counselor is unable to direct such practice, the student should be encouarged to enroll in a "How to Study" course, where individual attention to this problem should be given. Instructors of these classes should be informed as to the counselor's findings, in order that more effective training may follow adequate individual diagnosis.

SPECIFIC SUBJECT-MATTER DISABILITIES

Special difficulties of this nature are easily noticed and diagnosed. Symptoms appear in failing or low marks in course work and in complaints made by the student himself. Another diagnostic aid is the achievement test, which should be administered in cases of failure in special fields such as English, mathematics or foreign language. Where there is a discrepancy between classroom marks and achievement test scores, the causes for failure must be discovered elsewhere. A conference between counselor and course instructor may be helpful. In cases of low aptitude, the program must be better adjusted or remedial training provided. Just as we find persons with outstandingly high aptitudes along certain lines, so also there are others with specific disabilities. To bring all the individual's traits up to a common level is inadvisable, if not impossible. The student with little aptitude for mathematics should be encouraged to avoid an occupational choice requiring more than a mininum amount of this ability and to capitalize on those other capacities which he possesses to a greater degree. In some cases it may be advisable to encourage some improvement, where the low ability is apt to be a definite handicap. Where the college freshman's knowledge of English usage is poor, improvement is often effected by registration in a sub-freshman English course. Such procedure is warranted when desire to improve is evident. Here, again, the "How to Study" course may be a boon to the counselor. Individual help with specific subject-matter difficulties is occasionally rendered. Tutors are sometimes necessary.

CHAPTER X
TREATMENT OF VOCATIONAL PROBLEMS

The counselor must systematize his approach to the treatment of vocational problems. He should acquire a maximum of information regarding the world of work (especially detailed knowledge of source material) and he should become skilled in the techniques for disseminating this information. In addition, he must be able to interpret available occupational knowledge in such a way as to assist the student as an individual. In other words, the counselor must individualize vocational guidance services just as the school must individualize its educational program.

A. TECHNIQUES FOR SECURING AND IMPARTING OCCUPATIONAL INFORMATION

NOTE.—These techniques should not be used unless students have first been diagnosed and counseled regarding their aptitudes for job training and placement. It is decidedly unfair to stimulate students to think of their occupational future unless they have first been given an understanding of their own assets and liabilities. As a result of diagnosing and counseling, students will be able to narrow their search for occupational information and also will be prevented from making unwise choices which can lead only to failure and disappointment. Personnel workers should be the first to abandon group methods of instruction, which are based upon the naïve assumption that teaching can ignore individual differences. For these reasons, therefore, individual diagnosis and treatment should precede, or at least parallel, the dissemination of vocational information.

1. Analysis of Occupational Census Data.—It is obvious that the U.S. Census of Occupations is a mine of information in spite of the fact that there are serious technical difficulties standing in the way of a clear-cut analysis of these data. The Committee on Social Trends has published a useful analysis[1] and the National

[1] *Recent Social Trends in the United States,* Chapter VI, pp. 268–324, "Shifting Occupational Patterns," by Ralph G. Hurlin and Meredith B. Givens, one-vol. ed., McGraw-Hill Book Company, Inc., New York, 1933.

Occupational Conference in cooperation with the Personnel Research Federation[2] has carried this type of analysis still farther. Studies made by the Minnesota Employment Stabilization Research Institute should be consulted as a sample of what can be done with U.S. Census data for a given locality.[3] The Occupational Research Program of the U.S. Employment Service is now engaged in developing a periodic census of occupational trends through the analysis of millions of applications for employment and of job placements in public and private employment.[4]

Brief mention of some of the more striking findings will indicate the value of these studies as a means of keeping a counseling service abreast of developments in the labor market. The following two tables summarize the main facts presented in *Recent Social Trends:*

Type of work	Number of workers, 16 years and over		
	1870	1900	1930
Manufacturing, mechanical, construction	2,674,000	7,537,000	13,790,000
Agriculture and allied occupations	6,428,000	9,802,000	10,242,000
Trade and transportation	1,104,000	4,445,000	9,963,000
Domestic and personal service	1,168,000	2,726,000	5,448,000
Clerical service	206,000	781,000	3,935,000
Professional service	338,000	1,196,000	3,110,000
Mining	172,000	576,000	983,000
Public service (not otherwise classified)	73,000	260,000	692,000
Total	12,163,000	27,323,000	48,163,000

[2] *Occupational Trends in New York City*, published by National Occupational Conference, 551 Fifth Ave., New York, 1933.

[3] STEAD, W. H., and D. BJORNARAA, "Employment Trends in St. Paul, Minneapolis, and Duluth," *Bulletins of the Employment Stabilization Research Institute*, 1931, Vol. 1, No. 2, Minneapolis: University of Minnesota Press; and HANSEN, A. H., and T. M. SOGGE, "Occupational Trends in Minnesota," *Bulletins of the Employment Stabilization Research Institute*, 1933, Vol. 2, No. 3, Minneapolis: University of Minnesota Press.

[4] *Filling Nine Million Jobs*, prepared by the Division of Standards and Research of the U.S. Employment Service, U.S. Department of Labor, Government Printing Office, Washington, D.C., 1937; and *Who Are the Job Seekers?* prepared by the Division of Standards and Research, U.S. Employment Service, U.S. Department of Labor, Government Printing Office, Washington, D.C., 1937.

The preceding tabulation reveals marked increases in all occupational groups. Nevertheless, some groups have increased at a much more rapid rate than others. It is this shift in rate that points to the relative decline in importance of agriculture and mining and an increase in importance of most of the other groups. This shift is revealed by the following table showing the percentage distribution of gainfully occupied persons, 16 years of age and over, classified by occupation in 1870 and again in 1930:

Occupational groups	1870	1930
Manufacturing, mechanical, and construction	22.0	28.6
Agriculture and allied occupations	52.8	21.3
Trade and transportation	9.1	20.7
Domestic and personal service	9.6	11.3
Clerical service	1.7	8.2
Professional service	2.7	6.5
Mining	1.5	2.0
Public service (not otherwise classified)	0.6	1.4
Total	100.0	100.0

Even more striking shifts in relative importance appear when the above groupings are broken down into specific occupations. A word picture of the more striking trends toward increase is as follows:

Trade and transportation: salespeople, store clerks, insurance and real estate agents, commercial travelers, bankers and brokers, steam and street transportation workers, telephone and telegraph operators, street railroad operators, 802 per cent increase.

Clerical service: shipping clerks, office clerks, bookkeepers, accountants, stenographers and typists, 1809 per cent increase.

Public service: teachers, clerical workers, officials and inspectors, policemen and firemen, 848 per cent increase.

Domestic and personal service: launderers, laundry workers, barbers, hairdressers, boarding-house keepers, janitors, elevator tenders, servants including waiters, 367 per cent increase.

Professional service: technical engineers and electricians, craftsmen and designers, chemists and metallurgists, dentists, trained nurses, musicians and music teachers, artists and art teachers, actors, librarians, authors, 820 per cent increase.

Manufacturing and mechanical industries: semiskilled machine operators, and semiskilled assembly workers, 416 per cent increase.

The above shifts reflect the rapidity of technological advances being made in production with increased services in the areas of distribution and finance. Altogether, these advances make possible the employment of an increased proportion of the gainfully occupied in providing cultural, recreational and leisure-time services.

The facts about occupational trends are admittedly important as a means of revealing expanding occupational opportunities. Another purpose may be served by such figures if local school authorities will compare the expansion of vocational training facilities with the expansion in effective demand. Surveys of vocational choices made by junior high school and senior high school pupils and college students can also be compared with available opportunities as a means of determining the extent to which the educational and vocational guidance program is producing realizable vocational aims and ambitions among present-day students. All such comparisons as are here suggested will tend to reveal the unrealistic character of modern education. There is everywhere a striking failure to gear the educational machinery to the needs of an industrial civilization.

Another type of occupational study is helpful in permitting the school to give youngsters a realistic view of the world of work. This world of work, if viewed through the eyes of youngsters, appears to be an inverted pyramid in which job opportunities expand rapidly in number as one ascends the occupational scale from laborer to bank president or from unskilled work to the major professions. The cold facts, however, are quite the reverse. For example, the picture for Minnesota according to the 1930 census is as shown in the table on page 275.

2. Local Surveys of Job Opportunities.—Local surveys should be undertaken by school authorities in order to discover special types of training that should be provided by the school to meet local needs. For example, the Junior College at Rochester, Minnesota, has developed an effective training course in medical secretarial work to meet the needs of the Mayo Clinic. The Rochester, New York, Athenaeum and Mechanics Institute has also built its curriculum to meet the needs of local employers.

It is the duty of the vocational guidance counselor to undertake these local surveys with the help of job survey committees of teachers and businessmen.

Occupational Groups	Percentage Distribution, 1930
Professional workers	8.3
Proprietors and officials	8.8
Farmers	18.7
Farm laborers	11.9
Low-salaried workers (clerks, etc.)	14.9
Industrial wage earners	29.0
Servants	4.0
Unclassified workers	4.4
Total gainfully occupied 992,798	100.0

3. Personal Study of Occupations.—The counselor can frequently aid a youngster in his quest for occupational information by suggesting that a personal study be made of occupations that seem to interest him. Such personal study should include available information in the library, but it should also include interviews with actual workers and employers.

4. Occupational Bookshelves.—A bookshelf of occupational books should be maintained in the school library, as well as in the public library. Counselors will find librarians eager to prepare such bookshelves. The counselor should be prepared to suggest suitable books for purchase. The counselor should also keep abreast of new books and pamphlets by consulting current issues of *Occupations, the Vocational Guidance Magazine*, the *Occupational Index*, and the *Abstracts and Appraisals of Occupational Information*. All of these are published by the National Occupational Conference, 551 Fifth Avenue, New York. A basic reference book is W. E. Parker, *Books About Jobs: A Bibliography of Occupational Literature*. This book covers 8500 classified and annotated references and is published by the American Library

Association, Chicago, Illinois, for the National Occupational Conference.

The following references may be found helpful:

Bibliographies.

ALLEN, F. J.: *A Guide to the Study of Occupations*, Cambridge, Massachusetts: Harvard University Press, revised, 1925.

HAUSEN, M. Q., and M. R. LINGENFELTER: *An Annotated Bibliography of Vocational Fiction*, Columbus, Ohio: Bureau of Educational Research, Ohio State University, 1932.

Institute of Women's Professional Relations, *Occupations for College Women: A Bibliography*, Greensboro: North Carolina College for Women, 1929.

PARKER, W. E.: *Books about Jobs: A Bibliography of Occupational Literature*, Chicago: American Library Association, 1936.

———, and D. H. MOYER: *Vocational Information* (Vocational Series 1) Ann Arbor, Michigan: University of Michigan, 1928.

White House Conference on Child Health and Protection, *Report of Subcommittee on Vocational Guidance*, "Occupational Studies," pp. 89–137, New York: D. Appleton-Century Company, Inc., 1932.

Books and Articles Describing a Number of Occupations.

ADAMS, ELIZABETH: *Women Professional Workers*, New York: The Macmillan Company, 1921.

BINGHAM, W. V.: "Abilities and Opportunities—Some Meanings of Trends in Occupational Distribution," *Occupations, The Vocational Guidance Magazine*, 1934, 12: 6–17.

BINGHAM, WALTER V.: *Aptitudes and Aptitude Testing*, New York: Harper & Brothers, 1937. This book includes a comprehensive summary of abilities necessary for success in mechanical, clerical and business occupations and the professions of law, medicine, and teaching. The information is derived from research studies. The author also shows how a counselor may help students determine if they possess the necessary qualifications.

CRAWFORD, A. B., and S. H. CLEMENT: *The Choice of an Occupation*, New Haven: Yale University Press, 1932. This book is especially recommended for college men, particularly those who are interested in business or in one of the older professions.

FILENE, C.: *Careers for Women*, Boston: Houghton Mifflin Company, 1934. (Revised edition.)

FLEISHMAN, D. E.: *An Outline of Careers for Women*, Garden City, New York: Doubleday, Doran & Company, Inc., 1931.

HATCHER, O. L.: *Occupations for Women*, Richmond: Southern Women's Educational Alliance, 1927.

KITSON, H. D.: "Contemporary Biography for Use of Vocational Guidance," *Teachers College Record*, 1933, 35: 25–32.

LOGIE, IONE: *Careers in the Making*, New York: Harper & Brothers, 1931. A classification of current biographies as a source of occupational information.

OAKLEY, C. A., A. MACRAE, and E. O. MERCER: *Handbook of Vocational Guidance*, London: University of London Press, 1937. This book is one of the few books that attempt to give a picture of occupational requirements in terms of the human abilities necessary for success.

PRESIDENT'S RESEARCH COMMITTEE ON SOCIAL TRENDS, *Recent Social Trends in the United States*, New York: McGraw-Hill Book Company, Inc., 1933.

WILLIAMSON, E. G.: *Students and Occupations*, New York: Henry Holt & Company, 1937. This book is one of the few sources of information which lay proper emphasis upon the abilities necessary for success. Since major attention is given to types of work requiring college preparation, it is best adapted for use with senior high school students and college students.

As noted above, it is a rare thing for books on occupations to contain useful information in regard to the human abilities requisite for minimal success. Most books do give, however, statements in regard to abilities, but the statements themselves are exceedingly vague and general or are based on arm-chair speculation. The vagueness of statement is usually due to lack of precise knowledge regarding the *degree* to which any trait is really necessary. The statement that a given ability is required, without specifying the degree or amount, is not helpful, since almost every ability is required in some amount greater than absolute zero in almost every known variety of work. The result is that such statements, when made about any given job, are found to apply equally well to a vast array of jobs. For example, the reader is invited to speculate as to what occupation or job is meant by the following description:

ABILITIES AND QUALIFICATIONS REQUIRED

Any youth entering the _____ business will succeed in proportion as he:

has good health, strength and endurance
is interested in the work
is of a mechanical, or even inventive, turn of mind
likes to work with tools
has a good mind
is mentally alert
is industrious and persevering
gets along well with other people
is thorough, accurate and careful as a workman

While he must be able to use a wide variety of hand tools, no very great **manipulative skill is necessary,** such as is required in the machine **trades.**

When the above statement is presented to students especially interested in problems of vocational classification and analysis, a bewildering variety of answers is elicited and only rarely is the correct answer hit upon. The right answer is contained in the title of the reference given below as a footnote.[5]

5. Courses on Occupations.—These courses have been developed under a variety of titles, to serve as a means of occupational orientation. They are usually introduced at the junior high school level and may be repeated at the senior high school and junior college levels. The chief limitation of such courses is the apparent fact that immature high school students do not seem to acquire much useful occupational information.[6] Lincoln, however, has shown that her course in Occupations at the high school level produces significant gains, especially when the class meets five days a week.[7] Williamson[8] has shown that a course in Occupations at the junior college level may be so organized and conducted as to yield a significant gain in occupational information and in knowledge about how students may and should choose vocations.

It is possible that occupational information courses on the high school level could be equally effective were they organized to give a maximum of information about the traits essential for success. Most high school courses tend to neglect this vital information,[9] although Allen's group guidance approach is an exception.[10]

6. Vocational Information Conferences.—This technique brings to the school experienced workers, who lecture to groups of students or conduct round-table conferences in regard to a given

[5] *An Appraisal and Abstract of Available Literature on Plumbing*, National Occupational Conference, 551 Fifth Ave., New York, 1936.

[6] KEFAUVER, G. N., and H. C. HAND, "An Appraisal of Guidance in Secondary Schools," *Occupations, The Vocational Guidance Magazine*, 1933, 12:1, 53–57.

[7] LINCOLN, M. E., "Measuring Outcomes of the Occupations Course," *Occupations, The Vocational Guidance Magazine*, 1933, 12:4, 36–40.

[8] WILLIAMSON, E. G., "A College Class in Occupational Information," *School Rev.*, 1937, 45: 123–129.

[9] LINCOLN, M. E., and J. M. BREWER: *How to Teach Occupations*, Boston: Ginn and Company, 1937.

[10] ALLEN, R. D., *Inor Group-Guidance Series*, especially Vol. III, "Self-Measurement Projects in Group Guidance," New York: Inor Publishing Company, 1934.

vocation. The discussion usually dwells at length on such matters as duties and responsibilities, opportunities for promotion, training required, remuneration to be expected, etc. The technique itself is not enthusiastically endorsed here, because it tends to center attention on the occupation without indicating to the student the criteria whereby he can decide whether or not it is an appropriate opportunity. This is true because experienced workers are apt to stress their own personal experiences, since they lack the vocational and psychological knowledge necessary for a meaningful discussion of the qualifications required. Another drawback sometimes appears when a fluent and persuasive speaker injects an emotional tone into the presentation. It is a good technique, however, for enlisting the interest of businessmen and professional men of the community in the school's vocational guidance program.

7. Referral of Students to Experts.—Many guidance workers make extensive use of this technique. For example, a boy interested in journalism is sent to an editor for discussion of that field of work, or he may be sent to the head of the Department of Journalism in the college. Undue reliance upon this technique is inadvisable for the same reasons as listed for the preceding topic. It is helpful, however, for a guidance counselor to keep a list of such experts who are willing to be interviewed by inquiring students and who can be depended upon to do their part well. One definite advantage may be mentioned, namely, such an expert, if sufficiently interested and objective, can frequently give up-to-date information on recent changes and impending changes in the occupation. Another possible advantage is that the expert can judge the quality of samples of work produced by the student, such as art objects, musical performance, literary efforts, collections, etc.

8. Study of Classified Advertisements.—Mention should be made of the possibility of deriving useful information through a study of classified advertisements in the daily newspaper. Such a study should include "Help Wanted," as well as "Position Wanted," advertisements. The counselor should make such studies from time to time in order to keep abreast of trends. Study of classified advertisements by private educational and training agencies will also reveal the extent to which the local school system is failing to provide adequate vocational training facilities for its young people. When a school system fails to give sufficient training opportunities in the commercial field, private business schools will be on the job. When the school fails to give adequate training opportunities in the field of music, art, dancing, mechanics, etc., private schools will be found ready to give such service. In a sense, the failure of public education can be measured by the number and variety of private schools and private teachers competing in a given locality for the time and money of youngsters and older persons who are desirous of fitting themselves for the world of work.

9. Occupational Ability Patterns.—As a result of the research studies conducted by the Minnesota Employment Stabilization Research Institute, by the National Institute of Industrial Psychology in England and by vocational psychologists—from Muensterberg to Link, Burtt and Strong—we are beginning to get a quantitative picture of the pattern of abilities and interests characterizing successful workers in different occupations. The guidance counselor must keep abreast of these findings and be alert to translate them into improved diagnoses of the abilities and interests of youngsters seeking help in the choice of a career. Substantial progress has been made, so that the counselor is in a far better position today to render service of this type than could have been true ten or even five years ago. The factual basis is presented in outline form in several recent books[11] with which the counselor should be familiar.

The chief virtue of such patterns is found in the approach. It is essentially a psychological type of job analysis in which workers-on-the-job are measured to establish norms. The measurement techniques utilized in the job analysis are then available for use with individuals who may be contemplating the advisability of entering the same type of work. Thus, job analysis and man analysis are made in the same set of terms, so that the counselor is able to measure a given individual and com-

[11] PATERSON, D. G., and J. G. DARLEY, *Men, Women, and Jobs*, Minneapolis: University of Minnesota Press, 1936; EARLE, F. M., *The Choice of a Career*, London: Methuen & Company, Ltd., 1933; OAKLEY, C. A., A. MACRAE, and E. O. MERCER, *Handbook of Vocational Guidance*, London: University of London Press, 1937; KELLER, F. J., and M. VITELES, *Vocational Guidance Throughout the World*, New York: W. W. Norton & Company, Inc., 1937.

pare his pattern of abilities and interests with those of persons who have succeeded in the work. Further research will be needed to explore the full possibilities of this approach. We may look for additional data from the Occupational Research Program of the U. S. Employment Service, which is carrying on a most intensive and comprehensive study of workers and jobs.

Vocational psychologists in England have recognized the importance of this approach. As a temporary makeshift, they have prepared an elaborate occupational rating scale whereby each of 80 vocations has been rated with respect to 23 minimum abilities and other qualities required.[12] Counselors will find these results suggestive and valuable as a basis for interpreting the occupational significance of measurements and estimates of abilities and other qualities which are obtained through the vocational interview and testing situation. Admittedly, the "table of standards" is at the present time highly subjective. It is far less dependable than it would be if the minimum ability standards had been derived from actual measurements of successful workers on the job. Since it will be a long time before such elaborate objective approach will be completed, it is likely that this table will be exceedingly helpful as a point of reference.

B. TECHNIQUES FOR APPRAISING THE EFFECTIVENESS OF GUIDANCE PROGRAMS IN SCHOOLS AND COLLEGES

The attention of counselors is directed to a new series of guidance tests and inventories prepared by Kefauver and Hand as a means of appraising the effectiveness of guidance programs in schools and colleges.[13] There are five tests designed to measure a student's information and judgment with respect to the guidance services available in the following guidance areas: Education, health, recreation, citizenship, and vocation. A sixth test measures the gullibility of the student with respect to pseudo guidance and to false and misleading advertising. In addition, two inventory blanks are provided for recording a student's educational and vocational plans and his judgments of his own capacities.

[12] OAKLEY, MACRAE, and MERCER, op. cit., pp. 130–137.
[13] KEFAUVER, G. N., and H. C. HAND, Kefauver-Hand Guidance Tests and Inventories, published by the World Book Company, Yonkers-on-Hudson, New York, and Chicago, Illinois, 1937; Manual, six tests (two forms each) and two inventories.

The reliability coefficients for the six guidance tests (test-retest using the two comparable forms of each test) range from +.77 to +.89, with an average value of +.82. The probable error of an obtained score ranges from 2.0 to 3.0, with an average value of 2.5. Norms are not provided by the authors, presumably because they do not believe that guidance services are sufficiently well developed in most schools to warrant acceptance of present-day student performance as a standard. In all probability the publication of norms in the present unsatisfactory status of guidance services would tend to freeze or crystallize guidance services on a low level of efficiency. The purpose of the tests is to reveal present deficiencies so that administrators and counselors can organize a program that will become increasingly effective in the future. Some counselors may find them valuable as a device for collecting case-history data prior to the guidance interview.

C. TECHNIQUES FOR DIAGNOSING VOCATIONAL APTITUDES

1. Tests and Measurements.—It is well to mention again that the diagnosis of vocational fitness must be based upon a detailed knowledge of the personal assets and liabilities of the individual, interpreted in the light of occupational requirements. In presenting available tests and measurements in the preceding chapters we have already emphasized the educational and vocational guidance significance of information secured by their use. In this section, therefore, we shall merely point out types of vocational problems that can be attacked on a measurement basis. A more detailed treatment is available in Williamson and Darley's *Student Personnel Work*.

Counselors are frequently confronted by students who exhibit a discrepancy between a vocational goal and the abilities necessary to achieve that goal. It is obvious that measurement data will enable such students to compare themselves with norms established for workers in the vocation. Of more importance is the presentation of data that will enable the student to compare himself *in a favorable light* with workers in other occupations. In this way direct deflation is minimized and the attention of the student is directed toward lines of work in which there is a greater likelihood of success. Not only must the student's attitude be redirected in this way, but the counselor must frequently point out additional advantages inherent in the new goal. For example, it is sometimes helpful to point out to the student that it is better to be a first-class mechanic than to be a third-rate lawyer.

A different problem confronts the counselor when the student appears to have chosen a vocation that will not utilize his available talents to the utmost. Again, the counselor must direct the student's attention to types of work that will offer a more definite challenge to his capacities.

When instances of vocational indecision are dealt with, the counselor can frequently aid the student to make a decision by a detailed discussion of the student's make-up in relation to suitable or appropriate lines of work. It must be understood, of course, that the effective counselor never makes a decision for the student, but rather he aims to present available facts and probabilities in the hope that the student will come to recognize the desirability of a particular goal. In many cases, however, the counselor will restrain the student from making a hasty choice and will persuade the student to make a tentative choice or to delay a choice, pending further experience. In these cases some of the following techniques may be utilized.

2. School Curriculum.—The guidance significance of subjects in the curriculum has not always been apparent to counselors and students. If this possibility be utilized to the utmost, the counselor must have available a cumulative record of marks in previous courses. Relative success and failure in the pattern of courses taken will frequently suggest vocational possibilities that would otherwise be overlooked. "Hope springs eternal in the human breast," so the counselor may be forced to suggest further subject-matter courses as tryouts, pending more definite vocational decision. In doing so, the student should be persuaded to take courses pointing in several directions in the hope that further mediocre work along a given line may be counterbalanced by far greater success in other types of courses. There is every reason to believe that vocational adjustments would be facilitated if high school and college counselors would encourage student experimentation in course elections. To do so on any wide scale means the breakdown of rigid sequence requirements and the mere accumulation of academically respectable credits for graduation purposes. It will also require the introduction of an increased variety of courses into the school offerings. To

talk about the advantages of "general culture" and "general education" to the son of a skilled mechanic who secretly hopes to succeed in clerical work will not lead to an effective educational experience for the boy nor to a real preparation for one of the most important phases of that boy's life as an adult worker. General education and vocational training must be combined if the school is to meet the needs of youth. General education plus counseling is only a partial solution.

3. Extra-curricular Activities.—In general, school administrators and teachers are increasingly aware of the educational value of extra-curricular activities. Such participation is recognized as a means of reënforcing the appeal of classroom work, as for example, foreign language clubs, literary work in connection with the school paper, debating clubs, political science clubs, hobby clubs, etc. In addition, we would stress the vocational significance of such activities from the point of view of tryouts and training. The following summary may be suggestive:

Activity	Vocations Utilizing Experience Gained in the Activity
Athletics	Professional athletics, physical education positions, including coaching and camp work
Dramatics	Teaching dramatics, work on stage and screen
School paper and annual	Journalism, editor of house organs, etc.
School band and orchestra	Various positions in the field of music
School politics	Political careers
Debating	Public speaking aspects of a large number of positions
"Y" work and religious activities in the school	Positions in church work, boys' work, girls' work, social work
Foreign language clubs	Teaching foreign languages, and positions requiring knowledge of foreign languages
Other subject-matter clubs	Positions utilizing given types of subject-matter competence
Social activities	Positions requiring finesse in dealing with people, sales, politics, executive, etc.
Hobby clubs	Positions utilizing skills and knowledge acquired in a given type of hobby
Secretarial work, financial management and advertising work in connection with student organizations	Business positions

4. Vacation Job Experiences.—Many a student has laid a foundation for a wise vocational choice through vacation summer jobs. Many boys' club and girls' club workers got their start through jobs as counselors and instructors in summer camps. Vacation selling jobs (stores and canvassing) have produced workers fitted for various types of selling. Other things being equal, the student who has tried himself out in a variety of vacation jobs is in a position to select vocational training courses in a more realistic way than those who have never had such experience. It goes without saying, however, that vocational choices should not be based solely upon such experiences.

5. Hobbies and Recreational Activities.—Counselors will frequently find a valuable clue to possible vocational choices in a student's hobbies and recreational activities. These represent "drives" that may be converted into lifelong satisfying vocational activities. Strangely enough, many individuals do not recognize the vocational possibilities inherent in their own hobbies, because they recognize that they get fun out of their hobbies, whereas they have been schooled in the doctrine that one's occupation is work and work is a serious business without any fun element. This is why the counselor can frequently make an important contribution to the solution of a perplexing vocational problem by pointing out the desirability of utilizing a hobby in one's lifework. The following case will illustrate the possibilities. A high school graduate who had been engaged in credit work for ten years came to the university for vocational guidance service saying that he was unhappy in his work and would like to shift to a more congenial type of work. He was utterly at sea, however, with respect to alternative possibilities. A study of his life history revealed the fact that he was athletically inclined in high school and had continued athletic activities in the local "Y." He was also intensely interested in religious work and at the time of the interview was president of the largest men's Bible class in the city. Strong's Vocational Interest Test yielded C ratings in business occupations and science fields but high ratings in teaching and religious fields of work. As a matter of fact, he received an A+ rating as a Y.M.C.A. physical director. He was delighted with the suggestion that he might prepare himself to earn a living in "Y" work, since it had never occurred to him that he might capitalize vocationally on the two types of activity to which he had devoted most of his leisure time and attention.

D. TREATMENT OF VOCATIONAL PROBLEMS

It is difficult to distinguish between the diagnosis of vocational problems and treatment. As a matter of fact, the preceding section C of this chapter necessarily included suggestions on treatment. In this section, therefore, we merely list additional types of problems, together with suggestions for their solution. These problems are presented by a listing of frequent or occasional causes of vocational maladjustment.

1. Parents.—So much has been written about the "problem child" that it is time to shift attention to the "problem parent," who may be more responsible than the child for difficulties confronting the child. At least the vocational counselor must be aware of the fact that the solution of a student's vocational problem can frequently be achieved only through a direct approach to the parent. Parents may exhibit poor judgment in sizing up a child's talents (what parent is an impartial judge of his own child?) and hence may urge the child to choose a vocation beyond the child's level of ability. Parents are likely to be misinformed in regard to vocational requirements. They sometimes try to realize their own thwarted vocational aims through their children. In such instances a child may be forced into music as a career, or into art work, or a major profession, even though inclination and talent may be lacking. Or a parent may, through "emotional conditioning," exhibit a strong aversion to a particular type of work and go to extreme lengths to prevent the son or daughter from entering that work, even though it be a wise choice. Then again, there are instances of family tradition—the boys have always gone into business or into teaching or the ministry or the like. The boy tries to live up to the family tradition and, if he is not fitted for it, faces failure. These examples are sufficient to indicate that the counselor must frequently become the impartial interpreter of the student to his parents. Fortunately, parents are keenly interested in the welfare of their sons and daughters, a fact which makes it possible for the counselor to intervene successfully when the facts indicate the wisdom of intervention.

2. Teachers.—Teachers sometimes try to influence a student to enter teaching without due regard to the fact that the student's assets may point toward some other vocation. For this reason, the counselor may frequently need to stand between the student and teacher, aiding each to take a broader view of available occupational opportunities.

3. Classmates.—Some students select a vocation merely because a classmate chooses that vocation, without regard to whether or not that vocation represents an opportunity for success. Here is a striking example. A third-year student in architecture sought vocational advice because he was failing. He had entered architecture because his pal entered engineering. When quizzed as to why he did not enter engineering also, he replied that he knew he was not sufficiently capable in mathematics so he avoided that curriculum, but since the first two years of architecture and engineering were similar he entered the former (the math requirement being less severe) so that he could continue to be in the same classes with his pal. The counselor's duty here is to aid the student in seeking a more suitable vocation, but there is a further duty, namely, to aid in the development of an adequate secondary school guidance program to prevent the making of choices on such a flimsy basis.

4. Immature Judgment of Students.—When students, exhibiting immature judgment, are permitted to choose an occupation, it is likely that subsequent failure in the training situation will occur. Choices made without adequate knowledge of vocational assets, and on the basis of insufficient tryout experiences are not likely to be wisely made. Factors such as "social ambition," "rumors of fabulous salaries," "glamour of prominence," "white-collar complexes," coupled with "disdain for honest toil," are likely to dominate such choices. Proctor has shown that four-fifths of modern youth choose to enter the major professions and the executive levels of work which now engage only one-fifth of the working population.[14] Furthermore, his figures show that the same proportion of children with I.Q.'s under 100 choose

[14] PROCTOR, W. M., "The Use of Psychological Tests in Vocational Guidance," Chapter XV, pp. 170–180, in F. J. Allen's *Practice in Vocational Guidance, a Book of Readings*, published by McGraw-Hill Book Company, Inc., New York, 1927; PROCTOR, W. M., "Intelligence and Length of Schooling in Relation to Occupational Levels," *School and Soc.*, 1935, 42: 783–786.

these same levels of work. Such facts bear eloquent testimony to the widespread need for adequate vocational guidance programs in the schools.

5. Economic Pressure.—Financial limitations frequently prevent a student from choosing an occupational goal in harmony with proved assets. The cost of a medical education, for example, or of other types of training may force a student with limited means to forego a type of training for which he is best fitted. The alternative frequently turns out to be far less satisfactory. In any event, society is robbed of potential service of great value when such instances occur. The counselor can aid by putting the student in touch with sources of financial aid, if these seem adequate to meet the student's needs. An even greater service can be performed by the counselor, however, in aiding in the conduct of student personnel surveys designed to disclose the magnitude of this particular problem so that the resources of society as a whole may be tapped to provide training in accordance with talent, rather than in accordance with ability to pay.

6. Placement Facilities.—The problem of job placement has been sadly neglected by schools and colleges and by society as well. One of the valuable by-products of the depression is the recognition of the need for better job-placement facilities. It is gratifying to witness the development of a nation-wide system of employment offices under the auspices of the U.S. Department of Labor and the National Youth Administration. Vocational counselors can aid through bringing about a close tie-up between the schools and these new governmental agencies. The transfer of cumulative records from the school to the employment office will permit the latter to classify properly those who apply for work. Encouraging youth to utilize these new employment centers will also help. Finally, counselors can exert pressure to keep these new job-placement facilities free from the deadening influence of political patronage.

CHAPTER XI

TREATMENT OF PERSONAL PROBLEMS

A. EMOTIONAL PROBLEMS

In discussing the treatment of emotional problems, it is well to recognize that, *for the most part*, students with very serious conflicts and maladjustments do not come to counselors but instead go directly to a psychiatrist. For the most part, counselors are dealing with mild problems of maladjustment. Occasionally, however, serious maladjustments do come to the counselor's attention. In such cases he should be able to spot them at once and refer them directly to more competent and professionally trained workers. The counselor must recognize the fact that emotional problems may arise in any area of a student's life, not just in regard to schoolwork. Moreover, personnel workers should assume responsibility for emotional adjustments outside, as well as within, the school. Guidance is concerned with the individual as a whole, not just his learning of textbook material.

In most personnel programs, little information is available to the counselor prior to the interview and, therefore, he must diagnose this type of maladjustment during the course of the interview. In this connection it is well to recognize that the interview is, for the most part, an artificial situation and that the prestige of the counselor *in some cases* prevents a student from revealing worries and conflicts. For this reason a student's behavior during the interview may not be at all typical or representative of his behavior in the classroom or in his associations with other students. Many times the student will cover up an emotional problem which troubles him. He does not want to discuss such intimate problems with someone who, he feels, may hold it against him, may cause other teachers to give him low grades or may cause members of the administrative staff to take some disciplinary action against him. The last point refers particularly to problems involving sex adjustment.

In the interview situation the counselor should be on the lookout for symptoms or indicators of emotional conflict. Frequently, students evade questions asked by the counselor. Occasionally, students reveal this tendency to evade by begging the counselor to tell them point blank what vocation to choose. This overdependence upon the counselor may be, *but is not always*, an indication of lack of self-confidence. Sometimes students exhibit a flippant type of behavior during the interview or make defensive replies, indicating that they are on guard and wary of giving themselves away to the counselor. Occasionally, they show signs of being timid: they keep their eyes directed elswehere than toward the face of the counselor, they speak in a low voice and sometimes they blush easily when certain topics are mentioned, such as sex conflicts, social adjustment, lack of popularity and the like. Sometimes, students refuse to talk or they give an appearance of defiance, as though they were saying, "I dare you to get me to reveal what I am thinking." Occasionally, a student appears in a bizarre dress, being totally unaware that this is a marked deviation from the usual dress and that he stands out in an undesirable manner. Occasionally, the counselor will notice untidy hands or dress, probably resulting from habitual low social standards in the family. Occasionally, speech habits, faulty grammar, use of slang and even swearing may indicate an actual or a potential social conflict and a failure to be accepted by other students. All these symptoms serve as indicators of actual or potential conflicts with a student's social environment and his relationships to other students.

Many times students do not see themselves as others see them and, therefore, they are not aware that these peculiarities of behavior actually cause others to avoid them. In such cases the first step in treatment is for the counselor to describe such things to the student in a tactful way, to hold up a mirror for the student to see himself. Such a frank statement of the counselor's impressions, given in a courteous and friendly manner after rapport has been established, will aid the student in developing adequate sensitivity to social situations. Students appear to be grateful for such help.

Quite frequently, students with a worry or conflict come to the counselor ostensibly to discuss the problem of a vocational choice, but actually hoping that the emotional problem will clear up secretly if the vocational problem is cleared up, or that the counselor will discover the emotional problem indirectly and unaided. That is, they want the counselor to see what is wrong without waiting to be told what is wrong. A counselor who is not aware of this possible mechanism will turn the student away, thinking that solving the vocational problem is sufficient, when actually the serious emotional problem will remain untouched and the student will be dissatisfied with the counseling treatment.

In identifying these mechanisms and maladjustments it is well for the counselor to understand that he is simply collecting impressions and observations, and that he has, at best, only crude indications of the *extent* of a student's deviation from the average student. For this reason, it is a more adequate counseling practice to use tests of emotional maladjustment *prior* to the interview. For this purpose some of the adjustment inventories described in Chapter VI will provide a preliminary diagnosis of such problems. Such tests may be given to all students in the school as a group or may be given to students as part of their individual testing prior to counseling. Under such testing conditions there is much less undesirable emphasis on the content and purpose of tests, causing the student to be wary of answering truthfully. If a student takes the test *after* he has discussed his problem with a counselor, he may attempt to disguise his problem or he may overemphasize it in answering the questions.

It is necessary for the counselor to check his impressions made during the interview. For example, suppose a counselor asks a student during the interview whether he likes to be with other students. If the student replies affirmatively, the counselor still does not know the extent of his preferences for social contact or how his preferences compare with those of other students. If the student had taken the social preference test, we could compare him with other students in his class and thus determine the extent of his deviation, either above or below the average for other students. This would give us a more refined diagnosis of the student's social-mindedness.

It is well to emphasize again that asking personal questions during the interview may yield faulty answers because of the personality of the counselor; the student may conceal the true state of his feelings or may present them in too extreme a form. Moreover, the counselor has time to ask too few questions to get an adequate sampling of a student's actual attitudes and emotional habits and to get a measure of the extent of a student's differences from others. As has been shown by many surveys, nearly all students have some worries and some emotional problems. The problem facing the counselor is to determine to what degree a student's tendency to worry is being carried.

Thus, we see that tests of personality traits provide a satisfactory and effective lead to the counselor; he follows these leads to get the student to open up and to get at the details of the maladjustment and the causes. In this sense, personality tests need not be assumed perfectly valid as techniques for diagnosis of the maladjustment. Such tests are best used as indicators which the counselor follows up more intensively by questioning. He does not need to bore or frighten the student by catechizing him, when a simple test will provide more adequate preliminary diagnoses.

Now let us turn to what the counselor does after he has identified or diagnosed a personal problem, and after he understands fairly adequately the origin and ramifications of the problem. We shall divide our techniques of treatment into two general categories: first, those which help the student, psychologically, to master his own problems and to clear them up; and second, techniques for changing the external factors producing the irritation and thereby causing the maladjustment.

The technique of discussing and talking over the problems with the student and getting him to talk about them provides an emotional release or reduction of tension which is in itself beneficial. It is well for the counselor to remember that some students cannot completely solve their problems; but they can "get over" them emotionally so that they are no longer disturbed by the condition causing the problem. For example, a student may have a serious conflict with his father which causes the student to be so emotionally upset that he cannot study effectively. Now, it is possible that the conflict cannot be resolved, that is, that the father will continue to be irritable when he is with the son, but the counselor, by talking with the student, may desensitize the student to this irritable situation. In such a case the counselor has not changed the conditions causing the problem, but rather has changed the student's sensitivity to that condition. In addition to this type of treatment, the counselor should, after getting the student's consent, discuss the problem with the parent involved. A competent "outsider" is often needed to interpret to parents the psychology of their children.

Another effective technique is for the counselor, after understanding the cause of the problem, to explain to the student how his problem developed and how it reveals itself in his behavior. This explanation clarifies the student's understanding of his problem and, in most cases, gives him better control over his reactions to his problem and to its causes. In part, this reduces a student's fear and terror of his peculiar behavior, amounting in some cases to an incipient fear of insanity. Many students do not understand the psychology of insanity, and fear that any worry will inevitably lead to insanity. A counselor, if he is well informed, can reassure the student on this point. Many times this fear of insanity is associated with the presence in the family of some person who has been committed to a state institution. The student is afraid that he has inherited this tendency to insanity. An explanation of the psychology involved sometimes will relieve the student of this fear, but frequently such a student needs to be referred to a psychiatrist for more technical therapy.

Another technique is that of giving sympathetic encouragement to a lonely student who fears to reveal his problems to others for fear of censure or of being considered queer. An explanation of the psychology of abnormality will clarify this point for the student, particularly if he is told that, from the psychologist's point of view, most persons have some type of abnormality: that is, personality difficulties are a matter of amount or degree and not a matter of being normal or abnormal; there are deviations in normality; and very few people, if any, are perfectly normal. Sometimes, it is effective to remark facetiously to the student that there are only two types of perfectly adjusted individuals—those who are deceased and those who think they are Napoleon. This sometimes brings forth a laughter response and the student sees that he is not so badly maladjusted as he thought he was and that mild and temporary maladjustments may be characteristic of so-called normal persons. Of course, this technique will not work in the cases of those erratic individuals who get a tremendous kick out of discussing all their abnormalities with anyone and everyone. Such individuals are using their abnormalities as a device to get attention. The therapy for such individuals is more complicated and requires the services of a qualified psychologist or psychiatrist. It should be emphasized again that counselors should not attempt to treat serious emotional conflicts; that is the task of qualified psychiatrists.

In some cases, the counselor will have to take a hand in removing the external factors causing the irritation, for example, by removing financial factors which produce worry about getting through college or even a serious conflict at home. This may lead to an interview with the parents, to interpret to the parents their own son or daughter, and to explain the student's attitude to the parents from the standpoint of an impartial and disinterested outsider with the added prestige of being a teacher in high school or college. This prestige factor is very important in getting the parents to be receptive to any suggestions the counselor might make. If he can reassure the parents that further financial sacrifices on their part to educate their son are well worth the investment, then they may be willing to give more money and thereby relieve the student of part of his fears. If they understand from the counselor that they have been too severe or too lax with the student, then they may change the situation at home with regard to discipline.

The counselor may suggest how to make more effective social contacts to those students who have had insufficient training in home and high school. These undersocialized students will not respond to mass appeals to attend parties. They must be trained and encouraged to prepare for such participation in group activities. He may discuss such details as how to greet people, how to introduce people, how to shake hands, how to start a conversation, how to dress attractively, how to be well groomed and other details of this type. The effective counselor may need to stimulate the setting up of needed group activities for this type of student.

In treating problems of social maladjustment, the counselor may introduce the counselee to other students, or to the heads of student activities, or to faculty members. He may see that the student is given an invitation to a party. He may step in and actually make opportunity for the student's social adjustment. He may go to the head of the boarding house or dormitory or fraternity and talk to the supervisor or to other students asking for assistance in making the student feel at ease in social situations, thereby relieving his emotional tension.

But it is well for the counselor to remember that if such techniques of treatment do not work, or if the case exhibits very serious emotional problems, he should immediately refer the case to a psychiatrist or a qualified psychologist. There is nothing more dangerous than for an untrained counselor to attempt to handle a serious emotional problem with the naïve expectation that just talking to the student will cause the problem to disappear. Many, many counselors use but one technique, to tell the student, "Now, just quit worrying and everything will be all right." That is very much like telling a drowning man that if he will but swim to shore, he will be saved. Of course if the student quits worrying, everything will be all right; but the point is that he has a habit of worrying and he cannot break the habit without expert assistance. Thus, telling him to quit worrying will not help him; he needs assistance in regard to "how to quit worrying." Most counselors err in not recognizing serious maladjustments. It is safe to say that if a student's emotional tension is not reduced by the techniques referred to above, then he should be referred immediately. Indeed, if the student exhibits very serious symptoms or bizarre behavior in the first interview, he should be referred immediately and the counselor should not attempt to treat him at all.

It is well to remind the counselor once more that emotional problems may arise in any area of the student's life and that the counselor should keep in mind the various possible sources of such maladjustments. No student case has been adequately handled until the counselor has reviewed all areas of the student's adjustment. A short and incomplete list of these areas of possible maladjustment may serve as a suggestion of the types of data the counselor should collect and review before and during the case interviews:

1. Continued unfavorable comparison in the home with siblings who appear to be brighter and to be making better scholastic and social adjustment. In such cases the counselor must interpret the situation to the parents and help build up the student's morale by emphasizing outstanding characteristics of the student.

2. Peculiarities of personality, such as shyness, bizarre dress, obesity, etc. which may lead to the student's rejection by associates and classmates. A straightforward but kindly description of the student given by the counselor will often give him insight which will lead to effort and desire to avoid unfavorable social comparisons. Obviously, the counselor should not seek to achieve conformity at the expense of desirable initiative and individuality.

3. Worries ostensibly about ability or grades but in reality induced by conflicts in other areas of life. In such cases the causes of the problems may be so deep-seated and complex that only a competent psychiatrist can diagnose and treat the case.

4. Conflicts arising in the home between student and parents over finances, social habits, vocational choice, etc., etc. As a rule, parents will be very cooperative when they are convinced that the counselor has made a thorough diagnosis and has acquired an understanding of all factors entering into the problem. The counselor must interview the parents and discuss the situation frankly. But care must be taken to avoid disclosing confidential information revealed by either the parents or the student to the counselor.

5. Worries resulting from failure to achieve success in social and activity life in college commensurate with that achieved in high school. This painful deflation is usually concealed by students, with the resultant withdrawal from social contacts, or it may lead to an undesirable overcompensation in the form of political maneuvering, boisterous and adolescent "wise-cracking" or other attempts to "save face." A kindly but realistic revelation of the facts to the student, together with suggestions for attempts to achieve social status, will usually yield results. In many cases the counselor should personally introduce the student into group activities.

6. Worries about health. These should be handled in cooperation with doctors and sometimes with psychiatrists.

7. Worries about speech disabilities. These need to be treated with the assistance of speech pathologists.

B. FINANCIAL PROBLEMS

The techniques of treatment of financial problems are relatively simple and pretty widely understood and used. These techniques consist of referring students to specialized agencies for loans, scholarship, employment and N.Y.A. aid. The student should not be told merely to go to an office, but the counselor should write a personal letter or telephone to the agency, explaining the student's need and his potentialities. The counselor should explain that here is a student whose academic and vocational possibilities are such as to make him a worth-while investment for a loan, a scholarship or employment. Occasionally, the counselor may act as an employment officer himself and actually seek a job for the student, or a personal loan from among the counselor's acquaintances. The counselor may also write to other colleges and schools, recommending the student for financial assistance. But it is well to remember that agencies distributing financial assistance give most attention, not to the counselor's recommendation or to the counselor's general statement that this is a good student, but to the factual material on which the counselor bases his judgment. That is, an agency distributing employment or financial assistance would like to know the student's scholastic record, his test scores, what he does in the way of social activities and things like that. The facts are more important than the vague statement that this is a good student.

Of course, if financial and employment resources are not available, the counselor should stimulate an understanding of such needs and assist in organizing the proper resources. For example, women's clubs, service clubs and alumni clubs may be called upon to organize scholarship and loan funds.

C. HEALTH PROBLEMS

With regard to the health problem, here again the counselor is an amateur and should recognize his amateur's standing and not attempt to give advice on serious problems of health. Insofar as possible, the counselor should have before him a report from the health officer which gives the current physical status of the student. This report should be available before the first interview. During the interview, the counselor may ask questions with regard to eating habits, sleeping habits and tendencies to fatigue. Sometimes, just insisting that the student eat regularly or that he have fairly regular hours of sleep will clear up what otherwise is a situation leading to scholastic failure. But, for the most part, health problems should be referred directly to a health officer, with a note or a telephone call stating why the student is being referred, that is, what particular health problem the counselor had in mind.

D. SPEECH PROBLEMS

A student's speech may be an asset or a liability in social adjustment in college and in getting a job after college. After all, other people, including employers, want students to be able to speak fairly concisely, with grammatical correctness and a pleasing tone. Other students and even employers avoid students who stutter, stammer or exhibit other serious difficulties. Sometimes, these speech difficulties may disqualify a student who has high aptitude. For example, a student nurse was referred to a personnel officer because the patients complained that they did not like her and did not want her to be around them. This student had satisfactory grades and high, tested aptitude, and appeared to be very well qualified for nursing training. The head nurse who referred the student did not understand what the difficulty was. The counselor, in the first few minutes of the interview, noticed that the student had a very harsh, unpleasant voice, which became increasingly irritating as the student continued to talk. The counselor suggested to the student that perhaps this was what irritated the patients and that she should go to the speech clinic to have her voice examined and to be advised what speech exercises she might practice in order to cultivate a more pleasing voice. Her physical appearance and her dress were very satisfactory; it was just her voice that was a possible cause for the patients' reaction. The student did go to the speech clinic; the diagnosis revealed that her vocal chords were unusually thick and inflexible. The speech clinic gave her a number of speech exercises to practice. Three weeks later, she came back to the counselor saying that the patients no longer complained about her and that she was making a satisfactory record.

It is well for counselors to recognize that serious speech difficulties, noticeable to other people, call for the assistance of technically trained workers. Minor difficulties may be treated by the counselor; but, in view of the importance of speech in social and vocational adjustment, it is advisable for the counselor to refer students to a speech clinic or to a teacher of speech for specialized treatment. Those having minor speech difficulties, however, may be advised to enter public speaking classes.

E. PREVENTION

Every guidance worker must recognize and carry out his responsibility for doing more than to diagnose and advise the individual student. A very large number of student problems arise from certain sociological and educational conditions in the school itself or in the adjacent community. If guidance is ever to become more than remedial, workers must assume responsibility for clearing up the conditions which give rise to problems. This is the strategy of preventive work, so to organize and permeate the school and community with the personnel point of view, that many student maladjustments will be prevented from arising. The cooperation of community officials and of parents is just as necessary as is that of school teachers and administrators, and perhaps easier to secure. It is a basic principle in guidance, that such personnel work, the preventive phase, will result in a more effective educational system.

CHAPTER XII

GUIDANCE—A PROFESSIONAL SERVICE

As was stated in Chapter I, one of the outstanding characteristics of student guidance problems is the fact of complexity. Most students in need of guidance service exhibit, not one problem in a restricted adjustment area, but two or more problems in two or more areas of adjustment. For this reason, no single, specialized type of guidance service will be adequate to meet the needs of students.

The fact of complexity of problems requiring solution forces us to recognize the artificiality of attempts to distinguish between vocational guidance and other types of guidance. In fact, one of the weaknesses of the vocational guidance movement itself has been the attempt to develop a vocational guidance service as an independent agency in the educational system. No wonder that such guidance efforts have been looked upon as a fifth wheel in the educational vehicle! No wonder, too, that such guidance efforts have been as ineffective as a fifth wheel!

A view of guidance that recognizes its complexity and its intimate concern with every variety of student adjustment problems is rapidly coming to the fore. And with this change in point of view we are witnessing an increased acceptance of guidance as a central feature of an effective educational program. Increasingly, the educational administrator, the classroom teacher and the guidance specialist are beginning to speak the same language, because each is accepting a philosophy of education in which individualization is the cardinal principle. This is evident in the rapid spread of the personnel point of view in modern education.

But individualization cannot be accomplished without adequate means for diagnosing the assets and liabilities of each student. Since diagnosis is an essential first step in all effective teaching and training, it becomes self-evident that the primary aim of the school can no longer be confined to a "filling-station" function in serving the students. Instead, the school must "learn them" in order to teach them.

It is easy to accept the doctrine of individualization with diagnosis as its corollary. But the complexity of the guidance problems to be diagnosed makes it difficult to put the doctrine into everyday practice. This is so because the complexity of problems necessitates a parallel complexity in diagnostic techniques and methods of treatment. A superficial reading of the chapters in this handbook will reveal that fact.

It is too much to expect that each school administrator and each school teacher will become an expert diagnostician. For this reason, each unit in the educational system will require the services of a counselor who is primarily a trained diagnostician. And the counselor's effectiveness will depend upon the extent to which administrators and teachers will adjust their services to the needs of the individual student as disclosed by diagnosis. The counselor's effectiveness will also depend upon the extent to which the school can provide specialized professional services for the solution of certain types of problems. It is obvious that problems in the area of health must be diagnosed and treated by physicians and dentists, reinforced by nurses, medical technicians and dental hygiene workers. Experts in speech-correction work must also be available. Psychologists and psychiatrists must likewise be on call to handle emotional difficulties ranging in severity from mild disorders to the outright psychoses. In addition, the trained social worker is necessary for contact and investigatory work in the homes and existing social agencies.

But what about the qualifications of the counselor? Are his services so general in character that almost any well-educated and well-intentioned person can fulfill the requirements? The way the school answers these two questions will determine the quality of the program for individualization.

It is only recently that leaders in the guidance movement are concerning themselves with this problem. At the 1937 meeting of the National Vocational Guidance Association, a Committee on Qualifications of Guidance Workers submitted a progress report.[1] The report is noteworthy, because it proposes to

[1] SMITH, F. C., "National Vocational Guidance Association," *Occupations, The Vocational Guidance Magazine*, 1937, 15: 771. The Keller report itself will probably be printed in this same magazine in the near future.

establish minimum *measured* qualifications, rather than merely to specify the number and variety of professional courses to which a guidance worker should have been exposed. To carry out the recommendations of the committee will require extensive experimentation and a subvention is now being sought from one of the large foundations.

In the meantime, it is possible to outline briefly a job-specification picture of the qualifications required of a professionally trained general counselor.[2] The following description assumes that the general counselor must be qualified to develop and administer an adequate diagnostic service and, hence, must first qualify in the field of educational and vocational psychology.

MINIMUM QUALIFICATIONS FOR A COUNSELOR

Education.—Graduation from an accredited university graduate school with a Master's degree in psychometrics or its equivalent. Graduate training in as many as possible of the following specific fields: Tests and measurements—group and individual, educational and vocational; advanced statistical methods, industrial and personnel psychology, vocational psychology; abnormal psychology, social psychology; social pathology; social case work; personnel administration and management; occupational studies and job analysis; labor problems. The training in these specific fields will include classroom work, field work, and research.

Experience.—Two years' paid, full-time, recent employment in individual diagnosis work, carried on in connection with vocational rehabilitation, vocational and educational guidance, employment or personnel work and related types of service. Graduate training, in addition to the M.S. in psychometrics, in the same specified fields of study may be substituted for experience, year for year.

Intellect.—Scholastic competence (measured by grades and achievement tests) and intellect (measured by intelligence tests especially prepared for use at the college level) above the median of college seniors in first-class universities and colleges.

[2] Adapted from specifications prepared by members of the Occupational Research Program, U.S. Employment Service, and by the Division of Rehabilitation, Minnesota State Department of Education. See F. H. Finch, "Qualifications for Rehabilitation Counselors," *Occupations, The Vocational Guidance Magazine*, 1937, 15: 628–630.

Interests.—The counselor should possess vocational interests (measured by Strong's Vocational Interest Blank) characteristic of adult professional workers in the various personnel occupations.

Personality.—The counselor must be free from personality defects and personality-adjustment difficulties and in addition must be able to deal effectively with, and inspire confidence of, other individuals and groups.

Sex.—Male or female.

ADDITIONAL DESIRABLE QUALIFICATIONS

Education.—Graduation from an accredited university graduate school with the Ph.D. degree in technological psychology or its equivalent.

Experience.—Two or more years of recent employment in as many as possible of the following fields: vocational and educational guidance, vocational education, personnel work in government, business, or industry, psychometrics, clinical psychology.

Special Knowledge.—Knowledge of various types of jobs, job specifications and occupational information, derived from job studies and studies of occupational trends; knowledge of academic and vocational training agencies; knowledge of public and community agencies, such as employment services, rehabilitation agencies, health agencies, social agencies, psychiatric clinics.

The requirements outlined above are admittedly much higher than those that have prevailed hitherto. But this is necessary, in view of the progress that has now been made in the development of technical methods of diagnosing capacities, abilities, interests and other personality characteristics. Persons possessing these qualifications will be difficult to locate, however, because of the failure of graduate schools to modify degree requirements in accordance with present-day needs for professional practitioners. Intensive specialization in orthodox academic psychology, which is admirably designed to prepare Ph.D.'s to train other Ph.D.'s will not do. The inadequacy of such orthodox training is not only due to the depth and narrowness of training in research, but it is also due to the fact that such training itself seems to select a type of graduate student who is primarily interested in science and types of activity that will promote scientific progress. No one can have any quarrel with this type of training and the type of students selected for such training. The difficulty arises when the supply of such persons exceeds present-day research and academic teaching needs and the excess supply is diverted willy-nilly into the technological field, where different preparation and different personality characteristics are required. A more satisfying solution will come when departments of psychology, education, sociology and economics can be persuaded to work out a coordinated program of graduate studies designed to prepare persons for effective service in the broad area of human engineering. The professional training of the guidance counselor will have a definite place in such an educational program.

Discussion of the qualifications of guidance counselors naturally leads to a consideration of duties and responsibilities. These may be listed as follows:

1. Diagnostic Service.—(a) Cooperating with the teaching staff in giving a minimal battery of group tests to locate students in need of specialized guidance service in the major adjustment areas. (b) Providing teaching staff with diagnostic data to permit individualization in program making, classroom teaching, etc. (c) Providing means for further testing and diagnosis of individual students referred by teachers or coming voluntarily.

2. Treatment.—(a) Aiding students to formulate a suitable program for the solution of educational, vocational and social difficulties. (b) Securing the cooperation of teachers, parents, classmates, specialized guidance experts, community agencies, etc., as may be necessary to enable the student to carry out his formulated plans. (c) Follow-up service to provide the student with such additional diagnostic service as may be found necessary and to reformulate plans to overcome obstacles to satisfactory adjustment.

3. Analysis of Student Needs.—(a) Surveying student needs in the major adjustment areas, in order to locate problems requiring administrative action for solution, such as: Curricular changes, establishment of loan funds, scholarships and work opportunities, improvements in conduct of extra-curricular activities, more adequate provision for socialization activities, etc. (b) Surveying occupational trends and local employment opportunities and placing the findings at the disposal of teachers, students, parents, employers and community leaders.

4. Coordination of Personnel Services in the Interest of the Student.—(a) Developing a system of cumulative records and aiding administrators and teachers to use these data in making administrative decisions and in planning educational activities for the student. (b) Developing methods of securing the aid of the teaching staff in contributing valid data to the cumulative records. (c) Holding staff conferences to discuss the needs of particular students as a means of "educating" administrators, department heads, teachers and guidance specialists in regard to the meaning of "diagnosis" and "treatment."

The above suggested outline of duties recognizes the necessity for developing a student-personnel program as an intimate concern of all members of the administrative and teaching staff. It recognizes the futility of giving "guidance" in an office which is insulated from the operating staff of the school. It assumes that a properly qualified counselor will be the one officer in the school whose duty it is to enable the school to put into operation a thoroughgoing program of individualization. When such a program is functioning effectively, the guidance counselor can turn his attention to the development of improved diagnostic services and the conduct of personnel research studies to keep the school abreast of changes demanding readjustments in the school program.

INDEX

A

Abilities (*see* Primary abilities)
Academic achievement tests, 38–39, 95–156
  English, 114–122
  foreign languages, 141–147
  general culture, 153–156
  history and social studies, 147–153
  junior high school, 98–113
  mathematics, 122–130
  science, 130–141
  senior high school and junior college, 114–156
  (*See also* Tests)
Achievement tests (*see* Academic achievement tests; Vocational achievement tests)
Achiever (*see* Non-achiever; Super-achiever)
Activities, extra-curricular, 284
  recreational, 285–286
Adams, Elizabeth, 276
Adjustment inventories, 183–204
Adjustment Inventory (The), 185–189
Advertisements, source of vocational information, 279–280
Age of group tested, 44
Allardyce, A., 167
Allen, B. M., 146
Allen, F. J., 8, 276, 287
Allen, R. D., 4, 101, 278
American Council on Education Psychological Examination for High School Graduates and College Freshmen, 74–76
American Council on Education Psychological Examination for High School Students, 68–69

Anderson, H. R., 147–149, 153
Anderson, J. E., 31, 32, 70
Anderson, L. D., 51, 222, 224, 225, 229
Anderson, R. G., 71
Anderson, W. A., 105
Andrew, D. M., 66, 206, 209, 237, 240
Anecdotal method, 26–27
Aptitude Test for Nursing, 244–245
Aptitude tests, art, 210–216
  clerical, 206–209
  dexterity, 235–242
  engineering, 250–256
  law, 245–247
  mechanical, 222–234
  medical, 242–244
  miscellaneous, 242–256
  musical, 216–222
  nursing, 244–245
  scholastic, 35
  special, 35–38
  (*See also* Tests)
Aptitudes, poor scholastic, 265–268
  special, 46
  (*See also* Aptitude tests; Primary abilities; Tests)
Armsby, H. H., 256
Army Alpha Group Examination, Forms 5 to 9, 58–61
  (*See also* Revised Army Alpha; Bregman's Revision of Army Alpha)
Art Judgment Test, 210–213
Attitude inventories, 183–204

B

Barrows, W. M., 141
Beers, F. S., 51, 116, 119, 120

Behavior items, recording of, 21–27
  (*See also* Anecdotal method;
  Cumulative records; Rating
  of traits; Rating Scale)
Bell, H. M., 4, 184, 185, 189
Benge, E. J., 164
Berman, I. R., 66, 180, 224, 237, 240, 242
Bingham, W. V., 4, 9, 48, 49, 209, 233, 234, 276
Bird, Charles, 16, 85, 86, 259, 269
Bixler, H. H., 101
Bjornaraa, D., 272
Blackstone, E. G., 163–164
Blackstone Stenographic Proficiency Tests (Stenography test), 163–164
Blackstone Stenographic Proficiency Tests (Typing), 163
Boardman, C. W., 265
Branom, M. E., 105
Bregman, E. O., 62, 63
Bregman's Revision of Army Alpha Examination, Forms A and B, 62–63
Brennen, F. M., 220
Brewer, J. M., 278
Brigham, C. C., 212
Brown, A. W., 220
Brown, C. M., 13, 161, 162
Brueckner, L. J., 105
Burnham, P. S., 178
Butters, F. K., 133

C

Calibration of I. Q.'s, 72–74
California Test of Mental Maturity, Advanced Battery, Grades 9–14, 72
Carpenter, M. F., 114, 119
Carroll, H. A., 212, 213, 215, 216
Castle Mechanical Drawing Tests, 158
Census (*see* Occupational Census data)
Chapman, J. C., 85, 88

Chapman-Cook Speed of Reading Test, 85–86
Chave, E. J., 202
Chesney, A. M., 244
Chittenden, E. W., 122
Clark, W. W., 72, 111
Classmates, influence of, 287
Clement, S. H., 276
Clerical aptitude tests, 206–209
Cobb, M. V., 61
Cole, L., 269
Conflict (*see* Emotional problems)
Cook, S. A., 85, 88
Cook, W. W., 116
Cooperative Algebra Test (Elementary and Intermediate), 128–129
Cooperative American History Test, 147–148
Cooperative Biology Test for High School Students, 140–141
Cooperative Botany Test, 133–134
Cooperative Chemistry Test for College Students, 135–136
Cooperative Chemistry Test for High School Students, 134–135
Cooperative Contemporary Affairs Test, 150–153
Cooperative English Test, Series 1, 116–118
Cooperative English Test, Series 2, 119–120
Cooperative French Test, 142–143
Cooperative General Culture Test, 153–156
Cooperative General Mathematics Tests for College Students, 125–127
Cooperative General Mathematics Test for High School Classes, 124–125
Cooperative General Science Test for College Students, 131–133
Cooperative General Science Test (High School), 130–131
Cooperative German Test, 143–145
Cooperative Latin Test, 146–147

INDEX

Cooperative Literary Acquaintance Test, 120–122
Cooperative Modern European History Test, 148–149
Cooperative Physics Test for College Students, 138–140
Cooperative Physics Test (for High School Students), 137–138
Cooperative Plane Geometry Test, 127–128
Cooperative Spanish Test, 145–146
Cooperative Trigonometry Test, 129–130
Cooperative World History Test, 149–150
Cooperative Zoology Test, 141
Coordination of personnel services, 305
Copeland, H. A., 249, 250
Cornog, J., 136
Counselor, functions, 3–4
   qualifications, 301–304
   responsibilities, 304–305
   (*See also* Faculty counselor)
Courses, selection of, 257–258
Cowley, W. H., 4
Craig, H., 249, 250
Crawford, A. B., 178, 246, 247, 276
Cumulative records, 18–21
Curricula, selection of, 257–258
Curriculum, changes to fit student, 267
   use in diagnosing vocational aptitudes, 283–284
Cutright, P., 105

D

Darley, J. G., 4, 5, 7, 66, 180, 189, 191–193, 225, 241, 242, 280, 282
Dearborn Group Intelligence Tests, 71
Dexterity tests, 235–242
Diagnosis, of educational problems, 257–270
   techniques of, 6–51
   (*See also* Guidance)
Diagnostic service, 304

Disabilities, reading, 268–270
   subject-matter, 270
Douglass, H. R., 245
Drake, L. E., 82, 83
Drake, R. M., 219–222
Dvorak, A., 105
Dvorak, B. J., 36, 66, 179, 225, 237, 240, 242
Dynamicube Test of Power to Visualize, 250–252

E

Earle, F. M., 4, 51, 280
Eckert, W. J., 131
Economic pressure, 288
Edgerton, H. A., 77
Edmunds, J. M., 2
Educational level of persons tested, 45
Educational problems, diagnosing and treatment, 257–270
Elliott, R. M., 51, 222, 224, 225, 229
Elwell, F. H., 165, 167
Elwell-Fowlkes Bookkeeping Test, 165–167
Emotional Problems, 289–296
Engineering Drawing Aptitude Placement Test, 254–256
Engle, E. M., 159–161
Engle-Stenquist Home Economics Test, 159–161
English tests, 114, 122
Eurich, A. C., 87, 88, 91, 93, 94, 150, 213, 215, 216, 258
Experience of person tested, 45
Extra-curricular activities, in diagnosing vocational aptitudes, 284

F

Faculty counselor, role in mental hygiene, 12–18
Farnsworth, P. R., 213
Farwell, H. W., 131, 138
Fee, Mary, 188
Fernald, G. M., 83, 84
Ferson, M. L., 245

Filene, C., 276
Financial problems, 296–297
Finch, F. H., 72, 74, 265, 302
Findlay, W. G., 212
Finger Dexterity Test, 235–237
Fischer Mechanical Drawing Tests, 158
Fiss, C. B., 245
Fitzpatrick, F. L., 131, 140
Fleishman, D. E., 276
Foreign language tests, 141–147
Fowlkes, J. G., 165–167
Freyd, M., 165
Frutchey, F. P., 133, 135, 141
Fryer, D., 61

G

Garretson, O. K., 174, 175
Garrett, H. E., 165
Garrett, Mildred, 57, 268
Gaudet, F. J., 247
Generalized Attitude Scales, 202–204
Givens, M. B., 271
Goodenough, F. L., 31, 32
Gordon, R. B., 133
Graham, F. B., 101
Green, H. J., 66, 224, 237, 240, 242
Greene, H. A., 89, 91, 107
Guidance, coordination of services, 305
  effectiveness, 281–282
  professional service, 300–305
  purpose, 1–2
  three services to individual, 28–29
  traditional *vs* newer methods, 6–7
  types of service, 3–4
Guidance counselor (*see* Counselor)
Guilford, J. P., 22

H

Haggerty, M. E., 71, 91, 94
Haggerty Intelligence Examination, Delta 2, 71
Hammond, H. P., 124, 137

Hand, H. C., 278, 281
Hansen, A. H., 272
Hart, C. W., 153
Hartshorne, Hugh, 170, 171
Hatcher, O. L., 276
Hausen, M. Q., 276
Hawkes, H. E., 23
Hayes, H., 8, 9
Health problems, 297–298
Heidbreder, E., 51, 222, 224, 225, 229
Hendricks, B. C., 135
Henmon, V. A. C., 69–71, 81–83, 116
Henmon-Nelson Tests of Mental Ability, for College Students, 81–83
Henmon-Nelson Tests of Mental Ability, High School Examination, 69–71
Hespelt, E. H., 143–145
Hespelt, M. V., 143
Hildreth, G. H., 101
Hill, G., 150
Hines, Mildred, 237
History and social studies tests, 147–153
Hobbies, 285–286
Hollingworth, H. L., 7, 183
Holzinger, Karl, 38
Horn, E., 107
Horney, A. G., 135
Horton, C. W., 133
Hotelling, H., 38
How-to-study course, 263, 270
Hull, C. L., 36, 51
Humm, D. G., 197, 199, 200
Humm-Wadsworth Temperament Scale, 197–201
Hunt, T., 244
Hurlin, R. G., 271

I

Individual differences, 27–29
  (*See also* Measurements)
Individualization, 27–28, 300–301
Intellectual level of persons tested, 45

INDEX 311

Intelligence quotients, calibration of, 72–74
  table of equivalent, 72, 73
Intelligence tests, college level, 74–83
  secondary school level, 53–72
Interest inventories, 174–183
Interest Questionnaire for High School Boys, 174–175
Interests, inventories of, 39–40, 174–183
  special, 46
  (*See also* Tests)
Interview, 8–12
  supplemented by tests, 32–33
Interview Aids and Trade Questions, 167–169
Iowa Every-pupil Tests of Basic Skills for Grades Six, Seven and Eight, 107–111
Iowa Placement Examinations, New Series, Chemistry Training, 136–137
Iowa Placement Examinations, New Series, English Training, 114–116
Iowa Placement Examinations, Series M.T. 1, Revised, A. Mathematics-Training, 122–124
Iowa Silent Reading Tests, Advanced Tests, 89
Ishihara, Dr. S., 247, 248, 250

J

Job experiences, 285
Job opportunities, local surveys of, 274–275
Johnson, P. O., 133
Johnston, J. B., 4, 28, 35, 79, 265
Jordan, A. M., 105
Jorgensen, A. N., 89, 91
Judgments of students, 287–288

K

Katz, S. E., 197
Kay, G. M., 131
Kefauver, G. N., 4, 72, 74, 278, 281

Keller, F. J., 280, 301
Keller, Helen B., 84
Kelley, N. H., 89, 91
Kelley, T. L., 35, 36, 38, 47–49, 51, 98, 101
Kelty, M. G., 105
Kent, Grace, 229, 233
Kent-Shakow Form Boards, 229–233
Kintner, Madeline, 213
Kirtland, J. C., 146
Kitson, H. D., 276
Knight, F. B., 107
Koos, L. V., 4
Kuhlmann, F., 70, 71
Kuhlmann-Anderson Intelligence Tests, 71

L

Laffan, J. C., 22
Laird, Donald, 13
Landis, C., 197
Lapp, C. J., 131, 138
Larson, R. C., 217, 219, 220
Law Aptitude Examination, 245–247
Lawrence, D. C., 167
Learned, A., 153
Leonard, S. A., 116
Likert, R., 227, 229
Lincoln, M. E., 278
Lindquist, E. F., 107, 119, 147–149, 153
Lingenfelter, M. R., 276
Link, H. C., 225
Litterer, O., 86
Lloyd-Jones, Esther, 5
Logie, Ione, 276
Long, G. S., 66
Long, J. A., 127–129
Longstaff, H. P., 2
Lundholm, H. T., 124, 125, 128

M

McAdory, Margaret, 216
McAdory Art Test, 213–216

McBroom, M., 107
McCall, William, 72
McConn, Max, 51
McJimsey, R. B., 146
McLaughlin, Mary, 163
MacQuarrie, T. W., 233, 234
MacQuarrie Test for Mechanical Ability, 233–234
Macrae, A., 277, 280, 281
Maladjustments (*see* Emotional problems; Mental hygiene)
Maller, J. B., 197
Mann, C. V., 250–254
Marryott, F. J., 247
Mathematics tests, 122–130
May, M. A., 160
Measurements and norms, 27–51
  in diagnosing vocational aptitudes, 282–283
Measures of Musical Talent, 216–221
Mechanical ability tests, 222–234
Medical Aptitude Test, 242–244
Meier, N. C., 210, 213
Meikle, G. S., 204
Mental hygiene, role of faculty counselor in, 12–18
  symptoms indicating need of treatment, 16–18
  (*See also* Emotional problems)
Mercer, E. O., 277, 280, 281
Merrill, Maud, 56
Metropolitan Achievement Test, Advanced Battery, 101–105
Miles, W. R., 249, 250
Miller, L. W., 114, 116, 124, 136
Miller, W. S., 59, 65, 66, 71–74
Miller Mental Ability Tests, 71
Minnesota College Ability Test, 77–79
Minnesota House Design and House Furnishing Test, 161–162
Minnesota Inventories of Social Attitudes, 189–193
Minnesota Manual Dexterity Test, 240–242
Minnesota Mechanical Assembly Test, 222–225

Minnesota Paper Form Board Test (Revised), 227–229
Minnesota Reading Examination for College Students, 91–94
Minnesota Scale for the Survey of Opinions, 193–196
Minnesota Spatial Relations Test, 225–227
Minnesota Speed of Reading Test for College Students, 87–88
Minnesota Vocational Test for Clerical Workers, 206–209
Misumi, I., 213
Modern Foreign Language Study tests, 141–142
Moore, B. V., 9
Moore, M. W., 19
Moser, G. V., 144
Moss, F. A., 242, 244
Motivation, 261–262
Moyer, D. H., 276
Multi-mental Scale, 72
Musical Memory Test, 221–222
Mutilated Cubes Test of Power to Visualize, 253–254

N

Nash-Van Duzee Achievement Tests in Woodwork and Mechanical Drawing, 158
National Intelligence Tests, 71–72
Nationality of persons tested, 45
Nelson, M. J., 69–71, 81–83
New Stanford Achievement Test, Advanced Examination, 98–101
Newkirk and Stoddard Home Mechanics Test, 158
Nilsson, Sven G., 233
Noll, V. H., 131, 134
Non-achiever, 263–265
Norms, 46–47
  (*See also* Measurements and norms)
Northby, A. S., 124
Nursing (*see* Aptitude Test for Nursing)

INDEX 313

O

Oakley, C. A., 277, 280, 281
Occupational ability patterns, 280–281
Occupational bookshelves, 275–276
Occupational Census data, 271–274
Occupational information, bibliography, 276–277
　classified advertisements as source, 279–280
　conferences, 278–279
　referral to experts, 279
　techniques for securing and imparting, 271–281
　(*See also* Occupations)
Occupational trends, 272–274
Occupations, Census of, 271–274
　courses on, 278
　information on, 271–278
　personal study of, 275
　(*See also* Occupational information)
O'Connor, Johnson, 235, 237–240
O'Connor, W. L., 41, 101
O'Connor clerical aptitude test, 209
Ohio State Intelligence Test, 76–77
Ordway, S. H., Jr., 22
Orleans, J. S., 101
O'Rourke clerical aptitude test, 209
Otis, A. S., 65, 66, 68, 70, 71, 82
Otis Self-administering Tests of Mental Ability, Higher examination, 66–68

P

Palmer, F., 138
Parents, 286
Parker, W. E., 23, 275, 276
Paterson, D. G., 5, 7, 8, 22, 38, 51, 66, 77, 116, 119, 120, 170, 180, 206, 209, 222, 224, 225, 229, 237, 240, 242, 280
Personal problems, treatment of, 289–299
　(*See also* Emotional problems; Mental hygiene)

Personality inventories, 183–204
Personality problems (*see* Emotional problems; Mental hygiene; Personal problems)
Personality Sketches, 196–197
Personality tests and questionnaires, 170–204
Pintner, R., 51
Placement facilities, 288
Pond, Millicent, 209, 234
Powers, S. R., 130, 134, 140
Prediction of college scholarship, 265–266
Pressey, L. C., 63, 72
Pressey, S. L., 63, 65, 66
Pressey Senior Classification and Senior Verifying Tests, 63–66
Prevention of student problems, 299
Price, J. W., 141
Primary abilities, 36–38
　(*See also* Tests; Unitary traits)
Problems, educational, 257–270
　emotional, 12–18, 289–296
　financial, 296–297
　personal, 289–299
　vocational, 282–288
　(*See also* Student problems)
Proctor, W. M., 61, 287
Progressive Achievement Tests, Intermediate Battery, 111–113
Psychiatrist, in the school health service, 15–16
Puhr, M. F., 161, 162

Q

Quasha, W. H., 227, 229

R

Rating of traits, 22
　(*See also* Rating Scale; Behavior items)
Rating Scale for Students, 23–26
Reading disabilities, 268–270
Reading tests, 83–94
Records in guidance (*see* Anecdotal method; Cumulative records; Rating Scale)

Reeve, E. B., 161
Reliability of tests, 47–50
Remmers, H. H., 202, 204
Revised Army Alpha Examination, Form 6, Short Form, 61–62
Revised Stanford-Binet Scales, 54–56
Rosanoff, H. A., 198
Rosenstein, I., 179
Ruch, G. M., 68, 98, 101, 137
Rundquist, E. A., 193, 196

S

Sampson, H. C., 133
Schindler, A. W., 131
Schneck, M. R., 57, 165
School Inventory (The), 184–185
Science tests, 130–141
Scoring machine, 42–43
Seashore, C. E., 210, 213, 216, 217, 219, 220
Seashore Motor Skills Unit, 205
Segel, David, 96, 115, 116, 137, 252
Sex differences on tests, 45
Shakow, D., 229, 233
Shuttleworth, F. K., 171
Siceloff, L. P., 124, 125, 127–129
Siceloff, Margaret (McAdory) (see McAdory, Margaret)
Sletto, R. F., 193, 196
Smith, F. C., 301
Smith, O. M., 135
Snyder, L. H., 141
Socio-economic status of persons tested, 45
Sogge, T. M., 272
Sparling, E. J., 61
Spaulding, G., 142, 143, 145
Spearman, Charles, 36, 37
Special aptitude tests, 205–256
Specific Attitude Scales, 201–202
Speech problems, 298–299
Standard error of a score, 48
Stanford-Binet Scales (see Stanford Revision of the Binet-Simon Scales; and Revised Stanford-Binet Scales)

Stanford Revision of the Binet-Simon Scale, 53–54
(See also Revised Stanford-Binet Scales)
Stanton, H. M., 219–221
Staticube Test of Power to Visualize, 252–253
Stead, W. H., 272
Stenogauge, 164–165
Stenography tests (see Typewriting and stenography tests)
Stenquist, J. L., 159–161
Stoddard, G. D., 68, 114, 116, 122, 124, 136, 137, 245, 247
Stover, R. D., 245
Strang, Ruth, 5, 81
Strong, E. K., Jr., 45, 175, 176, 180, 181, 183
Strong's tests (see Vocational Interest Blank for Men; Vocational Interest Blank for Women)
Student guidance (see Guidance)
Student needs, analysis of, 304
Student problems, complexity of, 2–3
Study, difficulties in, 259
methods of, 258–263
motivating of, 261–262
planning of, 261
time record, 260–261
Sturtevant, S. M., 8, 9
Subject-matter disabilities, 270
Sullivan, E. T., 72
Super-achiever, 263–265
Symonds, P. M., 9, 51, 174, 175, 258

T

Tate, J. T., 138
Teachers, 287
(See also Anecdotal methods; Rating of traits; Rating Scale)
Teegarden, Lorene, 231
Terman, L. M., 54, 56, 58, 65, 70–72, 75, 98, 101

INDEX

Terman Group Test of Mental Ability, 56–58
Tests, achievement, 38–39, 95–156
  administration of, 40–41
  art talent, 210–216
  bookkeeping, 165–167
  clerical aptitude, 206–209
  color blindness, 247–250
  definition of, 31–32
  description of, 34–40
  dexterity, 235–242
  difference from interview, 32
  engineering aptitude, 250–256
  English, 114–122
  equivalent forms, 43
  foreign language, 141–147
  general culture, 153–156
  history and social studies, 147–153
  home economics, 158–162
  intelligence, 53–83
  interest, 39–40, 174–183
  law aptitude, 245–247
  mathematics, 122–130
  as measure, of growth, 34
    of present status, 33–34
  mechanical ability, 222–234
  medical aptitude, 242–244
  miscellaneous aptitude, 242–256
  musical ability, 216–222
  norms, 46–47
  nursing aptitude, 244–245
  personality, 40, 170–204
  persons for whom designed, 43–46
  for planning, 33
  purpose of, 31–34
  reading, 83–94
  reliability of, 47–50
  scholastic aptitude, 35, 52–94
  science, 130–141
  scoring of, 41–43
  shop course, 158
  special aptitude, 35–38, 205–256
  supplemental to interview, 32–33
  trade, 167–169
  typewriting and stenography, 163–165
  use in guidance procedure, 29–31

Tests, vocational achievement, 157–169
  vocational aptitude, 282–286
Tests for Color Blindness, 247–250
Thompson, L. A., 167–169
Thorndike, E. L., 36, 38, 71, 80, 81
Thorndike Intelligence Examination for High School Graduates, 80–81
Thurstone, L. L., 36–38, 40, 68, 74, 76, 201
Thurstone, T. G., 68, 74, 76
Thurstone clerical aptitude test, 209
Tiegs, E. W., 72, 111
Tiffany, L. H., 133
Tiffin, J., 153
Time record in study, 260–261
Tinker, M. A., 86
Toops, H. A., 51, 76, 77, 222, 224, 225
Trabue, M. R., 1–2, 66, 224, 237, 240, 242
Trade questions (*see* Interview Aids and Trade Questions)
Traits (*see* Behavior items; Ratings; Tests; Unitary Traits)
Traxler, A. E., 68
Treatment, of educational problems, 257–270
  of personal problems, 289–299
  three divisions of, 304
  of vocational problems, 271–288
Turney, A. H., 188
Tweezer Dexterity Test, 237–240
Tyler, R. W., 133, 135, 141
Typewriting and stenography tests, 163–165

U

Underhill, O. E., 130
Unit Scales of Aptitude, 71
Unit Scales of Attainment, Division 3, 105–107
Unit Scales of Attainment in Foods and Household Management, 161

Unit Scales of Attainment—Reading, 88–89
Unitary traits (see Primary abilities; Tests)

V

Vaillant, P., 142
Validity, of personality tests, 170–172
  of tests, 50–51
Van Wagenen, M. J., 71, 88, 89, 105
Viteles, M., 280
Vocabulary, 267–269
Vocational achievement tests, 157–159
  bookkeeping, 165–167
  home economics, 158–162
  shop courses, 158
  trade, 167–169
  typewriting and stenography, 163–165
Vocational aptitudes, techniques for diagnosing, 282–286
Vocational goal of persons tested, 45–56
Vocational information (see Occupational information; Occupations)
Vocational Interest Blank for Men, 175–181
Vocational Interest Blank for Women, 181–183
Vocational problems, diagnosing, 282–286

Vocational problems, treatment of, 286–288
Vocations (see Occupational information; Occupations)

W

Wadsworth, G. W., Jr., 197, 199, 200
Wallis, N., 213
Wells, F. L., 62
Whipple, G. M., 71
Willard, D. W., 58
Williams, R. H., 145
Williamson, E. G., 2, 4, 5–7, 35, 79, 96, 149, 189, 191–194, 196, 265, 277, 278, 282
Willing, M. H., 116
Wilson, E. C., 150
Wood, Ben D., 26, 27, 34, 42, 51, 80, 81
Woodworth Psychoneurotic Inventory, 183
Worries, 296
  (See also Emotional problems)
Worthing, A. G., 138
Wrenn, C. G., 258, 268, 269

Y

Yerkes, R. M., 61, 72
Yoakum, C. S., 61
Young, Kimball, 51

Z

Ziegler, W. A., 240
Zubin, J., 197